Pregnancy and abortion counselling

Joanna Brien and Ida Fairbairn

London and New York

First published 1996
by Routledge
11 New Fetter Lane, London EC4P 4EE

Simultaneously published in the USA and Canada
by Routledge
29 West 35th Street, New York, NY 10001

© 1996 Joanna Brien and Ida Fairbairn

Typeset in Times by LaserScript, Mitcham, Surrey
Printed and bound in Great Britain by
Mackays of Chatham PLC, Chatham, Kent

British Library Cataloguing in Publication Data
A catalogue record for this book is available from the British Library

Library of Congress Cataloging in Publication Data
A catalogue record for this book has been requested

ISBN 0–415–12278–3 (hbk)
ISBN 0–415–12010–1 (pbk)

Contents

Figures and tables

Preface

This book came into being through chance. We met at the 1993 British Association of Counselling Annual Training Conference and realized that we had much in common when we both attended the same three workshops out of a choice of ninety.

On the train journey back from Cardiff to London, fortuitously much delayed, we ended up sitting next to each other and shared our thoughts and feelings about our jobs and involvement with unwanted pregnancy.

Joanna had worked as a senior counsellor for fifteen years and, as well as counselling young people, was much concerned with improving practice, supervision and support for counsellors at London Brook. London Brook is a non-statutory voluntary organization for young people:

> The objectives of London Brook Advisory Centres (LBAC) are the prevention and mitigation of the suffering caused by unwanted pregnancy, by educating young persons in matters of sex and contraception and developing among them a sense of responsibility in regard to sexual behaviour.
>
> (London Brook: 1995)

At present there are seventeen centres spread throughout the capital. Venues vary from standard clinic sites to clinics held in a college, youth centres, a day centre for the homeless and a genito-urinary clinic. Over 15,000 young people visited London Brook last year.

Ida had been working with young people for a much shorter time. She had worked as a doctor at the Brandon Centre for two years. The Brandon Centre (formerly the London Youth Advisory Centre) is a well-established community-based clinic located in a large Victorian house in Kentish Town in London. Another voluntary, non-statutory agency, it is altogether a much smaller organization than Brook (570 people had appointments at the centre last year). It offers a complimentary service to young people with an emphasis given to individual psychotherapeutic work. The Brandon Centre service extends to a wide range of adolescent problems:

The principal objective of the Brandon Centre is to maintain and develop an accessible and flexible professional service in response to the psychological, medical, sexual and social problems of young people aged 12–25 years. It aims to relieve distress, mobilise personal resources and facilitate growth in adolescents towards responsibility and self-fulfilment. Furthermore, it aims to prevent or alleviate suffering caused by unwanted pregnancy and by mental ill health, psychological disturbance and maladaption in adult and future family relationships.

(Brandon Centre: 1995)

Ida was very aware of the lack of any training courses or written material that could have helped her as she started counselling young women who were unhappily pregnant.

This book was planned and conceived in the joint recognition of the need for support, information and guidelines to good practice for all those involved in pregnancy counselling. Although we have enjoyed the support and collaboration of our colleagues at London Brook and the Brandon Centre, we want to point out that this book represents our personal views, not those of the organizations.

It is written with several aims. Its starting point is the wish to educate helpers and increase their awareness of the issues involved in this widespread and important area of counselling work. We also hope that its publication will draw attention to the need for women to receive good pre- and, if necessary, post-abortion counselling. It is written in the knowledge that there is little material directed at those undertaking this work, that there are as yet no detailed written guidelines as to what pregnancy counselling is or how it should be carried out, and very little in the way of specific training. Counselling women who are unhappily pregnant is skilful work but often the work is unacknowledged. Silence and secrecy are often features of a woman's request for help and this isolates them from support. Pregnancy counsellors involved with women seeking abortion parallel this silence. We want to explore and examine the work we do openly; in doing so we can then support others' counselling work.

We are constantly aware that an abortion is the destruction of a potential child and have not tried to gloss over this issue or deny that this is the case. The personal anguish for clients is often great. We hold a strong personal belief that women have to make their own informed decision and that this can often be more easily achieved in a safe environment provided by a counsellor.

The book is written for established pregnancy counsellors who may value the opportunity to reflect on the complexity of their work, for all those embarking on this work and for the many health professionals who are so often at the front line. We hope that it will be useful to general practitioners and hospital doctors, nurses, both hospital-based and in the community, family planning staff, social workers, youth and community workers, and counsellors. We realize that some areas of the book will be of more interest to some disciplines than others but hope that readers will be able to dip into the book to find what may be particularly pertinent to them. However, by seeing all the ramifications of the issues around unwanted pregnancy, we also hope that there may be opportunities for learning and for understanding each other's roles.

Throughout the book we have chosen to refer to the counsellor as 'she' rather than 'he', simply in order to avoid clumsy constructions such as 'he/she', 'his/her'. What we have to say is of course equally applicable to counsellors of either sex.

The case examples we use to illustrate the points we make in the book are fictional, but are based on our joint experience as counsellors. They represent the sort of situations anyone working in the field will commonly meet.

The first three chapters set the scene, they explore factors that influence the decisions women take and that may make decision-making complex and difficult. The first chapter explores the range of pressures on individuals that cause pregnancies to be perceived as unwanted. Although ways of protecting against pregnancy are relatively safe and effective, the use of contraception is affected by conscious and unconscious factors and the chapter also aims to help workers become aware of such contradictions.

Pregnancy itself hampers decision-making. This is explored in Chapter 2. Chapter 3 provides statistics and information about trends, the law and methods of abortion.

The middle chapters contain the working bulk of the book. Pregnancy counselling is defined, and attention paid to who should receive and who should provide this counselling. Issues surrounding good practice are fully explored. We also consider the emotional aftermath of abortion and the various special situations that warrant extra care, such as work with young people. In a separate chapter we focus on termination for foetal abnormality as opposed to 'social' terminations and examine the similarities and differences.

The final chapter concentrates on the effects of this work on those who are providing counselling and medical or nursing attention. We are aware from personal communications, a questionnaire and workshops of the impact this work has on the professionals involved. Indeed it was our own experience of this impact that led to this book being created. We hope that you will find it helpful.

Acknowledgements

We would like to take the opportunity to thank all the people who have contributed to the writing of this book. We owe a great debt to our colleagues and friends at The Brandon Centre and London Brook. We are grateful to our families who put up with our engrossment in this project with as much patience as possible.

We appreciate the many people who wrote to us or responded to our questionnaires, attended our workshop and generally took time to discuss their work. We would particularly like to thank Gillian Ballance, Jonie Dimavicius from SATFA, Tania Glynn from The Red Admiral Project, Ruth Kaleb from Post Abortion Counselling Service, Chris Kell, Robert Kirkwood, Lyn Margerison from The Kennedy Galton Centre, Dr Linden Ruckert and Dr G. Zolese. The librarians at St Albans City Hospital and Hill End were also most helpful in finding papers.

Above all we would like to thank the young people who use the centres in which we work.

Chapter 1

Why do women get pregnant when contraception is available?

There were nearly 180,000 abortions in the United Kingdom in 1994 and yet free, effective contraception has been generally available since the mid-1970s. No contraceptive method can be 100 per cent reliable and good abortion provision remains a vital back-up for family planning services. Unfortunately, however, many abortions are avoidable and these abortion figures make uneasy reading to those of us concerned with women's health.

In 1991 in the UK, 'it was estimated in "Population Trends" that one in five pregnancies ended in legal abortion. Cumulatively, about one woman in three in the UK now has at least one termination before the age of thirty' (Guillebaud 1993: 400).

It is not possible simply to equate these abortion figures to 'unwanted pregnancies'; the relationship is much more elaborate. Some of the terminations may be carried out on wanted pregnancies, while many unplanned pregnancies go on to be wanted or unwanted babies. No one term can attempt to describe the different types of pregnancies that end in termination. They are commonly called 'unplanned', 'unwanted' or 'unintentional', and all hold a different significance. None of these definitions, though, can do justice to the complexity each pregnancy may hold, as these few examples illustrate.

A planned pregnancy may become an unwanted pregnancy due, for example, to changing circumstances, financial or medical reasons.

A woman may very much want to be pregnant but have an abortion as she does not want a baby. In this case she could be said to have a planned, wanted pregnancy but an unwanted baby.

A young girl may desperately want to be pregnant and to have a baby to love. In this case the pregnancy may be planned and wanted but later terminated due to parental pressure or the realization that a baby would not solve her problems.

A woman may very much want a baby but financial and social demands make her request a termination.

A young woman was made pregnant by her abusive stepfather; this was unplanned and unintended by her. However, the baby was very much wanted, mainly as a passport out of the intolerable home situation.

We feel the term 'ambivalent' best describes the pregnancy of most of the women we see for pregnancy counselling. We use the other terms with care in specific situations. This term, ambivalent, feels more relevant and, to a greater or lesser extent, is shared by all women as they embark on motherhood and face the changes this entails.

The reasons why women have an ambivalent pregnancy are myriad and encompass simple contraceptive failure, inaccessible services, ignorance due to poor sex education, risk-taking behaviour, cultural or religious opposition to birth control and complex unconscious factors that need to be heard and understood.

This chapter explores the origins of ambivalent pregnancy and for ease of reference has been divided into subheadings. It is of course impossible to neatly categorize these pregnancies as they are often the result of many influences. Nevertheless, one factor can often be seen to dominate. In a book designed for both counsellors and medical staff we hope that running through these causes will be a useful journey for both and a chance for mutual learning and understanding. We look first at the more obvious factors which are involved in generating pregnancies and are usually the concern of health care workers. We then move on to see how the woman's own internal difficulties, more commonly of interest to therapists, can be the source of pregnancy. Although we concentrate on the external factors initially, we are not blind to the emotional facets that are present in every woman and will have individual impact on the resulting pregnancy.

FERTILITY/LUCK

Pregnancy is the logical end result of unprotected sex. On average there is a one in three chance of getting pregnant if sex occurs around the time of ovulation. A fertile couple have a 10 per cent chance of a pregnancy if they have sex once a month rising to 30 per cent when intercourse occurs two or three times a week. Many couples take risks and 'get away with it'. The women who become unhappily pregnant could therefore be called unlucky. The couples who are most likely to be unlucky will be young, with increased fertility, and having frequent sex. Ironically, they may be the very couples who are most distressed by a pregnancy. However, we witness many 'unlucky' women who become pregnant at their one and only risky episode.

> Jane attended the clinic having missed a period. She was not really 'worried' but had been advised to attend by a friend. She had not had intercourse with her boyfriend yet, but they enjoyed heavy petting. On one occassion Jason had 'come between her legs'. This unlucky incident was enough to cause her unwanted pregnancy.

BIRTH CONTROL

There is still no Utopian method of birth control. Unfortunately, there is often an inverse relationship between the the technical effectiveness of the method (which is measured in pregnancy rates) and dangerous or troublesome side-effects. Many women choose not to use hormonal contraception or an Intra Uterine Device (IUD) which can offer the most protection. These women will include those who are concerned about their bodies and their physical well-being as well as others who have religious or medical objections. Couples may need to rely solely on natural family planning, withdrawal or barrier methods which entail much planning and forethought without offering the same security as hormonal or other methods, even when used consistently. Barrier methods bring their own disadvantages, expressed in the often stated remark about condoms, 'It's like making love with a boot on'.

No method of contraception is perfect and even with the best will in the world the most conscientious of couples can be let down.

FAILURE OF METHOD

The following table shows a woman's risk of pregnancy in one year.

As can be seen from the table there are considerable variations of the failure rates between those couples who use their chosen method carefully and those who are less stringent. For example, out of every 100 women who use a diaphragm carefully and consistently in the first year between four and eight are

Table 1.1 Risk of pregnancy in any one-year period

Method of birth control	Pregnancy risk
No contraception	over 80%
Sponge	10% with careful use (25% with less careful use)
Diaphragm and cap, with spermicide	4%–8% (10%–18% with less careful use)
Natural methods – charting temperature	2%–20%
Male/female condom	2% (2%–15% with less careful use)
IUD	1%–2%
Progestogene-only pill	1% (4% with less careful use)
Combined pill	< 1% (3% with less careful use)
Implant	< 1% for first year, 2% over 5 years)
Injectable	< 1%
Female sterilisation	0.1–0.3% failure ever
Male sterilisation	0.1% failure ever

Source: GP magazine November 11 1984

likely to get pregnant. However, among typical users who do not use the method so carefully every single time, between ten and eighteen are likely to get pregnant (Bounds 1994: 84–7).

No matter how effective they are as contraceptives, all methods become useless when they are not used or not used properly. Couples can be caught out by the demands of the diaphragm and condom which need to be used each time intercourse occurs. Regular pill taking may seem too complicated and be given up, as may the IUD because of side-effects or feared side-effects. Although some studies give the combined pill a failure rate of less than 1 per cent, this typically rises to 3 per cent because of less consistent use. At its worst, the pill failure rate is reported to be as high as 20 per cent (Guillebaud 1993: 401). Two examples of contraceptive failure are given here.

> Lesley could not take the combined pill due to medical reasons. She decided to use the mini-pill and condoms for contraception. Over the following six months she used both methods carefully. She came to the clinic as she was worried that she had had a condom accident earlier that month and had then missed a period. She had not come to the centre for emergency contraception at that time because she understandably felt that she was protected by the pill. She was upset to find that she was pregnant. She had been doubly unlucky in that the mini-pill had failed her too although she had followed instructions carefully.

> Andrea had had an IUD fitted two years earlier and had been happy to 'forget' about contraception. She was shocked to discover it had failed her and that she had become pregnant. She had believed the IUD could offer complete protection and was very angry and disappointed to have been let down like this.

FAILURE OF PROVIDER

Family planning providers may inadvertently also be one of the accessories in causing accidental pregnancies. John Guillebaud in his book, *Contraception Your Questions Answered*, gives a startling still unfinished list of more than thirty ways medical and nursing staff fail their patients, leaving them at risk of unwanted pregnancies (Guillebaud 1993).

When a packet of pills is given to a young woman without an explanation of what to do if she misses one, or condoms are handed to a young person for the first time without instruction, pregnancies are bound to occur. We need to be sure that people are given adequate information both verbal and written, in a relaxed atmosphere. It is important that there is time for questions to be asked and to double-check what facts the doctor or nurse thinks the women are taking away with them.

It can be very salutary to ask a young woman who says she has already understood the method perfectly, what she would do if she misses a pill and to find in fact she has no idea of the correct action to take.

Sue arrived at a clinic requesting a pregnancy test. She had been taking the pill regularly and had not missed any and was very distressed to have a positive result. On questioning it turned out that she had been given a course of antibiotics that interfered with the take-up of the pill and left her unprotected. Sue had either not been warned of this or if she had, she had not absorbed this piece of vital information.

Mary was pregnant. She had been put on the pill but had unpleasant side-effects, irregular bleeding and some nausea. She had not been advised about this possibility and had been frightened, and so she stopped the pill mid-packet without thinking of alternative methods of contraception.

THE MEDIA

Whereas family planning staff may neglect to give information to a few individuals, irresponsible press reporting can have an enormous impact on abortion rates. In Holland, for example, following the pill panic in the early 1980s which was inflamed by media attention, it took some five years to restore the very low abortion figures (Doppenberg 1994). It remains to be seen how the pill panic of October 1995 concerning the newer 'third-generation pills' will effect the year's abortion figures in the UK. Dr Ann Szarewski, Senior Clinical Medical Officer at the Margaret Pyke Centre, was quoted on the front page of the *Guardian*,

> The effect of this is going to be absolute chaos. All these women who have been told this is the best pill to take are suddenly being thrown completely and told they are more dangerous . . . women will stop taking the pill in droves.
>
> (*Guardian* 20 October 1995)

Preliminary figures sadly seem to confirm this prophecy. The BPAS (British Pregnancy Advisory Service) report 'Outcome of the Contraceptive Pill Announcement' published in April 1996 estimates that there may have been up to an extra 3,700 abortions nationwide between December 1995 and February 1996. It found that more than 60 per cent of the women attending with an unplanned pregnancy had failed to finish their current pill's course following the CSM (Committee on Safety in Medicines) announcement. The report also found that 4 months after the announcement, 60 per cent of pill users attending family planning clinics were still concerned about continuing its use.

Kylie came to ask for a pregnancy test. The doctor was suprised as Kylie had been happily taking Femodene contraceptive pill for the previous two years. Kylie said she had stopped Femodene the day she saw a frightening headline in *The Sunday Times*, 'Teenage Deaths Linked to Contraceptive Pill' (*The Sunday Times* 7 May 1995). She had been so panicked that she had thrown the rest of her packet away. Unfortunately Kylie was indeed pregnant, and requested a termination.

ACCESSIBILITY AND SETTING

Particularly for the young, the accessibility of a clinic and the assurance of confidentiality are of paramount importance. Having to come for contraceptive advice is an agonizing hurdle for many, but by ensuring that the clinic is as welcoming as possible, unnecessary anxiety can be alleviated. Time should be allowed for people to have their concerns heard and for things to be explained in their language. Men can feel out of place in a busy clinic and they too should be encouraged and respected for sharing contraceptive responsibility. The health care worker acts as a guide, helping people decide on their chosen method rather than knowing what is best for them.

Providers must be able to give correct, up-to-date information in a way that can be understood and acted on. The way we give this information and how we behave in a consultation can determine whether a particular form of contraception can be used. For example, a doctor's concern about the possible abusive element in giving long-acting hormonal injectibles meant that she was unhappy about ever prescribing this even when women themselves thought it was right for them.

Clinics must be run at times that suit their clients and must be geared up to be free for emergency appointments. It is sad to be with an unintentionally pregnant woman who knew about emergency contraception and indeed tried to make an appointment but was thwarted by inflexibility and embarrassment at having to explain the emergency to an unsympathetic receptionist. At present there is a call to deregulate emergency contraception so that it will be available at the chemist. While this may mean there is less opportunity for the doctor to advise on future contraception, it would remove one of the obstacles to obtaining post-coital contraception and so lead to a reduction in the abortion rates. As noted in the *British Medical Journal*:

> About 70% of unwanted pregnancies are predictable because the woman realises that she is at risk after unplanned intercourse or an accident with a condom. In such cases emergency contraception offers a 98% chance of preventing pregnancy. . . . Surveys of women with unwanted pregnancies have shown that 70% knew about emergency contraception but only 3% tried to use it.
>
> (Owen Drife 1993: 695–6)

Most people see their family doctors for contraception and are happy to do so. However, there are many times when complementary services are vital. Again we have mainly the young in mind. No matter how reassuring the GP may be, girls remain frightened of confidentiality being broken. They are scared that they may meet neighbours while in the waiting room who will be able to guess why they are there, or will innocently tell their mothers that they saw their daughter at the doctor's. This situation is intensified in small communities. For example:

Phillipa was pregnant. She had had unprotected sex and had bravely made an appointment with her GP the next day for emergency contraception. She told her mum she was at her friend's. While in the waiting room she saw one of her mum's friends. She was terrified that the woman would see her and bolted out of the surgery.

The well-run family planning clinic within general practice also poses its own problems as then everyone will know exactly why a young woman has come. There is often much confusion in a young person's mind, sometimes mirrored by the doctor since the Gillick case (see Chapter 3), about their legal position and the right to confidentiality.

A survey organized by *World in Action* and the Family Planning Association in 1993 showed that 42 per cent of under 16-year-old girls thought it was illegal for them to get contraception and that their parents would be told. Apparently, one in three GPs thought the same.

Many young people find it difficult to negotiate the change to an adult relationship with their doctor who may well have known them from infancy and they would therefore prefer to go to an outside agency. A study in the *BMJ* confirmed that those districts where clinics played a large part in delivering a contraceptive service had a lower conception rate for teenagers. It concludes, 'Family planning clinics are an essential component of an effective contraceptive service for teenagers' (Allaby 1995: 1643). Since the cuts of the 1980s community-based clinics have been in danger with reduced funding, ever diminishing resources and threats of closure.

Penny was pregnant. She was under 16 and getting condoms from a clinic. Over the Christmas break she had a condom accident and needed emergency contraception. She came to the clinic but on finding it closed did not dare go elsewhere.

Anita was brought to the clinic by a teacher to whom she had confessed that she thought she was pregnant. Although Anita had wanted to use contraception she had been too frightened to go to her GP who was a family friend. She had been scared that he would tell her mother, particularly as she was not quite 16. She did not know about the young person's clinic and the confidentiality that it could offer. She knew she had taken a risk but had not found the resources to help.

The need for young people to be assured of confidentiality is absolute; young people are known to prefer to risk a pregnancy than run the risk of confidentiality being broken.

LACK OF KNOWLEDGE

There are many couples who do not want a pregnancy yet still have sex without using any contraception. Frequently women only come to the doctor or clinic for the first time when they are already pregnant or think they are. Approximately 25 per cent of first medical appointments at the Brandon Centre are for a pregnancy test (50 per cent are for emergency contraception). Ann Phoenix found that more than 80 per cent of her sample of teenage mothers had not planned to get pregnant and nor had they used contraception (Guillebaud 1993: 401).

One of the major influences on this seemingly cavalier attitude must be the myths and ignorance regarding sex that abound in Britain today. In this the media has an unenviable place. It glamorizes and tantalizes people with sexual imagery and at the same time seeks to condemn those who have broken society's code.

Young women still come to pregnancy centres saying that they did not know they could get pregnant the first time they had sex, or if they were drunk, under 16 or if they made love standing up, and frequently that they never believed that it could happen to them. It can be difficult to assess how much of this is true ignorance or a way of trying to excuse themselves from the consequences of their behaviour.

RISK TAKING

Risk taking is often part and parcel of being a teenager. The burden of needing to use contraception effectively each time sex occurs gives many golden opportunities for taking risks.

A model of looking at risk taking was developed by Kristen Luker in her book *Taking Chances: Abortion and the Decision Not to Contracept* which was the result of a detailed study of 500 women requesting abortion. She proposed the theory that many women execute a barely conscious weighing up of the costs and benefits of contraception or of becoming pregnant. The decision whether to use contraception will therefore depend on first, the estimated risk of pregnancy, which may be based on misinformation, and then the relative costs and benefits of these alternatives (Luker 1975).

Eileen was pregnant. She described her feelings thus to the doctor: 'I wasn't using anything, I didn't dare go to the surgery, I was sure he'd tell my mum. Anyway where could I hide contraceptives at home. We hardly ever did it anyway, I really thought I'd get away with it. Now I'm pregnant it's not so bad, Ian will stand by me and I didn't want to stay on at school anyway'.

People may of course sometimes be influenced by drugs and alcohol which can reinforce denial, trusting luck and the belief – 'It can't happen to me'. There may be very little realistic sense of the likelihood of their becoming pregnant, and this of course becomes self-perpetuating as the longer the luck lasts the more risks the couple may take. The end result of this can be a couple worrying that there is something wrong with them until they have a pregnancy which is then terminated.

Beverly and Charles arrived at the clinic and were shocked to discover that Beverly was pregnant. 'How could this have happened?' was the message they seemed to impart to the doctor – 'we've been having sex for the past six months and this has never happened before'.

A visit to the doctor for contraception can be embarrassing as well as an admission that having sex is a distinct possibility. This act can force a young woman to accept herself as a sexual person, a view of herself that she may be unwilling to face. When sex occurs unplanned and by chance she can continue to deny her sexuality. She may imagine that others will view this request to be a sign of promiscuity. She may not want to admit to 'being that sort of girl' and so will remain unprepared.

Frequently teenage pregnancies occur in the first few months of sexual activity, with the riskiest time being the first month. Younger teenagers often delay contraceptive use until they have become more sexually experienced and are fully able to acknowledge their sexuality.

Jenny came to the centre asking for a pregnancy test as her period was overdue. She was a sensible girl who admitted she 'knew' all about contraception but had gone to a party and had too much to drink. Before she knew what was happening she was having sex with a boy she hardly knew. She said that she had no idea she would end up doing that and the idea of being able to prepare herself was impossible. She was totally inexperienced and not in a position to negotiate her safety. The pregnancy test was negative and Jenny was able to use this lucky escape as a spring-board to more care in the future.

SOCIETAL PRESSURES

Society traps both sexes into behaving in stereotypical, role-related ways. Boys are encouraged by their peers to behave irresponsibly and to notch up their successes (this stereotype can be challenged through good sex education), and girls are expected by parents and society to control how far he goes. Even in the 1990s, the era of AIDS, a girl can still end up feeling like a 'slag' if she carries a condom. How can she deny that sex isn't a possibility when she carries her own condoms? This quandary offers a partial explanation as to why 50 per cent of under 16-year-olds do not use any contraception the first time they have sex (Johnson *et al.* 1994).

Sex, as we all know, is exciting and can easily become passionately out of control. As Christopher writes: 'sexual activity is often impulsive and not planned for, tied up as it is with powerful and often overwhelming drives and emotions (sex is hot) whereas the use of contraception requires forethought and conscious effort (contraception is cold)' (Christopher 1993: 441). A young couple may not expect to have sex but can be literally carried away by the intensity of sexual desire, and momentarily 'forget' anything else. Under the spell of moonlight and roses, they may find it downright boring or just too embarrassing to have to discuss contraception. Failure to use contraception is therefore definitely more likely at the beginning of a relationship!

Sometimes using no contraception can be a test of love and commitment. A couple may enjoy the romance that the willingness to accept all consequences will engender. Curiosity about sex or the wish to cement her relationship with her boyfriend may also tip a young girl into having unprotected sex.

A girl may also be put in an agonizing double bind by her boyfriend, who may demand sex, particularly if she is worried about her attractiveness to him. Paradoxically, peer pressure and the belief that all her friends are doing it may drive a girl to experiment sexually before she is ready. These young girls may be particularly at risk from an unintended pregnancy as they are less likely to have the maturity to organize contraception. Teenagers have the tendency to overestimate the sexual experience of their peers and frequently end up attempting to conform to a false norm.

> Christine was rather isolated and lonely, always on the outside of a group of rather precocious friends. She had unprotected sex with her 'boyfriend' at a very young age in order to feel part of the gang. She ended up pregnant feeling more alone and unsupported than ever.

Over the past thirty years in Britain, attitudes and beliefs about pre-marital sex have changed beyond recognition. During these years the advent of the pill as an effective contraceptive, free since 1975, gave women a right to sexual expression for the first time without the fear of pregnancy. This climate has led to ever-decreasing ages of first sexual intercourse. The median age that young women now experience sexual intercourse is four years earlier than for those born four decades earlier, falling from 21 to 17. The *National Survey of Sexual Attitudes and Lifestyles* showed that 18.7 per cent of women and 27.6 per cent of men aged 16–19 had experienced intercourse before the age of 16. Four decades earlier fewer than 6 per cent of 15-year-old boys and 1 per cent of girls of the same age had had intercourse (Johnson *et al.* 1994).

Concern over HIV, cervical cancer, emotional trauma, etc. has not turned the clock back, although there is certainly a powerful moral backlash including the American chastity or 'Proud to be a virgin' type campaigns.

Society has always been frightened of what it sees as wild adolescent sexual desires and their unacceptable consequences. Throughout history different strategies have been developed to try to minimize the dangers seen in early sexuality. In some parts of the world this has involved arranging very early marriage and, in others, extreme segregation of the sexes in adolescence. Such strategies are not commonly used in the West as they are impracticable in our culture. However, a relatively high proportion of the women we see will be under their influence.

In the West we have been dictated to in the past by a sexual morality that kept us controlled through fear, shame and guilt. This was fuelled by moral and religious teaching which taught that sex was something basically sinful. Sex was never for pleasure but purely for procreation. These unhealthy messages managed to control some of our natural desires but have a devastating side-effect. There are generations of people who are unhappy about their bodies and find sex dirty, and pass these messages on in turn to their children.

SEX EDUCATION

One way of challenging both the difficult aspects of sexuality and the damaging legacy of moralizing messages would be to face teenage sexuality and to encourage positive responsible behaviour in both girls and boys. At the moment we are struggling between the old repressive attitudes and the openness that facing sexuality dictates.

This division can nowhere be seen better than in our laws around the age of consent and the whole area of sex education which seems to have become the symbol of our present dilemma. On the one hand, we have the knowledge that many of our young people are sexually active and, on the other, the 'illegality' of a teacher directing a pupil to a family planning agency or giving any advice.

Sex education has become a battleground with the 'moral Right' believing that sex is solely a moral issue and that birth control, abortion and even education are major causes of teenage sexuality. They think that discussion may even encourage young people to behave in ways that might otherwise not have occurred to them. Liberal family planners argue that effective sex education, backed by good birth control and abortion services, enables young people to make informed decisions about their own sexuality. They point out that the American abstinence-based sex education movement, which asks for a pledge of chastity till marriage, can leave those who 'can't' totally unprepared and more at risk. As Doreen Massey, former FPA Director, points out: 'It is ironic that we should look to a country with the highest teenage pregnancy rate in the Western World for the way forward' (Massey 1994).

In England, in spring 1994 the controversy surrounding sex education raged on. This was further fuelled by the moralizing of the then Education Minister, John Patten, who even at one point suggested the streaming of children for sex education. Every day newspaper headlines reported an endless litany of uncertainty and editorials fell on one side or the other of the divide. Early in 1994 a book, *Your Pocket Guide to Sex*, was comissioned by the Health Education Authority and written by a popular agony uncle, Nick Fisher, who was in touch with the concerns and language of young people. This book was withdrawn (but later published by Penguin) after it had been descibed as 'smutty' by Dr Brian Mawhinney, the then Health Minister. In another incident a nurse was pilloried over answering questions honestly about oral sex in a primary school. There was a furious reaction to the fact that nurses were giving out condoms to underage girls in a deprived area in Birmingham where there was a high incidence of teenage pregnancy.

In the USA matters came to a head when the Surgeon General, Jocelyn Elders, was forced to resign by President Bill Clinton in December 1994 for what was reported as her saying that masturbation should be taught in schools. She was in fact asked whether masturbation should be encouraged as a way to prevent infectious diseases and said:

> As to your specific question in regard to masturbation, I think that it is something that is part of human sexuality, and it is part of something that perhaps should be taught. But we've not even taught our children the very basics. I feel that we have tried ignorance for a very long time and it is time we try education.
>
> (Roberts 1994: 1604)

The reality of this improvised answer to a question at a UN conference on AIDS disappeared in the climate of moral outrage.

The National Survey of Sexual Attitudes and Life-styles (Johnson *et al.* 1994) has now confirmed that those children who had received formal sex education in school had the lowest rate of sexual activity under the age of 16, that being 7 per cent for females and 10 per cent for males.

The data gained from this enormous study clearly refutes the assumption that sex education encourages young people to experiment earlier; in fact it appears to postpone sexual activity. The World Health Organization's authoritative review of thirty-five studies also showed that sex education programmes often either delayed the start of intercourse and/or increased the adoption of safer practices (Baldo, *et al.* 1993)

In England and Wales there has been new legislation in force from August 1994 regarding sex education in schools. The government states its intention to provide comprehensive sex education for all pupils during their school career. The guidance stresses the need for all sex education to be set in a moral framework and promotes marriage and fidelity: 'Pupils should be encouraged to appreciate the value of stable family life, marriage and the responsibilities of parenthood' (Department for Education 1994).

Sex education has not been made compulsory in primary schools. It remains the responsibility of the school governors to decide whether the school will include sex education within the curriculum. This policy allows the more conservative presence on the board of governors to have a very restricting influence over any sex education programme.

In secondary schools, governors must ensure that education about HIV/AIDS and other sexually transmitted diseases is provided for all pupils in sex education classes. These aspects are removed from the science curriculum.

However, parents have the right to withdraw pupils from any sex education other than that in the National Curriculum which now only includes biological facts about sex.

Family planners would argue that sex education should be an integral part of school life from infant school onwards and questions and discussion should be sensitively dealt with in an age-appropriate way. Sex education should no longer be merely biological but holistic and cover general life-skills. It should enhance the ability of young people to feel good about themselves and their bodies, raise self-esteem and encourage the learning of assertiveness and negotiating skills. It should give a foundation from which both boys and girls would learn about relationships generally, and how to respect the rights and feelings of others. From that secure base they would be able to progress to sexual relationships feeling sure of themselves and their contraception.

This is more than a pipe dream. We could learn some lessons from the Dutch, who have the lowest abortion rate in the world as well as the most sex education and the most sexually permissive laws. Teenagers in Holland have one-seventh the UK conception rate. In Holland, it is legal for a girl to have sex when she is 12 and yet on average Dutch girls have their first sexual experience slightly later than their British counterpart at 17½ as compared to 17.

Research from the Guttmacher Institute confirms that the characteristics of the countries with the lowest teenage pregnancy rates are liberal attitudes towards sex, easily accessible contraceptive services for teenagers and effective formal and informal programmes of sex education. The figures from the Office of Population Census and Surveys (OPCS) show that the UK still tops the table for teenage pregnancies in Western Europe and that the US has the highest teenage pregnancy rate in the world.

At a recent conference on teenage pregnancy, a Dutch speaker said:

the trouble with you is that sex is a secret, and that you don't want your children to have sex. In Holland, we enjoy sex and want our children to as well, therefore we talk about it and prepare them.

This attitude stands in such marked contrast to the embarrassment and shame that haunts many parents in Britain when they talk to their children about sex. The Schools' Health Education Unit (28 March 1994), which questioned 29,000 children, showed that while more than half the teenagers thought their parents should be their main source of information about sex, only 15 per cent of boys and 22 per cent of girls between 15 and 16 look to their parents for this information, compared with 34 per cent of youngsters who find out from their friends. The knowledge gained in this way is often full of misunderstanding and inaccuracy and usually leads to earlier sexual experimenting. When children are able to talk openly to their parents about sex they are less likely to experience early sexual activity and more likely to use contraception. The vast majority of young people, 70–80 per cent, would like to have more sex education and feel they do not know enough (Johnson *et al.* 1994).

Britain is a multiracial, multicultural society and obviously sex education must be sensitively applied so that it can be relevant to all young people's needs and identities. This must include those shaped by religion and ethnicity. In 1990 the Sex Education Forum found ignorance and uncertainty among schools concerning the religious and cultural beliefs of young people and those of their families, a significant barrier to the provision of sex education. This is the challenge that schools now need to meet.

It can be particularly difficult for children brought up under the influence of two cultures. While their families retain their traditional values, the children are assimilating Western ideas through friends, media and school.

Jasmine arrived in a state of terror. She was a 15-year-old Bengali girl and had been having illicit sex with her secret boyfriend on and off for the past year. The only time she could meet him was during school and she had been weaving a complicated web of lies to both school and home in order to meet with him about once a month.

Jasmine was unhappy at home, was failing at school and only felt wanted and happy for the brief times she was with him. Jasmine's pregnancy test was negative, it turned out that her periods were not yet properly established. The doctor tried to use the opportunity that this presented to discuss how Jasmine could protect herself in the future. It became more and more of a battle with each method of contraception being rejected. There was no way Jasmine could discuss condoms with her boyfriend; the pill was out of the question as it could be discovered. At one point during the consultation the doctor nearly ended up agreeing that maybe abortion was the only form of 'birth control' that was practical.

Eventually the doctor managed to suggest that perhaps all methods of contraception were unsuitable when a girl didn't feel it was right to have sex. This was met with extreme relief and the agony of Jasmine's dangerous position was fully revealed. There could be no immediate resolution to her dilemma but she knew she now had a safe place to come and talk. When she left, the doctor felt a little happier that they would meet again in a more thoughtful way so that perhaps the crisis of an unwanted pregnancy could be avoided.

OPPRESSION

Unwanted pregnancy can also of course be due to assault through rape whether by a stranger, marital or incestuous. These extremely distressing causes of pregnancy will be studied in more detail in Chapter 6.

EMOTIONAL CAUSES OF AMBIVALENT PREGNANCY

This section focuses on the more hidden causes and symbolic meanings of an ambivalent pregnancy. Pregnancy can be a sign of distress and may also have a purpose, it can often be an imagined solution to complex personal problems. It is important to make sense of the multifactorial unconscious or preconscious influences that can be involved in these pregnancies but also to avoid unhelpful generalizations. It is often possible to recognize patterns and hear the unspoken message that can be behind the pregnancy, both for the individual and for society. In this section we aim to give many clinical examples of relevant material so as to best illustrate each point.

Unwanted pregnancy in a teenager can have a huge significance. The battles of adolescence seem to frequently involve sex, pregnancy and abortion. This particular area of confrontation involves conflict and rebellion alongside the wish to remain connected and the painful search for independence and a separate identity.

As Petchesky writes:

Whatever the outcome, it is clear that at least during a particular stage, a pregnancy and its resolution represent a critical struggle for power and control between young women and their parents and between them and their male partners. Working through this struggle is an emotionally charged, powerfully affecting experience that usually leaves teenage girls feeling older, transformed, on the other side of childhood. Notice, however, that they are active participants in constructing the sexual terms of the struggle and not just passive victims.

(Petchesky 1986: 223)

Anna was just 16 when she came for a pregnancy test which confirmed that she was indeed pregnant. She was tearful and the doctor was acutely aware of her deep concern for this young girl. She described an extremely unhappy home situation, comprising of her mother, little half-brother and mother's boyfriend of one year whom she hated. Anna's own father had disappeared when she was 2, she had made a good relationship with her stepfather but he too had left three years ago. Anna had got on okay with her mother until about ten months ago. Anna thought this was when she herself started going out with James, whom her mother disliked. Anna said this was only because he was Black. Anna was hurt by this and was planning to leave home to get away from such racists. Anna's obvious love for James seemed an incredibly powerful statement of independence from the fetters of her childhood. However, focusing so intently on her mother in the session, she also showed how entangled this relationship truly was.

Samantha came requesting a pregnancy test which was positive. It transpired that her mother was dying of cancer and although Samantha had taken the pill reliably for the past year she had forgotten several in the last month since hearing the news. Samantha had always been close to her mother but now she was dying Samantha could hardly be in the same room as her. She went out constantly just to escape from the unbearable feelings. She wanted her boyfriend to be with her all the time, and could hardly stand it now when he went to work. Becoming pregnant shook Samantha but as she talked she came to realize how she had somehow hoped that a 'new life' would make things better, and allow her a way out of facing death.

After two sad sessions Samantha decided to have a termination. She decided that a new baby could not make up in any way for her mother's death. She wanted to but wasn't sure whether she could spend more time with her mum in her last few weeks. She was offered continued support.

Laura, aged 16, came to the clinic requesting a termination as she had had a positive home pregnancy test. She admitted to unprotected sex with her long-standing boyfriend. Laura's mother was a single parent herself who became pregnant with Laura when she was also just 16. They had been having many arguments recently and these usually ended with Laura's mum screaming that she wished she had never had Laura. She should have taken other people's advice and got rid of her. Laura was distraught at her pregnancy. For obvious reasons she had always been anti-abortion but now she also discovered that she wanted to continue her studies and not end up like her mother. She had her abortion without her mother's knowledge and with a lot of insight and sadness. She still comes to the clinic three years later and has had no further problems with contraception.

A pregnancy may be an attempt to get a distant parent's attention, perhaps the girl has already failed to do so through other methods. It is at least a very visible way of getting noticed, and there is the hope that this could be used to look at some of the underlying distress. When only the abortion is dealt with and not the underlying problems then nothing has changed for the girl and the opportunity for understanding and growth has been wasted.

Jill, aged 15, was brought to the surgery by her mother when she was already fourteen weeks pregnant. Jill's parents had divorced four years previously. While her mother fell into a spiral of despair with no space for anything but her abandonment, Jill's father, who had originally kept in close contact, was now heavily into new fatherhood with his second wife. Jill had apparently become more and more withdrawn during the past few months and was doing badly at school. It seemed to take the crisis of this unwanted pregnancy for Jill's mother to notice that her daughter was also suffering.

Christopher points out that:

a pregnancy may happen when the woman or girl is faced with a difficult or painful choice e.g. staying on at school, going to college, finding a job, or where there are conflicts with the partner or the family (particularly in the case of teenagers). Thus a woman may hope that the pregnancy will free her from taking responsibilities for the choice or will resolve conflicts with the partner or family. However, once the pregnancy has occurred, the reality of coping with a child may be too great and abortion requested.

(Christopher 1987: 279).

Sally had planned to travel for a year before going to university. She had been excited about it all year, the chance to travel being her crutch as she prepared for 'A' levels. She was surprised to miss a period and find that she was pregnant a few days before she was due to leave. She acknowledged being careless recently about condom usage. She decided to have a termination and left for India a little later than planned. She spoke in her session before the termination of how scared she was about going and surviving in India on her own but how she had felt unable to share this 'weakness' with her family and friends. A pregnancy would have successfully sabotaged this trip meaning she no longer had to face the difficulties about leaving home.

One of the most poignant reasons for a pregnancy is when a baby is seen as being able to give the answer to feeling unloved and uncared for. The future baby (and the baby in fantasy which never seems to grow but always remains a baby) is seen only as a passive recipient for the girl's desires and needs. The baby fails to be seen as separate, so by identifying with the baby, a girl can give it everything she never had.

For a girl having an idea of a foetus being part of herself, of her own nourishment, and inseparable as a distinct being, may blur her own boundaries; having a baby to nourish and nuture may be like nourishing her still infantile self or being nutured again by her own mother. In this way she may express the need to remain mum's cared for and dependent child.

(Group for the Advancement of Psychiatry: 11)

Young women may come to the centre requesting a pregnancy test. They usually wish to have their 'baby' but sometimes the confrontation with reality may eventually lead them to request a termination.

Lesley, aged 15, and John, aged 23, arrived hoping that Lesley was pregnant. They never used any contraception and were disappointed that the test was negative. Lesley had been in care from a very young age and had no contact with her mother. Lesley told the doctor that her ambition was to be a mummy. When questioned, John, who had also been brought up in children's homes, said that he just wanted to be a mummy too! During the session the reality of having an actual baby was discussed and to the doctor's surprise, they suddenly decided that Lesley was too young to have a baby and that she should take the pill.

The very next month, however, they returned and this time the test was positive. They left the centre joyfully and have not been seen again. It seemed sad to the doctor that in this case the drive to repair something that Lesley had missed had been too powerful to challenge in the short time allowed. The doctor was also aware of all her own prejudices and concerns about being a mother so young. It could just be possible that having a baby would prove a route through which Lesley would be able to discover who she was and be able to move on.

Anne-Marie was 14. She had been subjected to an apalling childhood, and her needs had never been attended to. She had been on the pill for six months when she suddenly decided to stop taking it as only a baby now could make her feel happy. She wanted to give it everything she had been deprived of and she wanted a baby to love her. In fantasy she wanted to punish her parents by showing them how it should be done.

There are however, many other instances when getting pregnant and having a baby is a 'positive' conscious choice in a young girl who has suffered from social disadvantages, poor education and has little prospect of fulfilling employment. There may seem little point in delaying motherhood if you have no hope of much else from life.

Some women have a remarkable sense of fatalism, as though there is no point using contraception anyway as what will be will be. They have lost or never had any sense of power or control over their lives, and a pregnancy can just seem to happen. This needs to be understood and challenged to make any effective birth control acceptable.

Maureen came to the centre with her 6-month-old baby Zoe. She had come requesting a termination during that pregnancy but was too late in attending for this to be performed. Her baby's arrival seemed to make no difference to her life-style, which included all-night raves and drugs. After delivery Maureen had attended the clinic once only as she had a pelvic infection. At the time she agreed she wanted to avoid another pregnancy and would start on the pill. She did not attend for a further supply although she was sent several reminders.

This time Maureen was sixteen weeks pregnant and she asked again for a termination. While Maureen gave every impression of not minding at all what was happening to her body, the doctor who felt she had informed Maureen fully about contraception, was upset and angry that she had been put in a position of having to arrange a late termination. Later the doctor was able to reflect on the damage that Maureen herself must have suffered which caused such intense splitting-off of parts of herself and subsequent coldness.

Some women may be concerned that they are infertile and this can precipitate a pregnancy needed for its reassurance value.

Nancy had been through a turbulent adolescence, lack of caring for herself during her teens had resulted in two terminations and an episode of gonorrhoea. She had taken on board the messages that her fertility could be affected which she felt would be a deserved punishment for her past mistakes. She was now 23 and in a steady relationship. She was no longer able to stand the agony of not knowing if she could get pregnant, nor was she able to verbalize the distress, so she started having unprotected sex while her boyfriend still thought she was taking the pill. She got her answer to her doubts when she became pregnant and after some initial euphoria had to face up to the fact that she was still not yet in a position to be a mother. She decided to have a termination and also for the first time started being able to reflect and talk about herself.

Suzanne and John came to the centre together to discuss contraception. They had complaints about every 'conceivable' method and had given up using any. Eventually, Suzanne told the doctor about a riding accident that she had when she was a little girl. She remembered doctors talking about internal damage and thought she could never have a baby. She had been to her GP to ask for fertility investigations but had been told to wait until she wanted to get pregnant.

During the examination Suzanne was able to talk about the fears of the damage done to her 'insides' and seemed to relax visibly as these were discussed and her fears allayed. The doctor, however, thought Suzanne's uterus was slightly enlarged and Suzanne then admitted that her period was overdue. It transpired that she was already pregnant. This was an enormous shock to her and she decided to have a termination because she did not want a baby now.

For other women a pregnancy can give reassurance of femininity, attractiveness and proof of sexual initiation. As Dinora Pines writes: 'there is a marked distinction between the wish to become pregnant and the wish to bring a live child into the world and become a mother' (Pines 1993: 97).

Achieving pregnancy may be the only way a woman can feel purposeful or loved by her boyfriend. Equally, a man may need to prove his virility by making his girlfriend pregnant. This will more readily occur if he feels or is a failure in other areas of his life, and so therefore is related to low self-esteem, isolation, poor education and unemployment.

Simon arrived with his girlfriend Sheila. While he looked delighted, Sheila was upset when she discovered she was pregnant. They had been having unprotected sex as Sheila had been told Simon was infertile. Simon was the youngest of a large family, he had always been small, and was constantly picked on by his family and friends. He had done badly at school and was now on a youth training scheme that he hated. He seemed to grow visibly on hearing that he had managed to impregnate his girlfriend, as though now at last he had proved he was a man. Sheila decided to have a termination and the relationship broke up soon after.

RELATIONSHIP PROBLEMS

Problems in relationships may make themselves known through a pregnancy. As always, it seems that the risk of pregnancy is greatest at the most inconvenient times. This generalization includes those who are just starting out and do not think it worth using permanent contraception. The failing, unstable relationship is also a danger time since contraception is less likely to be used. Difficult feelings that truly belong to the relationship may also be displaced onto the contraceptive method so that it is no longer used.

> Marie stopped the pill as she didn't want to have sex any more with her boyfriend. However, she was unable to properly end the relationship. She unexpectedly agreed to sex one evening, which was unprotected and a pregnancy resulted.

Sporadic use of any contraception is also likely to occur in relationships in which both partners are fighting for control. In the commonest scenario a man may refuse to take any responsibility for contraception. The woman may then feel powerless and resentful and this resentment in turn can lead to difficulties in choosing and using any contraception.

> Rosemary and Jim had two young children and had, they thought, completed their family. Rosemary had been on the pill for many years and she thought it time Jim did something. Jim initially agreed to have a vasectomy but eventually chickened out. Rosemary was furious and refused to go on taking the pill. Their relationship deteriorated and sex became less and less frequent, occurring only during the safe time of the month. The impasse ended when Rosemary became pregnant.

A pregnancy may be used to try and trap the other into commitment when there are fears about the future. Sometimes an insecure man will try to keep his partner permanently pregnant in order to keep her dependent. It can be a last-ditch effort to try and patch up or keep a relationship alive, only to be despaired of a short time later.

> Sharon came requesting a termination. Over the past few months, Paul had been very moody and 'always ready to pick a quarrel'. Sharon somehow hoped that having a baby would make everything all right again. However, the news of her pregnancy didn't have the desired effect on Paul. He called her a 'cow' for trying to trap him and ended the relationship. Faced now with an unwanted pregnancy, Sharon asked for a termination.

The quality of the relationships a woman makes tells a great deal about how she feels about herself, and this will affect whether contraception is used. Birth control cannot be seen in isolation; when people are not able to plan for their future generally, they are less likely to use contraception. Risk factors that make it more likely for a woman not to bother and to forgo adequate contraception are loneliness and low self-esteem. When one feels empty through perhaps missing a good enough early experience, sex can be one way of trying to fill the hole and gain love and acceptance. In the neverending search for perfect love, promiscuity can develop with increasing pregnancy risks.

Sheila was only 15, yet had been coming to the centre for contraception for over two years. She would regale the doctor with stories of her latest conquests. There was always a new boyfriend who she was convinced loved her like she had never been loved before. Meanwhile the previous love would be tipped into oblivion. The doctor became more and more concerned over the risks of both pregnancy and sexually transmitted diseases (STDs) that Sheila took. While Sheila proudly tried to prove her control over all these men, the doctor could only see her as an immature victim. It was always hard to talk, there was always so much to do in the sessions, such as checking for pregnancy or discussing HIV. There were occasional quiet moments when Sheila would wistfully speak of her dad who hadn't cared about her and had left home when she was little. She described herself like a half circle and it was only a man who could make her feel whole, like she was a person.

There was a turning point when she eventually arrived pregnant and deserted by her last boyfriend. She was now able to face with the doctor the lonely emptiness that had led to such self-destructive behaviour and was symbolized by the abortion. She now was able to ask for the counselling help that in the past she had so scornfully rejected. She arranged her own appointment with the centre counsellor and was then able to use the sessions to acknowledge her inner desolation and then to painfully make a start at recovering a true sense of self.

SEXUAL PROBLEMS

This section includes both individual sexuality and sexual problems that may develop in the relationship. Childhood messages about sex leave their mark; it can be difficult to think about contraception if a woman believes that sex is dirty and not for pleasure but purely for having babies. A woman may believe mistakenly that there is no point using contraception if sex is scarce or if she has no enjoyment. Occasionally the contraceptive itself may also create problems.

Sally came to the centre with her boyfriend Tom. She was pregnant and they were very unhappy. They were both inexperienced and had planned to use condoms for contraception. However, Tom lost his erection when he put one on. They had taken some chances as they both felt too embarassed to return to the clinic to ask for advice.

Denise was seen in the surgery one evening and eventually managed to talk about the severe vaginismus that was preventing her from having intercourse. During the consultation Denise spoke of her fears about being too small and that she felt she could be ripped apart during penetration. The doctor examined her and during this Denise visibly relaxed and agreed to explore herself. She was amazed and delighted by her findings and the reassurance and left looking much happier with an appointment for the following week.

The doctor thought she had done a good piece of work and was surprised to see her booked in as an emergency the next day. Denise had in fact been able to have intercourse without any problems, except that it was unprotected that evening and she now needed emergency contraception. The doctor's initial pleasure was somewhat tempered by the thought that this episode could have had tragic consequences were it not for Denise's common sense, as the doctor had certainly not been thinking about contraception in the previous consultation.

In this chapter we have explored some of the many influences that can be at work when a woman is unhappily pregnant. These are complicated and need attention on many different levels. 'The Health of the Nation' states its objective to reduce the number of unwanted pregnancies and to ensure the provision of effective family planning services for those people who want them. We hope that by facing the problem in this multifaceted way we can meet the challenge and prevent some of the misery of abortion both for society and individual women.

Chapter 2

The changes that occur when a woman is pregnant

Pregnancy is a healthy condition and can bring with it a greatly enhanced sense of physical well-being. However, these positive changes may be undermined by a woman's emotional state. The physical, emotional and psychological alterations that occur when a woman has conceived, even in the first trimester, are significant and can bring profound and lasting changes. These changes can hamper decision-making. Counsellors need to be aware that women are not only in a new and stressful situation, but that they are also adjusting to the inescapable effects of pregnancy.

Even if a woman does not intend to continue with her pregnancy she, and those intimately connected with her, know that there is no possibility of her returning to having never been pregnant. Indeed, abortion is a procedure requested by women whose only alternative is to 'become' a parent. Whatever the ultimate decision, a major transitional event has occurred. This is often seen by women as more significant than living with a partner, leaving home, a first sexual experience or even marriage, though all these momentous events may lead to pregnancy.

Women are, it seems, designed to cope with change, and may be more tolerant of unpredictability than men. No woman can know when menstruation will flow or a spontaneous labour begin, until after the event.

The physical, emotional and social changes involved in pregnancy should not be minimized and need to be appreciated. Any alteration to the *status quo* is deeply unnerving. No matter whether a woman chooses to continue or end her pregnancy, a woman cannot 'rerun' the experience to see what would have been best. A woman with a pregnancy always faces some loss.

Often it is women who have the sole responsibility for making a decision that will alter their life and the life of a potential child. A woman needs to weigh up all the advantages and disadvantages of the situation and make a choice that she knows will have permanent consequences. This is inevitably stressful and emotionally taxing. This is especially so when she is saddled with all the upheaval that pregnancy brings.

PHYSICAL CHANGES

There is a unique partnership that happens between a woman's body and her pregnancy from the very early stages of pregnancy, in anticipation of implantation. The precise mechanisms that control implantation and maintain the early embryo are not known, though the hormones progesterone, secreted by the woman's ovaries, and human chorionic gonadotrophin (HCG), produced by the developing placenta, also help to make the lining of the womb receptive.

Women do not look any different outwardly when they are less than twelve weeks pregnant, but their bodies are undergoing dramatic physical alterations. Redman and Walker (1992) in their book *Pre-eclampsia the Facts* outline the many changes that occur in normal pregnancy.

When pregnant, a woman's blood has extra constituents pumped around the body. For example, iron that is needed to maintain the mother's blood levels is absorbed more efficiently from her diet, and other nutrients including protein and vitamin B12, are altered to favour the developing pregnancy. The placenta is more efficient at taking nutrients from the blood stream and can provide for the developing foetus even if there is a deficient diet.

A woman's cardiac output (the amount of blood pumped out of the heart) increases by about 30 per cent in the first ten weeks. To achieve this the mother's heart silently puts in an extra fifteen beats per minute. The pregnant woman makes more blood, by increasing the number of circulating red blood cells and in particular by boosting the plasma volume. This disproportionate increase in plasma dilutes the blood so that there is a lower concentration of red blood cells and haemoglobin which can therefore lead to anaemia. The blood's composition also allows clots to form more easily as an insurance policy against possible heavy bleeding during birth. The lungs and kidneys have an increased work-load, dealing with more waste products to collect and purify.

The immune system is modified, it continues to find and disarm harmful organisms (often less efficiently) but does not attack the different genetic material of the foetus. The pregnancy is protected, but this phenomenon is not fully understood and is still a medical puzzle. There have been various explanations which seem to indicate that the cells that make up an early embryo do not signal their difference or are provided with a mechanism to hide this difference and are therefore safe from the pregnant woman's immune system. An obstetrician, A. W. Liley, says that it is the foetus who: 'guarantees the endocrine success of a pregnancy and induces all manner of changes to the maternal physiology to make her a suitable host' (Liley 1972: 2).

There is a fall in the arterial blood pressure which drops when a woman conceives and continues to fall, reaching a low point at about twenty weeks and then slowly returns to normal. This fall in pressure is caused by a general peripheral vasodilation. This is also responsible for slowing down the circulation through many of the body tissues. An example is the characteristic change in the vagina from a dark pink colour to a dusky mauve – Chadwick's sign of pregnancy. This fall in blood pressure can also result in women feeling lightheaded and even fainting due to blood pooling in the lower limbs, (especially when standing still for a time) as there is then less blood supply to the brain.

Gordon Bourne, in his book *Pregnancy* (1984) provides a daunting list of thirty-six 'minor complaints' that women can expect when pregnant. Few women would be unlucky enough to have all of these; however, even a few could exhaust and slow a woman down. This could lead to extra stress and act as a disincentive from taking any action. To make a decision women have to weigh up their options and then act upon this decision. This requires energy and effort that can be lacking. We have grouped Bourne's list into two tables to illustrate this point.

We will look briefly at nausea and ptyalism, (a pregnancy symptom that is rarely talked about and may be culturally influenced). We then look at how a pregnancy can alter a woman's role, her psychology and her ability to think, her dreams and emotions, which can make her feel more isolated and introspective.

Nausea and vomiting

Perhaps the most well-known symptom of pregnancy, after a missed period (though bleeding can occur until late into a normal pregnancy), is nausea, with or without vomiting. This happens to the majority of women, quoted as 50–80 per cent in E. Sloane's (1993) *Biology of Women*, and can range from non-existent to extreme vomiting, continuing beyond the first trimester. Hyperemesis, as this is called, is rare (Fairweather 1968; Tylden 1968) but can lead to exhaustion and dehydration which needs hospital admission. Gordon Bourne states that:

> [Hyperemesis] used to be a common means whereby a woman with an unwanted pregnancy tried to obtain an abortion and as soon as she was convinced that the pregnancy would not be medically terminated the sickness would cease quite quickly.
>
> (Bourne 1984: 182)

Table 2.1 Physically debilitating and painful changes during pregnancy

Physically debilitating changes	Painful changes
Nausea, vomiting, hypermesis gravidarum (prolonged vomiting)	Pelvic discomfort
Insomnia	Sacroiliac pain (back)
Lowered blood pressure, fainting	Abdominal (broad ligament) pain
Stress incontinence	Carpal tunnel syndrome (affecting the wrist)
	Muscle cramps

Source: Bourne (1984)

Table 2.2 Physically and emotionally draining, and embarassing/annoying changes during pregnancy

Physically and emotionally draining changes	Embarrassing/annoying changes
Tiredness, weakness	Profuse vaginal discharge
Lassitude	Varicose veins
Constipation	Piles
Headaches	Cystitis
Shortness of breath	Heartburn
Frequency of micturition	Ptyalism (excessive saliva)
	Flatulence
	Pica (food cravings)
	Nasal congestion
	Gingivitis (bleeding gums)

Source: Bourne (1984)

Presumably this was before the 1967 Abortion Act and conjures up a tragic picture of desperate women trying to be too ill to continue with their pregnancy, and also leaves the impression that this condition was largely fabricated. Few who have experienced a degree of pregnancy sickness would doubt its reality and wretchedness. Nausea and vomiting can have a major physiological and psychological impact on some women, thus altering their lives.

There is no medical consensus on the exact aetiology of pregnancy sickness. Various theories have been put forward. The most common are an increase in circulating oestrogens, reduced stomach acidity, or changes in carbohydrate metabolism (pregnant women have a 10 per cent lower level of fasting blood sugar than normal due to the placental transfer of glucose) (Sloane 1993). Some theories attempt to link nausea with a high level of human chorionic gonadotrophin.

The biologist David Haig in a BBC *Horizon* programme (April 1995) outlined his fascinating view that the mother's pregnancy is not, contrary to popular opinion, a harmonious state; the mother physiologically protecting and nurturing her forming baby. He suggests the reality may be that the baby and mother are locked into conflict, with the placenta as the 'battleground'. This, he suggests, could lead at one extreme to the mother's body defending itself against the foreign tissue of the developing baby and producing a selective abortion. He postulated that if the pregnancy continued the mother would suffer pregnancy sickness. The mother's physiology tries to ensure that her baby's needs do not overwhelm hers and the baby's placenta in its turn tries to ensure sufficient nutrients and oxygen to survive.

The absence of nausea in early pregnancy has been linked to denial of the pregnancy (Deutsch 1944). Studies of the extent and severity of normal sickness and vomiting have suggested a connection between the absence of nausea and subsequent emotional disturbance in later pregnancy and after childbirth. (Uddenberg *et al.* 1971; Wolkind and Zajieck 1978). The opposite idea that nausea indicates mixed feelings, wanting and not wanting a baby, or even rejection of a pregnancy has also been presented (Hanford 1968).

Prolonged vomiting, hypermesis, has been viewed as occurring in women who lack external support, or have a history of miscarriage and previous induced abortion, which would fit David Haig's theory. A useful paper by O'Brien and Newton (1991) looks at the historical evolution of beliefs about nausea in pregnancy and charts the changing ideas about causes from 1929 to 1990. This divides theories into three separate camps, first, the Early Somatic Era up to 1929, which linked nausea and vomiting to the toxaemic effect of a pregnancy on a woman's body. Second, the Intrapsychic Era, 1930–80 where morning sickness was seen as neurotic in origin and third, the Metabolic and Social Stress Era 1981–to present day where a woman's metabolism and the stress of a pregnancy is thought to be the cause. Each of these ideas has its champions and many are being refined, however, a definitive cause remains obscure.

Many different remedies have been tried, from an infusion of ginger, eating dry toast before getting up in the morning, to pharmacological relief in the form of anti-emetics. The Thalidomide tragedy revealed the teratogenic potential of anti-sickness preparations and has led to many pregnant women avoiding their use and being wary of all drugs. Women who know they want to end a pregnancy can nevertheless be reluctant to take anything that could be harmful to a foetus. Women who tell you they must avoid all harmful substances could be subconsciously signaling that they do have an attachment to the pregnancy and need careful counselling.

It is difficult to counsel a woman who has to rush out to be sick or is physically exhausted by constantly feeling queasy. However, even with extreme nausea women do not, in our experience, give ending their sickness as a reason for requesting an abortion.

Ptyalism

The spitting of saliva into a handkerchief or receptacle such as a small bottle is a common feature of pregnancy in Africa and the Caribbean but is rarely mentioned here. Of the popular books on pregnancy only Gordon Bourne mentions and defines ptyalism as the 'hysterical inability to swallow the normal amount of saliva' (Bourne 1984: 184).

An increase in salivation does occur during pregnancy and is usually unconsciously swallowed. In a twenty-four-hour period 1.5 litres of saliva are normally produced. Whilst reading the last sentence you may be aware that you have become more conscious of the saliva in your own mouth, having just had the stimulus of reading about it. It is a curious fact that saliva production can happen consciously and unconsciously. This fact has been used to create a hypnotic state. The participant is asked to think about saliva in the mouth and ensure that saliva is present the whole time, and told that they will be unable to feel pain, and are then unable to do so.

It is possible that ptyalism is mainly recognized, or considered worth commenting on, if culturally expected and is ignored if not. In every culture there are myths, superstitions, beliefs and practices that surround pregnancy.

ATTITUDES TO PREGNANT WOMEN

Historically pregnant women around the world have provoked strong reactions and powerful attitudes. Adrienne Rich sums these up: 'Nowhere is the pregnant women taken for granted. She may be viewed as proof of her husband's sexual adequacy; dangerous to crops and men; an embarrassment; possessed of curative powers' (Rich 1977: 34).

Women's reproductive powers may be consciously envied or dreaded if not wanted, but today women are still presented with two opposing views of their bodies. On the one hand, the female body is seen as sacred, asexual, life-enhancing and giving. On the other, as impure, unclean, corrupt and contaminating. Menstruation has been believed to confer supernatural powers that were for the most part seen as harmful, for example, to sour milk and blunt tools (Weideger 1982).

The polarization is stark:

good	v.	evil
fertile	v.	barren
pure	v.	impure
restorative	v.	contaminating

It is very difficult to opt voluntarily for stopping a pregnancy if by doing so the woman is choosing the negative aspects of this list. She could see herself and be seen by others as choosing to be a non-mother, opting to be viewed as evil and barren. Often there can be a fundamental judgement that 'nice girls do not have abortions'.

When women see their body as an asset, they can be threatened by the pregnancy's potential to fatten their breasts, waist and abdomen making them less attractive to men. Women are prone to misrepresentation and negative feelings about their bodies. Clients' feelings of self-worth are often linked to how they think and feel about their body. A woman's self-image can fluctuate with her mood. In the 1980s Susie Orbach focused on a view of a woman's body as a commodity buying her power and acceptance, for with her body 'she gains a man, a family, a home and a place in the world' (Orbach and Eichenbaum 1982: 84).

This divide is further deepened by the biological father's physical distance from a pregnancy and birth; he does not have the experience of a growing baby which the mother has to accommodate. Paternity has to be assumed rather than being an incontrovertible fact. Women are often left 'holding the baby' but are socialized to be the gender that is nurturing, sacrificial and tender. In contemplating an abortion women can feel that they are going against nature and their own expectations of 'womanly behaviour'.

When a woman is to become a mother she has to adapt to all the practical and psychological alterations that this new role brings. Psychoanalysis has pointed out in numerous papers the complicated feelings that the woman has toward her foetus. Pregnancy may stir up and repeat buried feelings connected to her relationship with her own mother and the mothering she received.

On the other hand, the pregnancy can be seen as entirely wholesome and be imbued with good qualities so that the pregnant woman fears harming the pregnancy. Those who are pregnant can also feel warm and creative, responding to the idea of an unbroken bond with other women and especially their own mother. A new life resonates with the feelings and ideas that a woman has about her own upbringing and herself when a helpless and dependent infant.

These, at times contradictory and unconscious fantasies and the 'fluctuating identifications with the mother and with the mothered, with the victim and victimiser, with being creative and with being colonised' can help a woman's ability to be a parent or make the process harder, as Rozsika Parker describes (Parker 1995: 203).

A woman may hope that a pregnancy will announce her as an adult and yet find that being a mother telegraphs her need to depend on others. She may feel deeply unconfident of her own ability to be successful and have been relentlessly tested by her own parents.

Anne had already had one abortion that had deeply depressed her and led to her repeatedly cutting her arms. Now accidentally pregnant again, she was terrified of having an abortion and being tipped into the same anguish. Anne was at the same stage of pregnancy (nine weeks) when she had found her conflicting feelings unbearable and had an abortion in the hope of ending this pain.

She recounted that all those who were significant in her life, her parents and boyfriend, wanted her to have an abortion whilst work acquaintances had spontaneously celebrated the pregnancy. She wanted to secure or capture this precious approbation. It was rare for her to receive recognition of herself as a worthy person. This gave her a precious feeling of success and fulfilment. However, the thought of actually giving birth meant she would face the demands of being a mother. She expected her parents repeated warnings would be proved right, that 'a baby would be too much' for her and that she would fail. Anne's only recourse and the action she felt was safest was to deny that she really was pregnant. She knew intellectually this was little comfort but nevertheless wanted to organize an abortion quickly.

The counsellor took this client to supervision and found that she could remember nothing except that Anne was very angry and placed this anger on doctors and various other authority figures who, she felt, had denied her choice (of contraception) and had mistreated her. Anne seemed to split people into saints, providing unconditional acceptance of her, and monsters who rode rough shod over her needs. The counsellor felt unable to help and that she was effectively silenced. She could only feel the anger of the client and her own returning anger at not being able to help. In the next session the pregnancy counsellor tried to help Anne focus on what this pregnancy symbolized for her, what she was aborting, what were the hopes and fears encapsulated by the pregnancy? This allowed her to be more conscious of her predicament.

EMOTIONAL AND PSYCHOLOGICAL CHANGES

Pregnancy is not a static process and women can begin, almost in spite of themselves, to make an emotional investment in the foetus. Whatever feelings they have develop and change with the continuing pregnancy. At first the pregnancy is hidden, an unseen part of the client, a secret; the pregnancy can then be actually felt (movements) but is still invisible. Eventually it becomes a full-blown public pregnancy which is difficult to ignore and is recognized by others.

The focus for the pregnant woman has been seen as the pregnancy in the first trimester, the foetus mid-trimester and the baby in the final three months (Raphael-Leff 1993: 63–8). Pregnancy is seen as a time when women become more centred on themselves, have a richer fantasy life and 'loosening of associations and ego boundaries' (Muir 1982: 102). Similar points have been made by Benedek (1959) and Bibring et al. (1961).

Research into how women feel and think when pregnant has often been carried out with small self-selected groups of women. For example, research by A. Jarrahi-Zadeh et al. (1969) looked for emotional and cognitive changes in eighty-four White women. They identified various areas where changes might occur:

1 subjective awareness, increased tension and anxiety, or irritability;
2 depression, sadness, self-deprecating feelings and fearfulness;
3 obsessive concerns;
4 lethargy and 'morning sickness';
5 liability of mood;
6 mental function and fogginess.

Mental functioning was interestingly further divided into unclear thinking, change in the ability to think and concentrate and a difference in memory function and dreams. All these women were continuing with their pregnancies. They found evidence of an inability to concentrate, or plan ahead. Impaired ability in mental functioning could hamper women making the monumental decision to terminate or continue with a pregnancy.

We feel this is why women need time and a safe place to focus on their feelings and know that the counsellor is accepting of their muddled thinking.

This is important as the 'fogginess' of early pregnancy often leads to apathy and passivity; it is easier to hope your period comes, and to put off finding out where to go for pregnancy testing, than make the effort to take action.

Although the literature on the subject shows that women make a better or worse psychological adjustment to pregnancy (Kumar 1990), many writers are in agreement that women say they feel more moody, tearful, edgy and 'foggy' when pregnant. Some women oscillate between fear, hope and disappointment. Dana Breen explains that: 'The changes are of such magnitude, experience so strong, feelings so disturbing that she becomes, for the first time in her life preoccupied with making sense of her feelings' (1981: 11).

It is this wish to access feelings that can be picked up in counselling. If there is no one to listen to these difficult feelings, or provide firm boundaries as a committed partner can, then women are left to drift alone and can be prey to many fears and anxieties. Women have said to us, 'I feel as if I'm walking in glue'; 'It was too much to think about I just hoped the pregnancy would go away if I didn't talk about it'. These fears can often swirl around anxieties about an abnormal baby or themselves being unworthy mothers.

Some women show a marked decrease in libido in early pregnancy and less enjoyment of sexual intercourse (Kumar *et al*. 1981; Robson *et al*. 1981) and this could further isolate women from their sexual partners. A pregnancy often causes the woman to look again at a relationship, the partner can cease to be perceived as a lover or be seen in a 'rosy glow'. In addition, if a woman is not feeling sexual herself, then the often inevitable loss of closeness that sex can provide can lead to further alienation and isolation, so often described in pregnancy counselling by the client.

One psychological change that occurs in pregnancy is an increase in the vividness of fantasies, daydreams and dreams. A study of pregnant women's dreams reported that 40 per cent of these dreams were about the baby with only 1 per cent being reported in women who were not pregnant (Gillman 1973). Pregnant women's dreams can include images of 'dolls' (these can be actual dolls or, often, small pieces of different types of materials which can symbolize a baby to the dreamer); small animals; losing or neglecting babies or other people; searching for missing objects; discovering new rooms or structures. In these dreams opposites often figure: creation and destruction (with women facing abortion dreaming of killing or being killed or harmed), order and chaos, things that are tiny or huge. A client reported dreaming that she had given birth by mouth to a large baby that was laughing, she felt this meant that the baby was too developed and promptly re-swallowed it. The dreamer can, as in the latter dream, feel relieved or be made anxious and guilty by the fact that they could not look after their 'baby' in the dream. Clients can report being frightened by these dreams fearing they are a portent either of the future or foretell their lack of ability as a mother. It is possible that these dreams express fears and hopes that the pregnant woman has about being able to give adequate support to a child.

Dream images of new architectural structures also conjure up the new additions to their bodies which are secret, mysterious or scary or these structures can be described as crumbling masonry, erected scaffolding of work in progress, being repaired or tumbling down. These dreams can also be seen by the dreamer as worries about their own body coping with the physical and emotional changes. Psychoanalysts, such as Joan Raphael-Leff (1980) have written in detail about the analytical psychotherapy of pregnant clients and Dinora Pines (1972) noted that women's dreams are vivid with overt symbolism with hardly any attempt to 'censor' forbidden material. She concluded that dreams might function as a mechanism to work through all the contradictions.

There are also other complex alterations to a pregnant woman's way of thinking. J. T. Condon (1987), a consultant psychiatrist, argues that pregnant women undergo a shift in process of their thinking which becomes less logical, critical and more intuitive. This is described as 'primary process' thinking. This is a type of pre-logical cognition, current in early childhood, which ignores the reality principle; is concrete in nature and does not distinguish between wishing and what is actually happening. It is said to operate in dreams, fantasies and to occur in magical thinking. Children think in this magical way. A child, for example, may tell you that they did not kick you when they have just done so but did not mean to, or now wish they had not done so.

Women when pregnant are closer to their unconscious and that unconscious material emerges more easily and is felt and not analysed. In other words women are less defensive (Bibring 1959; Raphael-Leff; 1980). Bibring screened a random group of pregnant women for a psychotherapy research project and found to her surprise that many were diagnosed by psychiatric staff as 'borderline' psychotics because they exhibited 'magical thinking, premonitions, depressive anxieties, primitive anxieties, introjective and paranoid mechanisms frequently associated with the patient's own mother'(Bibring 1959: 115).

Joan Raphael-Leff has written that

> the pregnant woman has immediate and direct access to her well of fantasies, her earliest modes of symbolic thinking as she is 'in touch' with her unconscious and at times feels almost overwhelmed by the power of the irrational within her . . . she suddenly finds herself different from others and unable to communicate the 'mad' content of her experiences, which she recognises and is embarrassed by.
>
> (Raphael-Leff 1980 cited in Condon 1987: 330)

Women may talk in a way that is similar to free association with less obvious links between ideas.

It may be that mourning is inhibited in pregnancy and Emmanuel Lewis suggested that the reasons for this are complex, partly as pregnancy often involves mixed feelings. When a person is grieving the dead person is 'unconsciously imagined as being taken into their minds and bodies, the dead can be unconsciously felt as dead and yet be active inside us, imagined variously as alive and supportive or as damaged, burdensome and persecutory' (Lewis 1979: 27). Lewis suggests that if the woman is pregnant she instinctively protects her foetus from 'the dangerous summation of her confused mixed feelings if she blocks the process of mourning during a pregnancy. Women can then unconsciously equate her loved unknown fetus with the idealised dead person: she avoids mourning' (Lewis 1979: 27).

This suggests that the process of mourning whilst pregnant is difficult, even impeded. Maybe this accounts for the emptiness and delayed grief sometimes described by women after an abortion.

There is a crisis view of pregnancy, now widely accepted (Breen 1974) that stresses that some women may be overwhelmed by the tasks that are in involved (Oakley 1980; Pines 1972). Pregnancy is seen with some justification as being a time of heightened stress, the 'essential adaptation in her move towards maturation, is the achievement of a stable and satisfactory balance between unconscious fantasies, day-dreams and hopes and the realities of her relationship to herself, her husband and her child' (Pines 1993: 60).

The definition of a crisis is a sudden event that overwhelms the person's usual ability to maintain an equilibrium. Caplan (1970) noted that a crisis needs a novel solution that is outside the individual's past experience and requires creative and innovative problem-solving mechanisms. Crisis can create anxiety which affects both perception and understanding. Lazarus (1966) outlined four main coping behaviours: anticipatory action, attack, avoidance, apathy and inaction. The apathy of 'learned helplessness' (Seligman 1975) is sometimes seen. This is a psychological reaction to an unbearable situation. Vulnerable women may passively accept a painful situation rather than risk failure and greater damage to self-esteem.

Shock and an emotional numbness are often witnessed, with a lack of expressed feelings or a sense that the client is 'going through the motions' or is on 'automatic', as women have described this stage subsequently. Feelings of disbelief, anger, sadness and powerlessness often follow. Interestingly, J. Condon in his article for the *British Journal of Medical Psychology* (1987) makes the point that Caplan (1961) formulated his crisis theory from observations during pregnancy in the 1950s. This crisis has many causes, one may be the strange idea that there are two persons in one skin, that a pregnancy is both part of the woman and yet also has a separate entity. The understanding that pregnancy causes all the somatic and psychological changes can make the woman feel even more out of control and powerless. These fears can be heightened if the individual woman is stuck with the normal adolescent conflicts around identity, intimacy and isolation.

Though a pregnancy is proof that a woman is fertile and female and that she has had sexual contact, it is not proof that she is mature. The earlier stages of pregnancy are said by Dinora Pines to suggest similar worries that occur in adolescence about changing shape: some women are delighted, others have a libidinal interest in themselves, yet others show a 'marked increase in sexual investment in the self; a withdrawal from the object world and an increase in passivity' (Pines 1993: 63), some women may become more active to deny this passivity; others may have difficulty in accepting any dependency and envy their partner's freedom.

In adolescence it has been suggested that the increased awareness of the body stimulates an impulse to actually use the body to prove its worth. There can be a need to increase self-esteem by being seen as attractive and acknowledged by others as existing and being able to be a source of pleasure, as well as gratification for the individual themselves.

The idea of motherhood can refer back to the individual's own experience of being parented and their own ability to parent. The pregnant woman ceases to be her parents' child by carrying a potential child inside, she usurps her own mother and takes on this mantle with all its good and less good experiences devolved from her own upbringing, thus 'the problem is posed is she able to identify with the introjected mother or to rival her and succeed in being a better mother' (Pines 1993: 67).

Clients can be unprepared for loss (maybe she received no counselling, being rushed into a decision to please others or through lack of time), she may have had little time to anticipate loss and this makes it less likely that she will be able to cope with stress later. It is also apparent that a pregnant woman is going to lose the baby inside whether she continues or not.

The woman who is blasé about her pregnancy could be experiencing a 'blanket immunity' (Marris 1974) which is exploded by stress. Whereas if women can anticipate fear this may reduce the emotional shock. This also fits with Dana Breen's prediction in *The Birth of a First Child: Towards an Understanding of Femininity* (1974) that those women with extreme anxiety or hardly any anxiety have the most difficulty after having a child. We would extend this to after an abortion too. Of course other women may be able to balance and hold contradictory emotions and thoughts and still be disturbed or not after an abortion.

HEALTH AND POVERTY

The final influence to bear in mind is that women live longer but have more health problems than men. Women with children have been shown to have worse mental and physical health (Popay and Jones 1988) and are markedly affected by poverty with its 'draining effect, of guilt and worry, stress and anxiety combined with a poor diet, lack of recreational exercise, health damaging behaviour, housing and environmental hazards' (Payne 1991: 152–3).

Women can be prone to depression. Cynicism and detachment can allow them to give up any long-term plans. If your present situation is tolerable then you can contemplate the future, but if the present is grim because of poverty then women are forced to concentrate on 'getting through today', and have no energy to plan for tomorrow or take actions that will pay off in the future, such as taking contraception now to protect yourself tomorrow. Sarah Payne summed this up by saying that women are:

> paid less than men, receive fewer advantages, sick pay, occupational benefits and lower pensions . . . are less able to take on employment [and the work they do is] . . . paid at a lower rate . . . however, they perform the vast bulk of the domestic and caring work.
>
> (Payne 1991: 204)

All these affect pregnant women and can prevent them from seeking help immediately when they fail to have a period. Others may continue with monthly bleeding even though they are pregnant. Delays in seeking help, and procrastination, are to be expected as women are often in emotional turmoil and psychological upheaval. This is only made more difficult by having not wished for their pregnancy, a future child or even the manner in which they conceived and having an unsupportive relationship with the progenitor of their pregnancy, the father.

The pregnancy counsellor's work can be more effective if they have an understanding of the physical, psychological and emotional changes that pregnancy brings. Women dismayed to be pregnant are likely to find the negative aspects of pregnancy a further burden and this needs to be taken into account.

Chapter 3

Abortion: the historical, legal and social context

Abortion is a deeply emotive subject and has been the centre of many heartfelt campaigns, from those based on the belief that life from conception is sacred to those based on the belief that women should have absolute control over their own bodies.

The deliberate ending of a pregnancy continues to be the 'source of social and legal discord, moral uncertainty, medical and psychiatric confusion and personal anguish' (Callaghan 1970: 1). Opponents of abortion argue on moral, religious and even political grounds. Our personal belief is that the individual woman must come to her own decision, armed with all the relevant facts, and that she is entitled to help on the same basis as in any other situation where she seeks medical help that is freely available under the National Health Service.

Abortion is the most frequently performed operation in Britain inside and outside the NHS. Abortion is not seen by us as removed from accessible contraceptive services or comprehensive sex education to promote sexual health. We argue against a split in contraceptive and abortion services and for their integration at all levels. In March 1993, the Faculty of Family Planning and Reproductive Health Care of the Royal College of Obstetricians and Gynaecologists was established. This educational body hopes to be able to oversee the effective integration of reproductive health care within all the related disciplines. The separation of genito-urinary, abortion, sterilization and contraceptive services is not logical. It can lead to unnecessary gaps and fails to provide a 'one stop' service for clients.

It will probably never be possible to remove the need for abortion, even if contraception were to become 100 per cent effective, were reversible and had no side-effects, which is not the case at present.

It is now possible to separate sexual pleasure from pregnancy but however advanced or novel techniques of contraception have become (and many have not changed for hundreds of years) sex for pleasure has still not become entirely acceptable. In every country, for a variety of reasons, the view is held that being able to separate these two encourages promiscuity or illicit sex. For example, Brook Advisory Centres became infamous for letting it be known that they would see the unmarried in 1964, and a decade later under 16-year-olds (minors) even without parental knowledge or consent.

Although contraception has gained legitimacy due to society's changing views on sexuality and the intense pressure for reduction of population growth in developing countries, there is still disapproval. Marge Berer has succinctly explained this:

> A new morality is emerging, but it has only gone part way. The prevailing belief is that no matter how responsible an act it is to use contraception, it is only responsible enough if the contraception doesn't fail you, or you don't fail with it. In other words if you end up pregnant and didn't want to be, it's probably all your own fault. Needing an abortion is the main proof of irresponsibility. Hence as was true of contraception not so long ago, many people still think that abortion obtained 'too easily' implies that people especially women, have been able to get way with something.
>
> (Berer 1993: 41)

INDIVIDUAL BELIEFS

Some women we see for counselling are concerned about whether they have the right to 'take a life' and if they will be punished for rejecting a life. A woman's way of resolving the dilemma for herself is highly individual and often it is not possible for her logically or rationally to do so.

> A 16-year-old, who came with her mother felt she could not cope with a child but was ardently anti-abortion. However, she took comfort in a dream where her sister, who had died accidentally many years previously, reappeared and said she would look after the baby in heaven.

This dream allowed the client to have an abortion as she was benefiting her sister. Her mother's solution was different, that her daughter would, 'have the same baby the next time she was pregnant' which the client rejected as absurd.

All the major world religions are pro-natalist. A useful handbook, *Religion, Ethnicity, Sex Education: Exploring The Issues* edited by Rachel Thomson (1993) on behalf of the Sex Education Forum, gives an incisive perspective by allowing individuals of different faiths to set out their own views on sexual behaviour, contraception and abortion.

It is useful for counsellors to understand the prevailing religious views, cultural attitudes and mores but it should also be remembered that each individual client will have their own creed. Individual women's beliefs are often a mixture of morals (what is good), values (what weight should be given) and ethics (individual conscience) and the dictates of her own cultural and spiritual views.

The most common moral stand point is that where actions are deemed acceptable if they are seen to benefit the most number of people and do not deliberately harm others. Does the foetus have full, partial or no moral rights and who decides? If a foetus does have full moral rights then its life cannot be put in danger, which precludes invasive testing (for abnormalities) and abortion. If the foetus has no moral rights then it may have no value. This is an extreme position and is illogical if moral rights are then magically conferred at birth. For many people it seems the foetus has 'moral status but this develops with the developing fetus, and the issue is seen from the standpoint of the mother' (Abramsky and Chapple 1994: 12–13).

Women will have their own individual moral or ethical point at which they will cease to feel an abortion is permissible. For example, if the foetus is over 12 weeks, the mother may worry that the pregnancy will suffer pain or be used for experimentation.

Clients can come for counselling worried that a foetus will suffer during an abortion. An article that appeared in *The Lancet* (1994 344: 77–81) and was widely reported, proposed that a foetus of 23 weeks showed a hormonal stress response to invasive medical procedures (blood taken from the intrahepatic vein). This article raised the possibility that the human foetus feels pain *in utero* and may benefit from anaesthesia.

Some clients may concentrate on one aspect of this debate, whilst other clients take a wider viewpoint. Germaine Greer noted these complexities:

> Catholic opponents of reproductive freedom for women remain fixated on the minority of cases of induced abortion, incurious about the vast majority of cases, (referring to natural wastage, of miscarriages, and ectopic pregnancies and still births) unable or unwilling to understand the morality of actions taken because an individual came to the conclusion that she had no choice.
>
> (Greer 1984: 162)

People can feel strongly that abortion is not immoral or take the opposing view that it is so totally wrong that they are prepared to attack centres providing such help.

PUBLIC ATTITUDES

The British Social Attitudes surveys in 1983, 1986 and 1989 questioned the social circumstances in which an abortion might be performed. The percentage agreeing that abortion should be allowed within the law, has steadily increased.

In 1991 a Harris Poll showed that 4 out of 5 (81 per cent) agreed that a woman should have the right to choose whether to have an abortion in the first three months of pregnancy. One in 10 (10 per cent) said that that women should not have the right, while almost 1 in 10 (9 per cent) said that they did not know (Table 3.1). The latest MORI poll in August 1995 shows that 66 per cent of voters support 'abortion on request'.

The British media reflects society's own ambivalence about this subject. Various popular television programmes such as *Neighbours*, *Grange Hill*, or

Table 3.1 Percentage agreeing that abortion should be allowed by law under certain circumstances

Question	1983	1986	1989
The woman's health is seriously endangered by the pregnancy	87%	91%	95%
The couple cannot afford any more children	47%	58%	62%
The woman decides on her own she does not wish to have a child	37%	49%	54%

Source: British Social Attitudes Survey (Jowell 1990)

Eastenders run stories in which their female stars become accidentally pregnant, but most have ended up continuing with their pregnancies.

EARLY FOETAL DEVELOPMENT

It is apparent to us in our work as counsellors that although the majority of women do accept that in having an abortion they are preventing a life, their knowledge about the early development of the embryo and foetus may often be vague.

Counsellors need to inform themselves about the early foetal development so that they can answer basic questions. In the first weeks of human life the embryo is indistinguishable from other early life forms. It is at a month from conception (not to be confused with the date from the last menstrual period) that the embryo is recognizable as a mammal. At five weeks the crown (head) to rump length is 5–8 mm. The embryo has a primordial (primitive) brain, a heart, limb buds, eyes and ears, and the beginnings of the internal organs. By eight weeks the foetus is recognizable as human to the eye, is an inch long and Alessandra Piontelli was struck by the 'individuality of movement of each fetus and their preferential postures, attitudes and actions' which he felt showed clear individual initiative and a choice of movement (Piontelli 1986: 456) as revealed by early ultrasound scans. Brain development is slow but the precise moment of awareness is difficult to determine. Twelve weeks from conception the foetus is fully formed and is about 8.5 cm (3.5 inches) long. The foetus can move around but this is rarely felt by the mother, the head is now rounded, the neck and facial features are formed. The external sex organs are sufficiently formed to enable the sex to be determined.

The foetus is unable to survive independently and will not be able to for approximately twenty-four weeks. During the rest of the pregnancy the internal organs develop and grow.

The ethical, religious and moral debate centres around three main areas: judgements about when life begins and what value individuals and societies have placed on human life, and then if the mother and foetus have equally valid rights.

The knowledge of viability has influenced the history and legal aspects of abortion and will continue to do so.

THE 1967 ABORTION ACT

The 1967 Abortion Act transformed women's ability to get help with terminating a pregnancy. Before 1968 women resorted to using abortifacient drugs and vaginal douches, metal and wooden objects and sometimes what became known as 'back street' abortions to interrupt their pregnancies, even though the consequences could be pain, infection, infertility and in some cases death. Madeleine Simms commented that the Abortion Act was the 'consequence not the cause of women's determinations to control their fertility. Each abortion was an unwanted birth averted. Until completely safe and effective contraception is easily available to all, women will continue to seek and to obtain abortions irrespective of the state of the law as the historical evidence shows that they have always done.' (Simms 1980: 8)

The 1967 Abortion Act, amended by the Human Fertilisation and Embryology Act 1990, lays down the principal conditions which allow a registered medical practitioner to perform an abortion once two independent doctors have agreed that:

(A)*   there is a threat to the life of the pregnant woman, greater than if pregnancy were terminated; or

(B)*   the termination is necessary to prevent grave permanent injury to the physical or mental health of the pregnant woman; or

(C)   the pregnancy has not exceeded its twenty-fourth week and that the continuance of the pregnancy would involve risk, greater than if the pregnancy were terminated, of injury to the physical or mental health of the pregnant woman; or

(D)   the pregnancy has not exceeded its twenty-fourth week and that the continuance of the pregnancy would involve risk, greater than if the pregnancy were terminated, of injury to the physical or mental health of any existing child(ren) of the family of the pregnant woman; or

(E)*   there is a substantial risk that if the child were born it would suffer from such physical and mental abnormalities as to be seriously handicapped.

*   There are no time limits for clauses A B and E.

This is the wording on the legal document signed by two medical practitioners which is commonly known because of its colour as the 'blue form' HSA (previously green HSA1).

Although the Abortion Act states that a woman must fulfil one or more of these criteria it includes no guidelines to the way in which terms such as 'substantial risk' or 'grave permanent injury' should be defined. However, it has been established that the actual or reasonably foreseeable environment can be taken into account in determining the risks to a woman's mental and physical health and that Clause (D) includes children under a woman's care, such as step or adopted children.

The 1967 Abortion Act did not set out a time limit for abortions. However, the Infant Life (Preservation) Act of 1929 which aimed to protect a pregnancy over 28 weeks as being 'capable of being born alive' did provide the relevant legislation. (Section 1(2) Infant Life (Preservation) Act 1929). In practice a time limit of 28 weeks was imposed except if an abortion was necessary to save a woman's life because of grave abnormality.

The Human Fertilisation and Embryology Act, 1990 further reduced the time limit from 28 weeks to 24 weeks for the most widely used clauses, (C) and (D). Abortions over 24 weeks are only permitted if a woman's life is in danger, or in order to prevent grave or permanent damage to her physical or mental health, or if a child born as a result of continuing the pregnancy would be seriously handicapped.

Only a tiny minority of abortions are performed over 24 weeks compared to the total number of abortions (Table 3.5).

An abortion has to be carried out in an NHS hospital or place approved by the Secretary of State for Health. All terminations are notified to the Chief Medical Officers of the Health Departments for England, Wales and Scotland. These notifications are processed and the statistics published by the office of Population and Census Surveys (OPCS).

Northern Ireland

Abortions are illegal in Northern Ireland except when necessary to save the life of the mother or where continuing the pregnancy would involve serious injury to her physical or mental health. The law is contained within a framework of common law, statute and case law, such as the Offences Against the Person Act (58 and 59), the Criminal Justice Act (Northern Ireland) and Bourne case law. A few hundred abortions are performed annually.

The age of sexual consent is one year higher than in the rest of the UK. In 1993 Brook Advisory Centres successfully opened a contraceptive centre in Belfast which has proved popular, offering a two-and-a-half-hour session giving help to as many as thirty-five people. This centre opened to furious opposition and was picketed; this escalated when protesters closed the centre's shutters with 'superglue'. There have, thankfully, been no direct threats to staff or young people.

Catholics in Northern Ireland are more liberal than their southern counterparts. However, from both countries numbers of Irish women have made the journey to England for private abortions. The recorded numbers of women travelling to England rose to a peak of 4,154 women in 1991. In 1994 1,678 came from Northern Ireland alone. The true number is undoubtedly higher as some women will give an English address and manage to get NHS help.

Abortion for non-UK nationals

The number of women coming to England for an abortion from the rest of the world has fallen dramatically from a peak of 53,007 in 1973 and now stands at under 4,000 per year. (Other European countries 2,467; rest of the world 747, 1994 OPCS AB 95/8) (Table 3.6).

NHS help is only available to those countries with reciprocal health arrangements, for students and refugees, who must have conceived in this country (the need for treatment must arise whilst living here) and are resident here for at least six months and intend to continue training on a recognised course or to live here. Residence is the central qualification rather than nationality. It is important that hospital reception staff, medical secretaries or even admissions officers are aware of the regulations. The Department of Health has a special section of staff who can advise on complicated cases. We have encountered racism where women with 'foreign names' are asked to bring passports or simply told they cannot get NHS help because it is assumed that they are not entitled if their English is poor.

The private sector

The Secretary of State for Health approves private sector premises to carry out abortion under the 1967 Abortion Act as amended. One of the preconditions of approval is that places are registered with the local health authority under the Registered Homes Act 1984.

The private abortion sector is regulated by a set of assurances given to the Secretary of State. These assurances lay down the requirements with which clinics, private hospitals and pregnancy advisory bureaux must comply. The main system of guidelines and assurances was reviewed and updated in 1994. One of the principal changes was to raise the limit for surgical daycare from 12 to 14 weeks. A recent development is the licensing of mifepristone for abortions from 13–20 weeks gestation.

The Secretary of State registers pregnancy advice bureaux where women have a private consultation. One of the requirements is that bureaux should offer counselling to women seeking abortion.

ABORTION STATISTICS

Once women have decided to have an abortion they expect an easy and early access to a safe service.

In 1994, 156,539 women in England and Wales and 11,376 women in Scotland had abortions and were resident in the UK. A further 10,377 abortions were performed for non-resident women. This makes a total provisional figure of 178,252 for the UK.

The tables that follow are all taken from the abortion statistics (OPCS Monitor AB 95/8) for women resident and non-resident in England and Wales in 1994. These are compiled from the statistical information that has to be recorded with each legal abortion.

During 1994 a total of 166,876 abortions were performed (Table 3.7). This was a decrease of 1.1 per cent (1,835) from the 1993 figures (168,714) and the fourth successive fall in abortion numbers.

Between 1993 and 1994 the overall abortion rate per 1,000 women aged 14–49 resident in England and Wales decreased by 1.0 per cent. These figures show that 87.43 per cent (145,906) of women have an abortion under 12 weeks gestation, 66.14 per cent (110,384) are single and 53.27 per cent (88,908) are aged between 20–29 years (Tables 3.3 and 3.7).

The 1982 RCOG study into late terminations examined the abortion rate in correlation to the provision of abortion and found that there was a strong correlation between good NHS provision and low abortion rate. This was confirmed by Kendall rank correlation test (Albermann and Dennis 1984).

Table 3.2 Abortion rate per 1,000 women aged 14–49 resident and non-resident in England and Wales 1994

Year	14–49	Under 16	16–19	20–24	25–29	30–34	35–39	40–44	45–49
1994	12.18	5.23	22.03	25.40	18.64	12.59	8.03	2.97	0.24

Source: OPCS, Monitors AB 95/8
Note: Rates for 'all ages' are calculated on the basis events at all ages (including those under 14 and over 49) in relation to the population of women who are 14–49. The rate (per 1,000 women) for the under 16 age group is based on the population of women aged 14–15 and for the over 45 and over age-group the rate is based on the population of women aged 45–9. The denominator is the mid-1994 estimated resident population figures.

Table 3.3 Abortion statistics by gestation and marital status for women resident and non-resident in England and Wales 1994

Gestation weeks		Marital status	
>9	66,882	Single	110,384
9–12	79,024	Married	36,135
13–14	8,789	Widowed	499
15–16	5,120	Divorced	7,615
17–18	3,056	Separated	6,424
19–20	2,022	Not stated	5,819
21–22	1,294		
23–24	594		
25 +	94		
Not stated	1		

Source: OPCS, Monitors AB 95/8

Table 3.4 Abortion statistics by parity and age for women resident and non-resident in England and Wales 1994

Parity (number of existing children)		Age	
		Under 16	3,399
0	89,262	16–19	26,797
1	29,283	20–24	48,522
2	29,032	25–29	40,386
3	12,631	30–34	26,879
4	4,325	35–39	15,029
5 +	2,232	40–44	5,377
Not stated	111	45 +	480
		Not stated	7

Source: OPCS, Monitors AB 95/8

Table 3.5 Grounds for abortion (legal reasons for approval) for women resident and non-resident in England and Wales 1994

Grounds	Number of abortions 1994
Risk to life of woman	147
To prevent grave permanent injury to physical or mental health	3,233
To physical or mental health of woman (to 24 weeks)	160,515
To physical or mental health of existing children	15,086
Of the child being born seriously handicapped	1,848
In emergency – to save life of woman	1
In emergency – to prevent grave permanent injury to physical or mental health of woman	1

Source: OPCS, Monitors AB 95/8

Note: Total = 180,831. This is higher than the total number of abortions as more than one reason is given in some cases.

Table 3.6 Women from other countries having abortions in England 1994

Country	Number of abortions
Total – all non-residents	10,337
British Isles	7,123
Scotland	363
Northern Ireland	1,678
Irish Republic	4,590
Channel Islands	349
Isle of Man	143
Other European Countries	2,467
Rest of the World	747

Source: OPCS, Monitors, AB 95/8

Table 3.7 Legal abortions: age, residence, purchaser and rates per 1,000 women in England and Wales 1994

Age	Total terminations	Residents of England and Wales					Non-residents of England and Wales
		Total number	Rate	NHS	NHS agency	Non-NHS	
All Ages	166,876	156,539	12.18	85,243	19,551	51,745	10,337
Under 16	3,399	3,246	5.23	2,274	517	455	153
16–19	26,797	25,223	22.03	15,757	3,929	5,537	1,574
20–24	48,522	44,871	25.40	24,683	5,789	14,399	3,651
25–29	40,386	38,081	18.64	19,423	4,514	14,144	2,305
30–34	26,879	25,507	12.59	13,131	2,797	9,579	1,372
35–40	15,029	14,156	8.03	7,136	1,471	5,549	873
40–44	5,377	5,008	2.97	2,613	486	1,909	369
45 over	480	440	0.24	222	47	171	40
Not stated	7	7		4	1	2	–

Source: OPCS 1994

Note: NHS Agency refers to abortions paid for by the NHS but performed under an agency agreement (i.e., agreement by health authority to pay for abortion which will take place in a private clinic)

There is, for us, an unacceptable national variation in the percentage of women obtaining free help. This differs between Regional Health Authority Areas, and within the same Health Authority areas. The Northern Region with 85 per cent of their abortions funded by the NHS is one of the highest, with South West Thames providing the lowest figure at 43 per cent (1992 figures).

It is not always the area with the greatest number of abortions that funds the highest number of abortions, i.e., Trent RHA 7,885 abortions, 71 per cent on the NHS, and Northern Region RHA with 5,874 abortions, 85 per cent on the NHS (1992).

This is true of Scotland too, a new survey of gynaecology consultants has shown that abortion makes up 12 per cent of all gynaecology outpatients (both daycare and overnight stays) but is unequally distributed. The survey of 132 consultants (92 per cent response rate) showed similar variations between regions and among individual doctors. In one region a third of the consultants who responded would not accept abortion referrals, and in two regions referrals of women over fourteen weeks were refused. Provisional figures for 1993 showed that the 11,001 abortions performed in Scotland were carried out in NHS premises, giving the high proportion of 94 per cent funded by the NHS (Furedi and Paintin 1994).

This unequal distribution is far from ideal; women have an understandable expectation that where they live will not affect their abortion request. Local Health Care Commissioners or providers are faced with setting their own standards. There is a hope that this system will improve abortion provision for women. The 1994 figures show that the number of NHS-funded operations is increasing (though the total number of abortions has decreased in the last three years).

The Royal Commission on the National Health Service in 1979 recommended that 75 per cent of abortions should be provided within the NHS. In the last two decades the figure has remained static at around 45–50 per cent, recently rising to nearly 63 per cent in 1993 (62.2 per cent). From 1994 OPCS figures will clearly table whether abortions are funded by the NHS or are private (Table 3.7).

Private charity clinics have filled the gap since the 1967 Act and have generally had a high reputation for medical care and sympathetic treatment. It was in 1981 that BPAS first negotiated a contract with a local Health Authority (Birmingham which had one of the lowest NHS rates of abortions) and this began Agency Arrangements. Shortly, GP's who are fundholders will be able to 'buy' their own abortion provision from providers. At present about 40 per cent of the population has a GP who is a fundholder. The proportion can vary from 4 per cent to 87 per cent (Paintin, 1996: 128). This may prove beneficial where the GP is sympathetic to abortion but a further hurdle for women who have unsympathetic GPs. In theory the GP will be directed to pass women to the local health authority for help with an abortion but in practice this may cause further delay (HSG (95) 37). We have experienced Health Authority Departments not following this guidance and each purchaser and provider behaving differenly. Occasionally we hear horror stories, women have reported that their GP has told them abortion is illegal; not available on the NHS; impossible over twelve weeks of pregnancy; that two or more abortions are not permissible; or that the GP cannot afford to refer them for help. The number of abortions which have been paid for on the NHS but performed in the charitable sector has slowly risen from 1.8 to 5.5 per cent in 1991 and more rapidly to 7.5 per cent in 1992 (Savage 1994: 9). The latest OPCS figures (1994) note a 5.9 per cent increase in terminations purchased by the NHS, this compared with a fall of 11 per cent in non-NHS or private abortions. Increasingly, health authorities are turning to two main charities, BPAS and Marie Stopes (part of an international organization) and have found that these institutions can supply a cheaper provision to the NHS and at the same time release hospital gynaecology beds.

These block contracts are cheaper than the health authority paying for individual extra-contractual referrals. The present Government has instituted a system designated as 'safe haven' where extra-contractual referrals, (often to other hospitals with which the health authority has a contract or more commonly to the abortion charities) can be made if there is no service effectively available in the usual NHS hospital. This situation can arise where there is a four–six week waiting period to see a gynaecologist or where there are internal rules such as no second or third abortions, no 'social' terminations over twelve weeks or no abortions for women who have not contracepted.

We have some anxieties about the loss of expertise in the NHS, if this trend continues, with the totally separate provision of abortion in private charity centres although this may help to improve NHS funding of abortions.

ABORTION METHODS

In this section we look at the various available methods of abortion: medical termination (mifepristone), vacuum aspiration, dilation and evacuation and induced labour (prostaglandin) and two-stage process for late abortions. We outline in layman's terms how these are conducted and go on to discuss the possible risks and complications. This is deliberate as counsellors need to be able to communicate accurately, but in simple language, what happens and what can be expected.

The 1992 figures for England and Wales show that a total of 152,786 terminations were carried out using vacuum aspiration and/or dilation and curettage/evacuation. The number of medical abortions using mifepristone was low at 1,565. Those inducing labour with prostaglandins and other agents were 5,946.

The current figures from the Scottish Office show a significant increase in the number of terminations performed by medical method: up from 12 per cent of all terminations in 1990 to 27 per cent in 1994. This corresponds to a decrease in the use of vacuum aspiration from 84 per cent to 67 per cent.

Medical abortion using mifepristone (RU486)

This drug binds tightly to progesterone receptors in the woman's body and effectively blocks its action; without progesterone a miscarriage follows. Medical abortion involves three visits to the hospital or approved clinic. RU486 is taken by mouth at the hospital and women usually stay under medical supervision for two hours. Some women will miscarry at this stage (the endometrium begins to erode and the implanted embryo is expelled along with some of the lining of the womb).

A prostaglandin analogue is given, as a pessary that the woman can place in the vagina herself when she returns to the clinic less than forty-eight hours later. Bleeding usually starts fairly soon and the woman may have painful uterine contractions before 'miscarrying'. This usually takes place over about six hours.

Women need a follow-up appointment at the clinic a few days later, when an ultrasound scan is taken to establish that they are no longer pregnant. Medical abortion needs to be performed early before the woman is nine weeks pregnant (sixty-three days from LMP). Around 5–10 per cent of women miscarry with mifepristone alone, there is no 'turning back' at this point and Diana Mansour at Margaret Pyke Centre in London has evidence of possible limb deformities if a woman failed to miscarry and continued (Abortion Services in England and Wales, paper given at this conference 1994, London).

This drug, developed by Roussel-Uclaf, is expensive (1991 UK NHS rate for RU486, £42.90 per 600 mg and the prostaglandin pessaries, usually Gemeprost, in England cost £21 each). A study of the relative economic costs to the NHS of a medical abortion versus surgical vacuum aspiration, including the cost to the woman herself (travelling, child care etc.) carried out in Aberdeen, concluded that a medical abortion under eight weeks used 8 per cent less resources (£343 v. £374) and 18 per cent less of the woman's resources when compared to vacuum aspiration (Henshaw *et al.* 1994: 64–8).

Women may choose this method because it is non-surgical, does not require general anaesthetic and can seem more natural. On the other hand, for young people, especially those who have not experienced any contraction-like pain, the method can be frightening. The number of visits it requires may also be off-putting, especially if no one else must know about the pregnancy. The complication and risk rate is similar to that for surgical abortion. The method has a 5 per cent failure rate, when a surgical abortion would be needed, and a 1 per cent intervention rate because of bleeding, pain or retention of products of conception. Women who do experience pain should be advised to avoid asprin for 8–10 days as there is a theoretical risk that it can inhibit the prostaglandin action, and increase blood loss.

Mifepristone is also used to halt cancers (breast, meningioma, reversing symptoms in Cushing syndrome) and induce labour. Research is being carried out into other uses (primarily for glaucoma, ulcers and wound healing) and there is a possibility that the drug could be used as a contraceptive, or as a very early interrupter of pregnancy. In the USA there has been no research as the anti-abortion lobby has blocked use of the 'death pill' (Sloane 1993).

Vacuum aspiration

The most commonly used method of abortion in the United Kingdom, used in over 80 per cent of abortions is vacuum aspiration under a general anaesthetic or, more rarely, with a local preparation applied to the cervix. Women who are given a general anaesthetic will be unconscious for around ten minutes during which time they will be unable to feel anything and have no memories or feelings. A cannula (a narrow flexible hollow tubing) is passed up the vagina and carefully into the womb and vacuum aspiration is used to remove the pregnancy. This process takes several minutes. The contents of the womb should be checked following aspiration to ensure that the expected pregnancy has been removed, and to ensure that the pregnancy is not ectopic.

The woman will be taken to a recovery room but rarely remembers being woken up and will wake up, with hearing often the first sense to return. Some women feel 'woozy', others are crying or giggling. Most women will bleed and may have accompanying period-like or even contraction-like pain. Bleeding can be anything from non-existent, merely dark brown staining to a bright red blood loss continuing for ten days gradually decreasing.

The next period will occur fourteen days after the first ovulation. This is a very important point to stress, as women need to know they will be fertile *before* their next period. The next menstruation will be between two and six weeks, normally about a month later.

Dilation and evacuation

This method could be used under twelve weeks but would generally be used from fourteen to eighteen weeks from last menstrual period. The gynaecologist makes a clinical decision based on experience and training. It is always performed under a general anaesthetic. Greater dilation of the cervix is required and a cannula of greater diameter (12–21mm) is directed into the womb. The foetus is larger, the placenta formed and evacuating forceps are used as well as suction to complete the process. The cervix needs to be carefully dilated to avoid cervical tears. When a pregnancy is over ten weeks in first pregnancies and in all pregnancies over twelve weeks, various cervical preparations can be used prior to the abortion to dilate the cervix (prostaglandin pessaries), materials that swell with moisture (Laminaria tents) or mifepristone by mouth (Mansour and Stacey 1994). Identifiable foetal parts are removed. This technique requires skill and is seen as being technically and aesthetically difficult.

Late two-stage dilation and evacuation

This is done for pregnancies over twenty weeks and involves a two-day stay in hospital. First the woman is given a general anaesthetic and the cervix is dilated, often using laminary tents, the membranes are broken and then the cord is clamped and cut. The next day the woman is again anaesthetized and the foetus is removed using forceps. Two stages are necessary because the foetus is easier to remove after maceration has set in following the cutting of the umbilical cord. Women are often seen the next day for a dilation and curettage (D&C) under general anaesthetic.

Induced labour or prostaglandin abortion

This is still the more commonly used method for abortions over fourteen weeks. To start contractions the prostaglandins such as Gemeprost can be introduced either via the vagina or by a needle into the amniotic fluid. The woman may also be given drugs (syntocinon) intravenously via a drip to maintain the process. A prostaglandin abortion happens whilst the woman is fully conscious and can take up to twelve hours to complete. The contractions may be painful and women need to have adequate analgesia and privacy as with labour. The woman will eventually 'expel' the foetus.

If the abortion is taking place later than twenty weeks urea can be added to the syntocinon to ensure that the foetus is not alive on delivery. Diana Mansour reports that an alternative method of ensuring the same end is for 'the gynaecologist to inject potassium chloride directly into the fetal heart' (Mansour and Stacey 1994: 36). It is now possible to use a combination of mifepristone followed 2 days later by misoprostol tablets intra-vaginally. This is a simpler, possible safer method of inducing a mid-trimester abortion and may become more available.

RISKS TO HEALTH

Women need to be informed of the small health risks involved in abortion which are dramatically increased when the abortion is delayed beyond the first trimester. Some women will assume that if they have complications this means that the operation has been done badly.

The physical complications of a surgical abortion can include uterine perforation (3/1,000 abortions by dilation and vacuum aspiration, Mansour and Stacey 1994: 37), haemorrhage, the anaesthetic risks, damage to the cervix and infection that may, if untreated, lead to infertility. In practice, if the abortion is carried out in a well-equipped clinic before twelve weeks gestation, there are very few complications. From twelve to eighteen weeks prostaglandin abortion is associated with more reactions to the drugs used and haemorrhage than dilation and evacuation while this method has more risk of uterine injury (ibid. 1994: 37).

The mortality rate, in the UK, is less than 1 per 100,000 abortions and less than 0.5–2 per cent of women are readmitted to hospital with pain, bleeding or fever, usually due to incomplete abortion or an infection. Infection will often cause women to have lower abdominal soreness and a temperature. If the infection is diagnosed and treated there are usually no long-term problems. All women requesting abortion should be screened for sexually transmitted infections, especially Chlamydia Trachomatis, as untreated severe infections can lead to blocked fallopian tubes and possible infertility.

The risks to women are increased in the case of late abortion. After twelve weeks gestation the:

> rate of complications rises to 3 to 5 percent and the mortality rate increases to 9 to 12 per 100,000. There is no reduction of the woman's fertility or any increase in the risk of spontaneous abortion, preterm birth or fetal loss in a subsequent pregnancy.
>
> (Llewellyn-Jones 1994: 105)

Chapter 8 looks in detail at the possible emotional sequelae of abortion. How each individual can be helped by the pregnancy counsellor to decide what is the best course of action is the subject of the following chapters.

Chapter 4

Counselling: definitions and constraints

In this chapter we want to look at the availability of counselling, who should provide and who should receive this counselling, and what constitutes pregnancy counselling. We also look at issues that are fundamentally related to good practice; legal matters related to pregnancy counselling, confidentiality, and cross-cultural considerations.

THE AVAILABILITY OF COUNSELLING

We believe that adequate counselling should be offered to all who need to make a decision concerning a pregnancy. Counselling provides time for exploration, discussion, information, explanation and advice.

> A woman considering abortion should be able to discuss and explore her difficulties in an informal and unhurried manner. She should be told the nature of the operation (risks and alternatives). She should thus become more fully aware of the implications of the continuation, or alternatively the termination of her pregnancy and be helped to arrive at a wise and independent decision as to what her real wishes are.
>
> (Lane Committee, Section K, 1977, HC(77)26)

The Lane Committee, which was set up to look at the working of the Abortion Act in 1974, found that facilities for counselling were inadequate and they are still patchy, twenty years later. For example, of three South London hospitals one offers pregnant women counselling by a social worker; another by a lay counsellor; and the third offers no counselling at all. The difference is not due to the needs of the population they serve, which is similar in population size, demography and deprivation, it simply reflects the lack of a thought out provision for pregnancy counselling.

WHO SHOULD PROVIDE COUNSELLING?

Isobel Allen's study, *Family Planning, Sterilisation and Abortion Services* (1985) stated there was clear evidence of professional inability to sort out who needed what kind of counselling:

There was no generally accepted standard of practice and no agreement on aims and objectives of counselling of this kind. Techniques had been borrowed from a number of different disciplines and there was evidence that there was very imperfect understanding among professionals on both practice and purpose.

(Allen 1985: Introduction)

A wide range of health professionals and lay people undertake pregnancy counselling today, not all of whom receive counselling supervision or are trained counsellors. The Department of Health has never given detailed advice as to who should provide counselling or how such help should be provided. This has meant that systems have evolved and reflect the priorities that professionals have attached to counselling. A London hospital that still does not offer counselling prior to abortion will ask the obstetric and gynaecological social workers to see women afterwards, which they feel leaves them to 'pick up the pieces'.

Today there is a fresh emphasis on primary care in the community and general practitioners would seem admirably suited to provide pregnancy counselling. The GP may know a woman well, be familiar with her circumstances, have a sympathetic attitude to her possible embarrassment in owning up to an unwanted pregnancy and give her the time she needs while minimizing any interruptions (phones ringing, etc.). Other general practitioners can be less sensitive or have their own strong emotive reactions.

In order to avoid the situation where a woman either receives counselling from every professional she meets or none at all, thought needs to be applied to the aim of counselling, and who is best placed and/or trained to deliver this service.

Ideally, a pregnancy counsellor needs the foundation of a training in counselling, preferably to diploma level. Training to this level involves at least 400 hours of staff contact either as a one-year full-time course or a two- to three-year part-time course. Diploma courses carefully recruit and select their counselling students using procedures designed to ensure that the student has sufficient ability to cope with emotional stress, is able to reflect, can demonstrate self-awareness, maturity and academic skills.

Courses recognized by the British Association of Counselling (the nearest the emergent profession gets to a regulatory body) require students to counsel 'real' clients (not role play). Supervision is mandatory and involves a high degree of self-examination and the the ability to monitor, evaluate and be accountable for counselling work (see Chapter 9).

Diploma students are expected to undertake written work, at least 10,000 words, and the appropriate research 'to clarify philosophical and theoretical concepts and their application to practical counselling work' (BAC 1990a: 6). A core theoretical model would be explored in some depth on a diploma course (psychodynamic, person-centred, etc.) and compared with other theories. Counsellors are expected to be professional and to monitor their skills, and take part in on-going self-development and training. In addition to this training, pregnancy counsellors need the experience of working with a wide range of individuals who are coping with crisis.

It is important that the pregnancy counsellor is able to allow the exploration of feelings without reacting or being defensive to the client's judgements or assumptions. In this way the counsellor does not add to the stigma, isolation or anxiety that a woman may be feeling. Ending a potential life is still seen by most people as shameful and taboo; if clients feel the counsellor is not 'on their side' this can inhibit decision-making or add to their tension by increasing feelings of guilt or rejection. The counsellor does not assume what the woman will or will not want, feel or think.

The personal qualities of the counsellor are especially important when time is at a premium. For this reason training could be offered to those who show perceptiveness and sensitivity for this demanding and rewarding work, whether they are lay people, nurses, doctors or social workers.

The appropriate qualities are difficult to acquire through training alone, however comprehensive, unless the counsellor's disposition naturally encompasses the personal attributes of resilience, empathy and integrity. Counsellors need to demonstrate empathic concern so the client feels valued, 'looked after' and respected. When the counsellor can be realistically hopeful and resilient, avoiding false optimism, her persistence can reassure a client that this person at least is not going to 'give up' or abandon her.

Doctors, both general practitioners and family planning doctors, are also often expected to undertake the legal decision-making (does the woman have grounds under the 1967 Act?) and to separate this from the exploratory role of counselling. Clients can see the doctor's role as hierarchical and authoritarian. When a client has negative feelings about the abortion that their doctor has taken the trouble to agree and arrange they may feel unable to return for post-abortion counselling.

Women themselves often find it difficult to believe counselling will help, especially after they have allowed a permanent and irreversible event such as an abortion to happen.

WHO SHOULD RECEIVE COUNSELLING?

We feel, as the Birth Control Trust does, in their 'Model Specification for Abortion Services' that:

> Counselling should be available and, in about twenty per cent of cases, will need to be in depth. It must be possible for those who remain ambivalent to see the counsellor on subsequent occasion(s) to enable them to come to an appropriate decision. [It is estimated that ninety per cent will choose to have an abortion, about eight per cent to continue with their pregnancy, one per

cent will have presented too late for an termination and one per cent will not be pregnant.]

(Birth Control Trust 1994: 5.4)

Hare and Haywood (1981) in their study of women's needs for pregnancy counselling found that: 48 per cent had made a clear decision; 32 two per cent were ambivalent; 20 per cent were unprepared and needed time to consider their decision.

This leaves an estimated 52 per cent of women who could benefit from counselling. However, the other 48 per cent of women who have made a decision often benefit from counselling. They can use the counsellor as an invaluable resource to gain more understanding of how their pregnancy occurred, and how to prevent another unwanted pregnancy. It has been argued that only women who want to see a counsellor should do so (Allen 1982) and some of the pregnancy advisory services have recently switched to seeing only those women who ask to see a counsellor. Paradoxically, it may be those women who 'know what they want, and don't want to talk about it' who will use the session, if offered, to explore relevant issues. We feel that if the counsellor has the skill and ability to match her counselling to the individual, then she can respond to the situation and avoid being intrusive. The client after all may only require information.

In 1994 Brook undertook a survey of their clients' expectations of counsellors and counselling (unpublished) and the most common statement was that women want someone to demonstrate that they 'understand', 'I only want to be listened to'. After counselling, clients recorded that they actually received less advice than they expected but were understood, heard and enabled to talk. A total of 96 per cent found the counselling helpful.

Marcus (1979) identified five pregnancy counselling goals:

1 increase contraceptive uptake;
2 reduce repeat terminations;
3 consider alternatives;
4 improve medical follow-up rate;
5 reduce negative feelings relating to the abortion.

All of these are worthwhile goals, though Marcus' research found that only the last goal was achieved with any reliability.

WHO ARE THE CLIENTS?

Any woman can be unhappily pregnant and benefit from an opportunity to talk. For many women this may be the only time they see a counsellor, and some women are unused to communicating complex feelings in words.

Clients who can especially benefit from counselling and have been reported to be more likely to suffer psychologically after an abortion (Allen 1982; Ashton 1980) are:

1 adolescents;
2 those who have not started or completed mourning past losses;
3 those suffering from depression, or with a history of mental health problems;
4 those with a history of gynaecological problems;
5 those with a history of repeat abortion, still births, difficult births, miscarriages;
6 those who are highly anxious or show a marked calmness which is inappropriate to their situation;
7 those whose feel or have felt unwanted, e.g. 'in care';
8 those who have been emotionally, physically or sexually abused;
9 those with eating disorders, addictions and compulsive behaviours;
10 those having terminations for medical reasons.

Adolescents can present the counsellor with sharply delineated views and feelings; they tend to be dissatisfied with the choice of abortion, viewing abortion as 'wrong' and perhaps because of this often present late. Research shows they can report greater severity of psychological stress, and deserve careful counselling (Franz and Reardon 1992). We have devoted part of Chapter 6 to the counselling of young people.

Women making a difficult decision about a pregnancy have to struggle with complex emotions that also affect those close to them. Some people will be lucky enough to have friends and relatives who are able to listen and share some of these conflicting feelings whilst at the same time containing their own feelings and ideas. Some women will have their difficulties compounded by other peoples' reactions.

Men can feel emotionally pregnant but can never experience pregnancy, abortion or birth at first hand. This fact is often reinforced when they accompany women for counselling or consultation and staff seem uninterested in them. When men are excluded from the counselling session, this naturally heightens a sense of being discarded. There is no monopoly on hurt and often both men and women accuse each other of being selfish and 'not being there' for each other.

Women and men can be isolated by the crisis of an unhappy pregnancy, especially if accompanied by shame, which can go back to early childhood feelings of weakness and vulnerability. Clients can lack human or financial resources and this can deplete the energy needed for creative thinking and atrophy the ability to act, seek help or make a decision.

WHAT IS PREGNANCY COUNSELLING?

It is commonplace for the term counselling to be very loosely used even amongst health professionals so that part of a consultation may be labelled 'counselling' when it would be more accurate to describe it as advice or even information-giving.

We believe the main purpose of pregnancy counselling is to provide people with time to look at their pregnancy and situation, explore all possible options and make an informed choice when they feel ready to do so in as non-threatening an environment as possible.

Pregnancy brings with it enormous physiological, emotional and psychological changes, as outlined in Chapter 2, making thinking and acting decisively more difficult as the body adapts to its pregnant state. Pregnancy itself is complicated and involves conflicting feelings and paradoxes: women often feel isolated yet have a constant companion, one who has not been invited or has become unwelcome, and yet has decided to stay; who is invisible and yet is felt often as a presence extremely early in a pregnancy. This other being that is conceived as part and not part of a pregnant woman cannot be universally defined, as everyone has their own individual way of seeing a foetus.

Individual descriptions range all the way from clients saying 'it's only blood isn't it?' to others talking of a fully fledged baby complete with gender and personality. An abortion involves letting other people physically invade the client's body and take away whatever the client has constructed as being her pregnancy. Simone De Beauvoir wrote about these feelings:

> In her heart she often repudiates the interruption of pregnancy which she is seeking to obtain. She is divided against herself. Her natural tendency can well be to have the baby whose birth she is undertaking to prevent: even if there is no positive desire for maternity, she still feels uneasy about the dubious act she is engaged in.
>
> (De Beauvoir 1992: 507–8)

Set against this is the harsh reality of an abortion where the foetus is treated medically as waste, in the same way that other unwanted tissues are, and is incinerated.

Pregnancy counselling involves a confusing mixture of assessment, counselling, information-giving, practical help (arranging their chosen help, referrals for counselling, or other professional help) or even, on occasion, advice and guidance, which would come outside the British Association of Counselling's definition of the term counselling. It is messy and consequently difficult to neatly define pregnancy counselling, as so many areas overlap and there are different strands which interweave. There are however, some key issues which all counsellors must address.

Checking the facts

Counsellors first need to check facts, for example, has there been a reliable pregnancy test or examination? Home tests are accurate, but anxious women can read them wrongly or use them too early to get an accurate result. Sometimes an ultrasound scan is needed if a woman has, for example, had amenorrhoea due to oral contraception, or is found by examination to be more or less pregnant than her dates. An ultrasound scan though is only accurate to plus or minus a week; the optimum time for assessing gestation is sixteen weeks from the last menstrual period (LMP).

Pregnancy counselling requires accurate detective work so that the woman, or couple, has all the facts. If a client makes a statement such as 'I can't be pregnant', this assumption has to be checked. The false premise may be that the client has decided that her sexual behaviour is 'safe' rather than that she has not had any sexual relations. All this may sound obvious, but can be crucial.

Kelly (15 years old) was running away from home, when an educational social worker turned up to speak to her mother as Kelly was climbing over her garden wall. It had transpired that her teacher had felt she had to inform the 'authorites' when Kelly, unable to concentrate on her school work through anxiety, had confessed that she was pregnant. Kelly told the counsellor that she 'must be pregnant as she had not come on'. Kelly was not in fact pregnant; she had not had a test or examination. For this young woman, this negligence was tragic. Her relationship with her mother worsened, a fragile trust was shattered because by Kelly's actions she had revealed that she might have been pregnant and had been sexually active.

Pregnancy tests

Before counselling begins the doctor may be in the position of breaking 'bad news'. This is always difficult and letting someone know of their unwanted pregnancy is no exception. There is no easy or right way of doing this and the way it is done will be individual to each woman. Hearing the result will affect each woman in her own way but sometimes the immediate trauma can be moderated by sensitive care.

Some women come prepared for a positive result and only want confirmation of their worst fears. Other women who seem prepared to hear that the test is positive are still overcome by the painful realization that they are indeed pregnant. Others, though concerned enough to have a test, have not allowed the reality of the situation to sink in. They will not let themselves think about the possibility of the pregnancy until they have a confirmed result.

The time before undertaking a test can be used to encourage the woman to talk through the possibility of being pregnant. This helps the woman focus on and acknowledge the seriousness of her situation. This anticipatory concern can pave the way for dealing with a confirmatory result. Even when the result is negative this time can be spent as a prelude to further discussion about never 'wanting to go through that scare again' and the contraceptive choices available.

Women can be in such an agony of apprehension that they need to know, and are unable to respond to anything but 'knowing'. It can be uncomfortable to be in the position of knowing the result before the woman does. Sometimes it can feel right to watch the test together sharing the moment of confirmation.

Fourteen-year-old Tania came for a pregnancy test. She had been having unprotected intercourse but had since broken up with her boyfriend, and missed a period two weeks earlier. It was highly probable that she was going to have a positive result. She had come on her own and had not felt able to talk to anyone about her worries. She was unable to think what she would do if she were pregnant, and was quite distraught. The doctor was extremely concerned about doing the test when she was on her own. After a long discussion she agreed to come back the following day with her older sister. The test was indeed positive and it was clear that the older sister could help Tania through the next few days.

The doctor felt in this case it had been right to ask the client to come back. She did not consider how she would have felt if the girl had never returned or if her sister had not been helpful.

'Chris just wants a pregnancy test. Can you do it for her? She doesn't mind what the result is?' The doctor agreed to do the test without preparation and Chris's screams of pain still resonate inside her. Chris never came back and the doctor resolved not to repeat this casual telling again.

Giving information

Difficult information (such as the results of a pregnancy test, the method of late abortion or being told there is a four-week wait for a gynaecologist) can be startling. Various defence mechanisms can be stirred up, which attempt to control anxiety by in some way disassociating the person from what is happening. In this way they are protected from having feelings or thoughts which are too disturbing. Women disassociate in many different ways, by day-dreaming, by watching themselves as if on film, giggling, being so numb that they have no reaction, by dwelling on one aspect of their predicament (for example, getting help without a parent knowing) or by having other people present (small children, partners). As in all counselling it is useful to be reminded that this is a familiar reaction to any information that has to be internalized before a client can react. A counsellor will usually spot if the client has no reaction; but if a women nods and smiles, it is possible to miss the fact that she has 'blanked out' and is not hearing or retaining any information.

Recap essential information, and give your name and where and when you can be contacted, underlining that sometimes people cannot take everything in at once and may need or want to see you again. Written information, though useful, will be no help if a client is illiterate. Conflicting information affects an individual's confidence in their helpers and themselves, so if you work in a team it is important to check that information is consistent.

When a client is reluctant to give any information, or is suspicious, it is important to resist withdrawing from the session in return. Focus on the individual's motivation for this behaviour. Tell the client that it is their prerogative not to talk, or give any information. Usually this ability to hold back will increase a feeling of safety for the client who may choose to talk later in the session.

Few people can concentrate for longer than twenty minutes, even when they are in good health, happy, motivated and stand to benefit from the information received. The attention span is drastically reduced in a stressful situation. Factual information needs to be repeated to be retained. There is also a tendency to recall negative facts. We all define words differently and attach our own values; 'sometimes' can mean 'often' or 'rarely'. The counsellor needs to be as unambiguous as possible and use the client's own words and phrases. The counsellor avoids giving information that the client has not asked for, and allows sufficient 'thinking time' for the client to come back with their questions.

Family and friends

When a pregnant woman comes accompanied (by friends, partners, key workers) it needs to be established that you can see them together. Some people will come strongly attached to a parent or friend, others will be at the opposite end of a scale and refuse to look at the accompanying person and the atmosphere is tense or hostile.

When seeing a couple it is useful to allow each of them to express their feelings whilst helping the other partner to hear what is being said. To foster this clear communication the couple can be asked to repeat in their own words what the other has said, and to face each other. The couple may also benefit from indentifying if they are making this decision as a couple or individually. This can highlight conflict and opposing wishes, and gives both a chance to be supported by the counsellor.

However, it is important to see the client alone, briefly, to check for coercion. It can be a mistake not to see a woman alone.

Celia, 15 years old, had been examined and was twenty-two weeks pregnant. Twelve weeks previously she had been taken to the family GP, as her mother knew she had not had a period for some time. Celia had a well-established menstrual cycle. Celia's mother was anxious, as she had conceived Celia at a similar age, of course she was also keen to have her fears allayed. Celia was not seen alone, and was asked in her mother's presence if she 'could be pregnant' Celia felt obliged to deny vehemently that this was possible.

Celia had a good relationship with her mother and knew she was trusted. Her mother had made it clear that she did not want her to have sex, but had also told her that if she needed contraception she must come and tell her. Celia chose to lie rather than hurt her mother, listening to the 'feeling' message rather than the rational one. The GP advised that the amenorrhoea was common at this age, and to return if necessary. Her mother left much more cheerful and relieved. Celia came to the centre because of strange 'fluttery feelings' in her tummy which turned out to be foetal movements.

The counselling approach

The most suitable counselling approach is one that lessens threat and enables the focus to be kept on the client's needs. It has proved notoriously difficult to evaluate the effectiveness of counselling. Available research has shown that the client's feeling of being 'understood' is the decisive factor in the relationship, not the method or technique that is used. We feel this is the core requirement for pregnancy counselling (Ashurst and Ward 1983; Corney 1990).

Techniques that have been developed for time-limited counselling can be effective as these make the most of the 'honeymoon' stage of counselling. The pregnancy counsellor works at being as understanding as possible of whatever the client brings, before there is time for transference to develop (although this can happen before meeting) so that the client can get the maximum benefit from being supported by the counsellor.

Whatever the theoretical background of the counsellor there are several important areas that need to be covered. In every case the counsellor, whatever additional roles (such as doctor, nurse, social worker), will need to set the boundaries of the counselling relationship, offer uninterrupted time, preferably of a stated length, and outline the total duration of time available for counselling, (the number of sessions for the client to explore their feelings around pregnancy) and to make clear the limits of confidentiality and access to the counsellor.

The counsellor's task is to create a sufficiently welcoming space, rapidly build a working relationship and demonstrate respect for the client. The counsellor needs to establish that the client understands what help is being offered and what that individual client wants. The counsellor also provides help by staying with the client's ambivalence whilst she is making a decision. Once the client has decided to continue or terminate the pregnancy, the counsellor helps the client to accept and deal with the possible consequences of this decision.

RESOURCES AND SETTING

The setting in which the counselling takes place naturally affects what is offered; this needs to be clearly established with clients and any limitations specifically spelled out.

Ideally, a pregnancy counsellor should have the resources to to see clients (male or female) at any point during a pregnancy or after an abortion or birth, regardless of the decision the individual has made. In reality, the resources may be unavailable; the counsellor needs to understand that if, for example, they can only see a client once without the possibility of on-going counselling, then the intensity of the session has to reflect this and the client needs to be told of the various alternative therapy and counselling resources available in the area. The duration and frequency of counselling sessions, the skill and competence of the counsellor, as well as the ability of the client to pay for help or travel will vary and has to be taken into account. When a service is not free, is a long way from their home or at an unsuitable time (e.g., daytime for a single working parent) this does not provide open access and will impose restrictions for some clients.

Clients can have problems getting appropriate help.

Gloria, 28 years old, had an abortion in October. She was shocked and hurt to have conceived whilst using contraception. This was compounded when she was told by her partner and brother that she should have an abortion, which she felt told her respectively that her child, and therefore herself, was unwanted, unloved and that she could not cope. She duly had an abortion. Gloria spoke of various kinds of emotional and physical abandonment that had occurred throughout her childhood and left her unable to trust others or herself.

Although she had received counselling from the family planning nurse who was a trained counsellor she had brought along her partner, and her hurt and humiliation did not emerge. She felt unable afterwards to go back to the family planning clinic as this had not been suggested and the counsellor had not helped her express her feelings. She went to her GP, where there was a counselling service, and was told that the practice counsellor was 'full up', a further rejection. Gloria was prescribed anti-depressants with which she tried to commit suicide. At hospital she was seen routinely by the psychiatrist who suggested that she come in for an in-patient stay to get away from her problems. She saw this as too drastic, implying that she was mentally unwell. She returned to her doctor a couple of months later for further anti-depressants but did not manage to tell him that she was having increasingly aggressive feelings towards her partner who had moved out. She felt desperate.

This sad series of events might have been avoided by sharper pre-abortion counselling and the offer of further on-going help. Even though the practice counsellor was full up Gloria could have been assessed and referred for post-abortion counselling, as there was a specific service devoted to this in her area.

There is unfortunately no nationally or locally organized network of information for counselling referral that covers individual counsellors, counselling agencies and statutory agencies (a need that could be met by an enterprising computer company as any information needs regular updating). Counsellors need to badger their employers to provide such information.

The actual setting where the counselling takes place should set the scene. If possible, the room should be welcoming, with soft lighting and easy chairs. Often, however, the counsellor will be seeing a woman in a clinical setting, a stark room which is multi-purpose. Any agencies or purchasers of counselling services need to ask themselves, 'Would I feel comfortable in this setting to talk about painful feelings connected with pregnancy?' Rooms with all the paraphernalia of a baby clinic, (wall displays promoting breast feeding, special baby scales) can be upsetting; those with no windows, or where cardboard boxes and other junk are stored, can be unsettling as they can give the message that the session is as unimportant as the discarded rubbish.

Whatever the resources, it is always possible to take down the posters or buy a bunch of flowers. We aim at neutrality. The chairs that are available should be on the same level, so neither of you are looking up or down at each other. Everyone has their own distance from others that they feel comfortable with, if chairs can be moved, this gives the other person extra control; seemingly small things increase a feeling of trust and safety, reducing a climate of threat.

Safety for the client and counsellor needs to be considered. Can you both call out to other staff? Do you need a personal alarm? Is there a way of signalling for help? If your client can hear others outside the room she may fear that others can also hear and this may increase her feeling of anxiety. A radio in the waiting area is an effective way of blocking out conversation but not a shout for help.

THE LAW AROUND CONSENT

It is important for pregnancy counsellors to be aware of their legal position and that of the staff with whom they work.

Consent

A doctor has to have the consent of a patient before undertaking any treatment, whether or not the doctor feels a refusal of treatment is wise or unwise. Linda Heywood, barrister, spelled out that the intent of the law is 'to prevent interference of one person with another person's wishes and allows the patient full self determination' (Heywood 1994: 63).

To be valid consent must be given voluntarily and be informed consent. The patient, or client, must have sufficient information, provided in a way that they can understand, to form an opinion. The information must include the relevant risks and benefits of treatment or non-treatment.

Thus anyone deemed competent, who is aware of the ramifications of treatment is able to give their consent, regardless of age.

British Law is primarily made up of case law, rather than statute, which means that a legal ruling on a new case can alter the law. A classic example is the case of Victoria Gillick who challenged the law when she did not want her daughters, who were under 16, offered contraceptive help without her knowledge (Gillick v Norfolk and West Wisbech [1986] A.C. 112, H.L.). For the following year it was unlawful to provide contraception to young people under 16 who refused to tell their parents they were requesting contraception.

The decision was reversed by Appeal in the House of Lords. The guidance the Law Lords gave established that 'giving contraceptive advice to young people under 16 years does not necessarily infringe parental rights nor are the doctors who act in good faith committing the criminal offence of aiding and abetting sexual intercourse with young people under 16' (Brook 1995: 5).

One of the Law Lords was Lord Fraser and his original judgement forms the basis of the revised guidelines issued by the Department of Health and Social Security and the Welsh Office in 1986 in England and Wales. Similar guidance was issued in Northern Ireland. In Scotland those under 16 can consent to contraceptive treatment if their doctor feels they are capable of understanding the nature and possible consequences of the procedure (The Age of Legal Capacity (Scotland) Act 1991 section 2(4)).

FRASER GUIDELINES

Contraceptive treatment for young people under 16.

2 In considering the provision of advice and treatment on contraception doctors and other professional staff need to take special care not to undermine parental responsibility and family stability. The doctor or other professional should seek to persuade the young person to tell parents or guardian (or other person *in loco parentis*) or to let him inform them, of advice or treatment that is given. It should be most unusual for a doctor or other professional to provide advice or treatment in relation to contraception to a young person under 16 without parental knowledge or consent.

3 Exceptionally, there will be cases where it is not possible to persuade the young person to do so. This may be, for example, where family relationships have broken down. In such cases, a doctor or other professional would be justified in giving advice or treatment without parental knowledge or consent provided he was satisfied:

1 the young person could understand his advice and had sufficient maturity to understand what was involved in terms of moral social and emotional implications;
2 that he could neither persuade the young person to inform the parents, nor allow him to inform them, that contraceptive advice was being sought;
3 that the young person would be very likely to begin or to continue having sexual intercourse with or without treatment;
4 that, without contraceptive advice or treatment, the young person's physical or mental health or both would be likely to suffer;
5 that the young person's best interests required him to give contraceptive advice or treatment or both without parental consent.

  (Health Circular HC(86) 1, Local Authority Circular LAC (86)3)

The full text is given as an appendix in Brook's excellent booklet, *Under 16s. The law and public policy on contraception and abortion in the UK, 1995.*

It is therefore possible for health professional working with young people in their best interests to provide contraceptions and other medical treatment. When a young person is able to fulfil *all* the criteria laid down in The Fraser Guidelines they are what has become known ironically as 'Gillick competent'. To establish that this is the case requires professional staff to be experienced at working with young people and has to be done on an individual basis. Confusion can arise when health professionals consider the young person to lack maturity or for their actions to be unwise. It does not alter the fact that young people can understand the consequences of medical treatment and give their consent.

A parliamentary question in 1987 clarified the position on abortion and consent:

Sir John Biggs-Davidson asked the Secretary of State for Social Services in what circumstances minors may be invited to give written consent to an abortion and to a general anaesthesthetic for such an abortion, without parental knowledge; and whether he will make a statement.

The Minister for Health (Tony Newton): 'Written consent may be given in the circumstances described if, in the judgement of the doctor concerned, it is in the patient's best medical interest and she has sufficient maturity and understanding to appreciate what is involved.'

(*Hansard* 10 February 1987 Vol. 110 No. 49 Col. 147)

This does not mean that a 14-year-old will easily be able to get help with an abortion. Many doctors would be unwilling to agree that such a serious procedure should be undertaken without a parent's knowledge, even if consent is deemed unnecessary.

Doctors need the written consent of one parent if they consider the young person is unable through lack of understanding to give their consent (Medical Defence Union: *Consent to Treatment* 1991).

In practice it is only in exceptional situations that a referral for abortion is made without parental consent and that a consultant agrees to terminate in these circumstances. If a parent disagrees with a young person's request for abortion the consultant gynaecologist will be guided by whatever course of action he or she considers to be in their patient's best interests.

A young person may be estranged from their parents and parental responsibility may be shared with the local authority. In such cases either can give consent if the young person is deemed unable to do so.

In England and Wales under section 33(3) of the Children Act 1989 and where the child is subject to a care order, the extent of parental responsibility can be determined by the local authority to protect the child's welfare. In Ireland parental responsibility passes from the parent of a child in care to the Health and Social Services Board. This Board takes account of the moral and religious views of the child's parents. The position in Scotland is different. The exact terms of a supervision requirement determine whether parental rights remain with the parents or with the local authority. A young person is still able to give consent. In practice, if the issue arises, the local authority should advise the child's parents, but if the issue is not resolved it can be referred to a Children's Hearing.

If a young person has been made a Ward of Court the designated officer of the court has to be informed before any treatment can take place, though help in our experience is unlikely to be refused if this is seen to be in the young person's best interests.

Putative fathers (whether married or not to their partner) do not have any legal rights to give or withhold consent for contraceptive advice or for an abortion to take place. This has been challenged in the past but so far case law has sided with the woman. It has been deemed that her rights are paramount over her partner's whilst the pregnancy is contained within the woman's body and the foetus cannot survive outside her body.

The Children Act 1989 does not change existing legislation or guidance about those who are under 16 and reaffirms the present situation that decisions about care or treatment must be in the young person's best interests. Anyone over 16, who is not a Ward of Court, can give consent to treatment and this is reinforced by statute (Family Land Reform Act, 1969 S, 8(1)).

ACCESS TO CLIENTS' RECORDS

Clients may want to have access to their notes. The Access to Health Records Act, 1990, which operates for notes written since November 1991, allows people to see their records.

A parent can request to view their child's medical records but a clause within the Act gives permission to refuse access. A health professional who believes that the child has only given permission under duress can refuse access if this is not in the client's best interests. This would arise if, for example, a 14-year-old had been coming for contraception and had explained that for cultural and religious reasons her family would find this behaviour so unacceptable that her life would be in danger if it were disclosed. Parents can be asked to make a written request to see notes as this allows them to 'cool down' and gives time for a careful assessment of the situation.

All clients' notes may be subpoenaed by the courts. Counselling notes would probably not be regarded as material evidence unless the counsellor had recorded verbatim what the client had said and this revealed current or recent illegal activity, such as abuse. Counsellors can write case notes in the third person. Audio or video tapes are admissible evidence and could be subpoenaed. The General Medical Council Guidelines, 1995, reminded doctors that: 'In the absence of a court order, a request for disclosure by a third party, for example a solicitor, police officer, or officer of a court, is not sufficient justification for disclosure without a patient's consent' (General Medical Council 'Confidentiality': 6).

In 1994 eight cases at the Old Bailey involving requests for confidentiality to be broken were contested. In half the cases the judge decided that the notes were not material to the case and they remained confidential. This is a grey area open to dispute and challenge. However, it is likely that each case will be assessed on its individual merits.

CONFIDENTIALITY

Counsellors need to work within the legal framework and their professional code of practice and will make every effort to protect client confidentiality.

Confidentiality is of particular importance for counsellors, as clients need to freely explore their ideas, fears, intimate fantasies and innermost feelings knowing that the counsellor will not pass on such sensitive information. This can only happen when the client can trust the counsellor and confidentiality builds this trust. For this reason it needs to be borne in mind that limitations on confidentiality may diminish the usefulness of counselling.

All clients value confidentiality, especially adolescents, as they are growing at such a rate that their physical and psychological boundaries are rapidly altering and they need the containment and security that a promise of confidentiality confers.

Confidentiality means:

1 that anything the client says will be treated with respect;
2 that there will be no gossip;
3 that any material the client chooses to share with the counsellor remains with the counsellor, their supervisor or within the organization;
4 the limits of your policy on confidentiality, for example, abuse or self-harm are made clear.

Young people

Most young people will not confide if they feel that their parents or carers will be informed; they would prefer to risk pregnancy, which seems to them a remote possibility. When a service is not confidential many will vote with their feet and not return. Research showed that almost 75 per cent of young people under age 16 and 50 per cent of 16–19-year-olds interviewed feared that their GP could not or would not preserve confidentiality regarding contraceptive service (Allen 1990). More recently 50 per cent of 15-year-olds thought doctors had to tell of a request for contraception (Teenage Opinion Survey, FPA, Brook, HEA, 1994).

Doctors' professional code says that they owe the same duty of confidentiality to under 16-year-olds as they do to any other patients. As already outlined, any competent young person, regardless of age, can independently seek medical advice and give valid informed consent to medical treatment (British Medical Association 1994).

However, hospitals and other agencies that try to maintain confidentiality can have complex situations to deal with:

Marsha, age 15, was adamant that she did not want her mother told of this pregnancy; her mother had gone to the police when she discovered she had a boyfriend and could, she said, be unpredictable and violent. Marsha told the pregnancy counsellor that she had visited a project after she had run away from home and a reconciliation had only recently taken place. She could not bear anything to jeopardize this truce in their relationship.

Marsha had been referred without parental consent after several meetings with the counsellor. The counsellor had pointed out that if her mother did discover the pregnancy then the relationship could be further damaged. Just what Marsha wanted to avoid. The mother discovered papers relating to the abortion and came into the hospital in a highly distressed state.

The hospital counsellor could not know what the reality of the situation was but did not want to take any action without speaking independently to Marsha. Her mother told the counsellor that Marsha was being abusive and blaming the mother for her abortion as she could not confide in her. The daughter had refused to give any contact address which left both the hospital and the original community counsellor who had referred her to the hospital with anxiety and guilt. Would insisting that Marsha's mother was told have helped? Or would this have only denied Marsha anywhere to turn to for help?

The major problems in maintaining confidentiality are in cases where the client is in grave danger, or if siblings or other children in the community are deemed at risk of serious harm. It is also difficult in situations where the client is a risk to themselves or other people.

No confidentiality policy can offer an absolute right to complete confidentiality. Counsellors need to examine carefully their practice and feel confident to account for any decisions they take. It is possible for a professional to be sued for negligence if information is not disclosed and harm ensues. At the start of their relationship with the client the counsellor needs to make clear the limitations on confidentiality for their particular setting. A drawn-up policy can be useful but guidelines can never cover every eventuality.

The British Association of Counselling's 'Code of Ethics' (published in 1984 and revised in 1990) gives detailed consideration to the importance of confidentiality for clients' autonomy and self-determination and provides guidance on the limitations of confidentiality (BAC 1990b: B4–B8.2).

Tim Bond's book *Standards and Ethics for Counselling in Action* (1993) and the shorter pamphlet by the same author 'Counselling, Confidentiality and the Law' (1994) covers the legal position for counsellors, which in the main is determined by the setting in which they work, and the particular issues related to the Children Act, 1989 and child abuse.

He outlines that an obligation to be confidential is legally enforceable, if there is a verbal contract to maintain confidentiality between doctor/patient or counsellor/client. The law can therefore punish breaches of this contract, leading to litigation. Tim Bond was unable to find a case in which a counsellor has been sued for a breach of confidentiality, and thus there are no legal precedents.

Pregnancy counsellors will often be working in a medical setting and may be able to assert along with doctors, as stated in the Human Fertilisation and Embryology Authority Code of Practice, 1991, that 'information should be kept confidential' and that a record should be kept of the counselling offered, whether or not the offer was accepted, rather than the content of the counselling. This code also states that 'if a member of a team receives information of such gravity that confidentiality cannot be maintained, he or she should use his or her own discretion, based on good professional practice, in deciding in what circumstances it should be discussed with the rest of the team' (3.24).

Midwives, nurses and health visitors are also reminded in Clause 9 of their confidentiality code that 'the responsibility to disclose or withold confidential information lies with the individual practitioner and that s/he cannot delegate responsibility' (UKCC 1992). This places a grave responsibility on the practitioners to decide when to talk to others.

However, the law does not guarantee confidentiality as an absolute right. Counsellors would be expected to have high standards of confidentiality and Tim Bond emphasizes that it is acceptable or 'defensible' to breach confidentiality only in certain circumstances.

Defensible reasons to breach confidentiality

1 When the client has given express permission.
2 When the confidential information is already public knowledge (although the definition of 'public knowledge' could be disputed).
3 When the disclosed information is of such public interest that this overrides the right to confidentiality. If, for example, the confidential information told to the counsellor needs to be passed on to prevent serious physical harm to others or illegal activity.

Essential or mandatory legal reasons to breach confidentiality

1 Information covered by the Prevention of Terrorism (Temporary) Act, 1989, Section 18 (Northern Ireland).
2 A Judge may require a counsellor to appear as a witness and disclose information given in confidence. A refusal would constitute contempt of court. Tim Bond (1993) gives an example of a psychiatrist who refused to give confidential information on principle and was allowed to do this as a 'matter of conscience'.
3 A counsellor's notes can be subpoenaed by a court. (Legal arguments could dispute that the recorded information is not material (relevant) evidence.)

4 When specifically obliged by an employer's contract, usually in regard to abuse.

Exceptional circumstances

The principle of 'exceptional circumstances' where a counsellor might wish to breach confidentiality is outlined in the BAC 'Code of Ethics' (1990b):

> Exceptional circumstances may arise which give the counsellor good grounds for believing that the client will cause serious physical harm to others or themselves, or have harm caused to him/her. In such circumstances the client's consent to a change in the agreement about confidentiality should be sought whenever possible unless there are also good grounds for believing the client is no longer able to take responsibility for his/her own actions. Whenever possible, the decision to break confidentiality agreed between a counsellor and a client should be made only after consultation with a counselling supervisor or an experienced counsellor.
>
> (BAC 1990b: B.4.4)

This is a wide definition designed to cover as many different settings as possible. Many counselling agencies have a clearly worded policy statement that is drawn to the client's attention at the start of a counselling contract, leaving no ambiguity. Barbara Rayment (1994) argues in her useful pamphlet on confidentiality that terms such as grave or serious harm have to be spelt out. She feels the client is helped by the counsellor being honest and explicit about the boundaries of confidentiality.

Barbara Rayment (1994) gives two examples of exceptional circumstances statements by counselling agencies. The first is used by 'Off the Record' in Twickenham which says:

1 Where there is suspicion that an individual might cause physical harm to themselves or others.
2 If a client is no longer in a fit state to make rational decisions or take responsibility for their actions.
3 A child or young person is in a life-threatening situation. A situation is life threatening if:

   a) The young person is now so physically damaged that immediate medical attention is necessary.
   b) The next time the young person meets the abuser there is a danger of physical harm or death.
   c) The young person is sufficiently scared that they will possibly take their own life, take a major risk (e.g. running away), or generally placing themselves in an unsafe situation.

or from 'No Limits' in Southampton:

By exceptional circumstances we mean:

a) When a young person discloses to their helper that they have been abused (physically, sexually or otherwise) and inaction could place them back into the same threatening situation.
b) When other young people are considered to be at risk, e.g., younger siblings are left in a so called threatening situation.

(Rayment 1994)

It is debatable whether it is better practice to simply state that a service is confidential, and then make rare breaches of confidentiality or have a carefully worded statement regarding 'exceptional circumstances' that is brought to the individual client's notice. Brook's outreach work with specific needs groups of young people (who had not attended a Brook centre) has shown that if exceptions to confidentiality are mentioned many young people feel they fall into the exception and state that they will not seek help.

No doubt these policies make the counsellor and other workers feel more secure and that they are not liable to a law suit for negligence and are not colluding or ignoring abuse, but what is most helpful for the client?

Those clients who have no choice about being involved in sexual activity, abuse or rape are faced with issues that centre around power, control and trust. Does breaching confidentiality further betray their trust? Clients coming for counselling choose an agency consciously and/or unconsciously and have taken perhaps the first perilous step to seek help. Asking for help is breaking the secrecy that has often been essential to keep the abuse hidden and therefore possible. Young people and children can seek out adult help hoping to tap into their ability to act and make things happen. This is highly sensitive work; any decision to breach confidentiality must be taken with the greatest care. If at all possible the client's permission to get the relevant help that will stop the abuse is sought, and thus confidentiality is maintained.

The Children Act, 1989, directed inter-agency communication in 'Working Together under the Children Act' (HMSO 1991) to collect and collate information about an individual who is suspected of being abused or discloses information about abuse so that a joint risk assessment could take place.

Counsellors are faced with a dilemma when a client expressly wishes information to be kept confidential around abuse. A client, for example, could state that they will commit suicide if confidentiality is broken.

The position differs for those counsellors working in statutory or non-statutory agencies, but allows for some professional discretion if this is in the client's best interests. The interpretation of this may vary and allows different guidelines to be drawn up by child protection teams.

Statutory agencies

The Cleveland Enquiry Report (HMSO 1987) looked at this fraught situation and identified that confidentiality could not be guaranteed. The following agencies have statutory power and responsibilities: local authority social services departments, the police and the NSPCC.

There is a qualified duty for local authority statutory agencies: education, probation, health authorities and general practitioners to 'assist local authorities with enquiries by providing relevant information and advice' (Bond 1993: 135).

Non-statutory agencies

Agencies that are *not* included in the Children Act are mostly all the voluntary organizations or, indeed, individual counsellors who, in effect, the client has employed (whether or not payment is made). Non-statutory voluntary agencies offer clients the flexibility to be different and are seen by clients as outside the 'system' and independent.

How a counsellor handles a necessity to breach confidentiality has to be based on individual discernment and experience. This would need to take into account the client's age, resources and the support they have both internally and externally. The decision would have to be shared with a senior colleague and supervisor. In cases of grave concern, advice from the counsellor's professional organization can be vital.

A breach of confidentiality should be minimized by restricting information so it is pertinent and given to those who are in a position to provide help. The client must be informed at all times. In the case of abuse the counsellor can expect to be invited to case conferences and will need to keep detailed notes.

It may be useful to have guidelines outlining good practice. The principles of confidentiality need to be raised during the selection, introduction and on-going training of staff. Complex issues will arise where conflicting needs are assessed. Counsellors and health workers need to be clear about exceptional circumstances so that high standards of confidentiality are maintained.

It is important that counsellors know their legal and organizational limitations and that the scope of confidentiality will be altered by the setting in which they work. Pregnancy counsellors need to have thought through the ethical complexities of maintaining confidentiality, the trust of their client and their responsibility to protect the client from serious harm.

CROSS-CULTURAL COUNSELLING

Special attention needs to be paid to any situation where there is an imbalance or difference between counsellor and client due, for example, to race, culture, disability, class or sexual orientation, as this can prevent a working relationship being established.

It is unusual to speak to a stranger about your private thoughts and feelings in any culture. A woman may never have received undivided attention. Women may perceive the counsellor's attempts to maintain eye contact as friendly and caring or as rude. The counsellor can be seen as an authority figure and the client could avert their eyes as a mark of respect and courtesy, or to signify that making contact is difficult, or it could be due to shyness. There is a myriad of possibilities. Problems will arise if the counsellor acts on her own assumptions and prejudices without being aware that this is happening. This is an area where there is no substitute for personal work and training to increase awareness.

An awareness of Equal Opportunities principles and knowledge of cross-cultural techniques need to be made explicit when a counsellor is interviewed, in induction training and should be embedded in a counsellor's practice.

A counsellor's awareness can be deepened if she is able to look at discrimination in society, both overt and hidden, and realize that 'better than' attitudes are endemic. These are attitudes born of fear and ignorance that conjure up how anyone can feel in relation to other distinct groups of people who are viewed as of lesser worth or importance and treated by the 'better than group' as 'worse than' themselves.

Most people are 'at home' with others of the same class, race, culture, age, sexual orientation and education as themselves. People cultivate and feel comfortable with people on their 'wavelength'. An additional factor that helps to keep the minority group oppressed or 'held down' is if the group is either less numerous or has less political power, and thus less authority. An accessible example is sexism.

Ideally, counsellors need to work on these issues personally, as counsellors have the same cultural stereotypes, fears about those from other cultures and races as everyone else. There is a training exercise that is illuminating where the counsellor imagines their perfect client sitting in the waiting room. One colleague initially imagined the client as having the same gender and age as herself then gradually shed all difference until the imagined client became a copy of herself. The counsellor was surprised and realized that this was the one client she would never see. It is an effort to reach out to others and tolerate their strangeness.

An understanding of our own responses to oppression and what has held us back from challenging or noticing it is a personal responsibility. As counsellors, our own position has changed from the classic liberal statement, 'I treat everyone the same', which ignores difference, to being able to explore and own guilt and the sense of helplessness in the face of discrimination.

This is an on-going process, with layers of misinformation to peel away that have been learnt or absorbed from parents, friends, the media and society. To alter attitudes as well as behaviour requires energy, the willingness and ability to experience the pain and vulnerability of our clients so that difference can be welcomed.

Various stages have been identified in working well cross-culturally, which involve the counsellor in a process of changing their behaviour. The first stage is when the counsellor becomes aware that minorities exist. The counsellor might at this stage talk in a simplistic way about minorities, what they are like and what they do, with no differentiation: 'they all have such marvellous faces' (about a group of West African women). This statement implies that these women formed a homogeneous group. Difference is effectively disregarded and the counsellor might say, 'people are people' and be unaware of themselves as a racial being.

The counsellor may then become aware of society's pressures on those who are different. The counsellor may want to refer the client on to a counsellor of the same minority if one is available.

In the second stage the counsellor may become depressed and guilty as she is forced to acknowledge that she is White (or whatever the counsellor's cultural identity is), and is more aware of the shortfall in the standards expected towards others as regards care and respect and the realities of life for those who do not form a majority. The counsellor could respond by overidentifying with minorities, being extra friendly or positive, or by retreating into her own culture and by stopping trying to improve her practice.

The next stage that has been defined is as a reaction to the second stage. The counsellor may feel angry and hostile towards minorities for 'making her feel guilty', maybe even becoming covertly or overtly anti-minorities and seeing any traits as negative and morally of less worth.

The counsellor moves forward after this backward step by becoming curious about minorities and is more interested in similarities and differences. She may become involved in more cross-cultural work, perhaps with those who are similar to her own cultural grouping.

Eventually the counsellor accepts that racial differences and similarities exist and approaches these with appreciation and respect, seeing difference as an enhancing factor rather than a deficiency. The counsellor now actively seeks cross-cultural work.

It is worth being aware that if client or counsellor is from a minority culture they will probably be quite experienced at communicating cross-culturally. It may be the majority-culture professional who feels inadequate and de-skilled (Ardenne and Mahtani 1989).

Counsellors, once they have realized how crucial this area is, need the courage to comment on the difference they and their clients are aware of. This has to be tentative because they could well be wrong. If she is White and middle-aged and is counselling a young Black man, the counsellor could say: 'I'm wondering as I'm White and middle-aged and you are a young Black man what you might need to check out with me . . .'

Counsellors can unconsciously be communicating that they are embarrassed or apologetic, expecting their client to reject them. This involves taking a risk and the time to work through painful areas that may be hurtful for our clients, rather than ignoring the whole issue and contributing, albeit unwittingly, to institutional racism where the issue of difference is made invisible.

Careful thought and acceptance need to be given to the stress caused to a minority client from previous racism, repeated rejections and the misinformation that the majority culture has about minority cultures. On one occasion a nurse became puzzled and irritated by the fury of a young Black woman who had reacted indignantly when she was handed black condoms. The nurse was especially put out, as she thought we were providing just what the client would need.

The nurse was helped to look at the assumptions she was making about the racial grouping of this woman's partner (that he was Black), and that Black men want to use condoms that are shaded black, as opposed to the range of other 'fun' colours on offer. A better approach would have been to offer the woman a choice of condoms, from which she could pick out what she wanted, rather than restrict and dictate her choice, which had caused understandable offence.

The counsellor needs to let the individual make the statement about what her cultural norms are. These will not be a textbook version of her minority's life-styles and attitudes. Just as the director of a period drama can make the mistake of furnishing the set with props from the exact historical period rather than a mix of furniture garnered from various generations, so culture is a rag-bag of different cultures and traditions. The counsellor should work on the premise that her own culture is not the 'norm' and its values are not intrinsically good or normal just because they are familiar. These assumptions are so deeply ingrained that they are often not noticed by the counsellor; people from minority cultures are still shouted at, or spoken to at a snail's pace, just because they are viewed as foreign, even if they speak standard English.

Professional health staff need, but rarely get, adequate support to learn from and discuss mistakes, so that they are able to be avoid being, often unwittingly, ethnocentric.

Chapter 5

Counselling: the relationship and practical issues

ESTABLISHING A RELATIONSHIP

The client may have experienced counselling before and 'know the rules' but still fear the novelty and embarrassment of revealing feelings to a stranger. A relationship needs to be rapidly established which is maintained by fostering an environment of trust and respect. Clients are often hesitant and can be reluctant, making the counsellor's task more difficult. When a client is reluctant, perhaps sent by someone else, this needs to be acknowledged by the counsellor.

Many clients will come from families where strangers are distrusted and may have vulnerable feelings woven around needing and asking for help. It may be that for your client to go for help outside the extended family is discouraged and can be seen as disrespectful, disloyal or even indicative of personal failure, 'I don't talk to anyone else, it's not done'.

The client can wish to be told what is the 'best way', to be literally taken in hand and guided step by step. Any unknown situation is scary, it is a human desire to wish to lessen the inevitable anxiety of beginnings.

The counsellor needs to follow the client rather than lead, noticing how the woman tells her story. Is she rushing, hardly waiting for any reaction or dialogue, is he looking through a thick fringe at the corner of the room, and twisting away from you in his chair; what are the messages that are being conveyed and how do you feel in response? The counsellor may be aware of areas that the client seems to be avoiding or that are missing. These hidden areas, that can be just out of the client's awareness, require effort and a high degree of attention to spot.

The counsellor works to get 'alongside' her client, pitching any questions, interventions or responses at a level that is comprehensible to the client. This level is neither too superficial nor too deep, but allows them to examine how they are feeling and thinking about their present situation. When the depth is too intrusive the client might say very little or feel unable to talk about connected worries or problems. When the depth remains too superficial the client can feel that they have not been understood. When a woman does not feel the counsellor 'is on her side', she can feel unable to tell the counsellor, for example, that this conception is the result of a rape. Especially if the woman does not define what happened as rape, but as something she is ashamed of that has happened many times before. Some of the skill of pregnancy counselling is knowing at which depth to work with whom.

RESPECT

Respect for the client is built first through non-verbal signals: the tone of voice used, gestures and courteous actions (such as closing a curtain if hot sunshine is on the client's back). As non-verbal signals are picked up before others, the way you look at the person and welcome them in, even showing them where to sit will indicate in a direct way what they can expect. The counsellor shows by the careful choice of words that she is trying to understand the emotional and practical reality the client is experiencing. This sounds routine, but is important in setting the atmosphere for the counselling process.

A relationship cannot be gradually built up over time or earned as in open-ended counselling. There is no time to correct mistakes or for either of you to go off at tangents coming back to the focus, so the onus is on the counsellor to concentrate and work hard. Accurate reflective feedback is needed so the client feels that the counsellor has understood. When the client's experience of the counsellor is, for example, slightly patronizing, indifferent or silent, this can prevent a bond forming. The client needs to experience the counsellor as flexible and able to keep pace with each individual.

TIME CONSTRAINTS

The time available varies greatly, counsellors who work at Pregnancy Advisory Bureaux and at Brook Advisory Centres (NHS funded non-statutory centres targeted at young people and seeing them for counselling and contraception) work as part of a multi-disciplinary team and have the luxury of seeing women for up to forty-five minutes. On the other hand, a hard-pressed general practitioner or family planning doctor will find themselves limited to a much shorter time in a busy clinic.

However short or long the time available, this time can be used positively. Rather than saying, 'we have only got ten minutes', an entirely different value can be communicated if the counsellor believes that the shortness of time will act as a focus and is beneficial and says, 'in the . . . minutes we have available what would be most helpful?' Women are often acutely aware of the biological time clock that has begun to tick from conception; only in a very few instances is help needed immediately (e.g., in labour, if a client is haemorrhaging). There is always time to look at options. An unhurried approach deflates panic and provides respite for the client from the pressure of time, and the counsellor from feeling they must help the client reach a decision or solve a crisis.

The pregnancy counsellor often sees women for just one session. Clients come with a specific decision to make regarding their pregnancy, and may not be seeking self-awareness growth, or change but a 'solution'. Anna Dartington has noted in her brief four session counselling with young people at the Tavistock clinic (psychotherapy treatment centre) that they are are 'not so much coming for counselling as to see what counselling is and what it "feels" like' (Dartington 1995: 253).

When material comes up in one session the counsellor needs the experience and skill to help the client contain this material. Pregnant clients can reveal a mass of thoughts and feelings. Care should be taken so the client does not leave awash with unbearable feelings. The counsellor has to be aware of the limitations of the setting and of her or his own training and/or experience, and have realistic expectations of what can be effective in the short time available. The counsellor needs the integrity to help the client to focus on what is most useful or helpful at that time. The client also has a chance, if the session is carefully paced by the counsellor, to comment on how they have experienced the counselling session, and this can be beneficial if a referral for further long-term work is made. The client is then more aware of the counselling process and what was and was not helpful. It is the counsellor's responsibility to bring the session to a close within the stated time limits already agreed with the client.

ASSUMPTIONS

The counsellor needs to be as conscious as possible of assumptions that she or other staff may be tempted to make.

Thea was a grumpy 14 year old who was underdeveloped and could have passed for an 11–12-year-old. Her feet did not touch the floor as she sat in the chair. An accompanying worker, who was the only staff member who could be spared, said in presenting Thea, 'I hope you will talk some sense into her, she's a baby herself'.

Thea came to see the counsellor accompanied by a key worker in her children's home. Thea was not sure why she had been sent and didn't know what a counsellor was except she expected to be 'told what to do'. She tucked noisily into a half-eaten MacDonald's hamburger.

Once we started, Thea was passionate about wanting to have a baby that she saw as hers and 'no one else's'. She was not able to be realistic about how and where she could look after a child; she hugged herself and her eyes shone. Her own childhood had been full of separations and Thea had gone voluntarily into care as her mother's mental health led to periods of neglect and unpredictable behaviour.

It would be easy to assume that Thea could not cope and consciously or not, direct her into having an abortion. Crucial here is to have an open mind and not to assume that her delight in being pregnant will mean that she will want to end up having a baby or, if she did, that she could not be an adequate parent. Thea needed to have her dreams of a safe, happy family heard as well as the reality of her life in a children's home with its lack of continuity of care, privacy or individual attention that was mirrored by her original deprivation.

It may be that this worker had not wanted to explore her own frustration and hostility about what Thea wanted to do. She felt that Thea should be sensible as, in her opinion, continuing with a pregnancy would lead to a repeated cycle of deprivation. The worker recognized that she was powerless to prevent this cycle. Feeling helpless is often frustrating, demoralizing and can stir up hostility and resentment. Helpers often do not want to recognize their own anger and can blame others or transfer their anger. The worker could be exasperated that a counsellor was appearing to sanction a 14-year-old continuing with a pregnancy and irritated with the client for wanting to continue.

CHECKING UNDERSTANDING

The counsellor needs to establish whether their client wants and understands what counselling involves. Sometimes a woman will tell the counsellor that she has, 'Done all that already' (counselling) but on closer investigation this turns out to have been prescriptive help, 'You shouldn't continue your pregnancy with a diagnosis of HIV'; admonition, 'An abortion will damage your future fertility'; or gushing sympathy, 'Oh, you can't cope with three children under 5'. Such experiences limit a client's capacity to think and feel for herself and add to guilt or anxiety.

The counsellor needs to monitor whether counselling is appropriate. Is the client so preoccupied with an intense internal world that they cannot reflect or think? How much support does the client have externally? Sometimes counselling cannot be used by the client, for a variety of reasons which may not be immediately apparent, for example, the client may be so emotionally damaged or deprived that they have no basic trust, or are in shock and numb.

Occasionally, clients will have lost or never gained the confidence to question and will accept unchallenged whatever is said, so that there is no dialogue with the counsellor.

Meg had taken some amphetamines in early pregnancy and had asked her GP about the possible harmful effects, the doctor had laughed and told her there were only some defects reported in rats. This had devastated Meg who had interpreted the laugh as sinister. She was already feeling that her pregnancy could not be normal and now feared she was carrying something damaged and akin to vermin.

Other clients can seem attractive and exciting but these characteristics are 'stuck on' and beneath this façade clients can feel deeply empty. The client may well not know how they feel and not know how to set boundaries, ask questions or even have a self, on whom to reflect. This can lead to all sorts of misunderstandings and confusions.

REFERRALS

Careful consideration needs to be paid to times when a referral on for more specific help is needed. Referrals are an art, and if well handled provide a bridge to further help. However, if handled carelessly they can imply rejection, the client can be left thinking, 'she can't help me', which could increase low esteem – 'I am not worthy of help', 'if I had been a better client she would have wanted to continue seeing me', or whatever the individual believes from their own past to have held the interest of parental figures – and any number of other negative assumptions.

The counsellor needs to be very clear about the purpose of the referral. The reason the referral is being made should be stated in such a way that the person being referred feels that they are receiving positive help. As mentioned earlier, there will be some clients who are seriously disturbed and who need prompt professional help. It is important to have worked out where these clients can be referred to in your local area, and to have made personal contact with other psychotherapists, psychiatrists and psychology staff.

Pregnancy counsellors are often working in a multi-disciplinary team and will be able to consult with the doctors in their team. There are also invaluable nation-wide directories, for example, *The Really Helpful Directory for Pregnant Teenagers and Young Parents* (Di Salvo and Skuse 1993). Personal knowledge of local counselling centres can be built up during your practice by visiting other counselling agencies in your area.

Counsellors can also see clients who at first confound them but whom they are subsequently able to help within the limitations of their service.

Beth, who had moderate learning difficulties, was 23 years old. She scowled and did not look at the counsellor in the waiting room and had to be pushed through the door. Beth's key worker came into the counselling room immediately behind Beth, showing a high degree of concern about her client, who was in a home and was pregnant. Beth had refused to talk to any staff for five days and they were at their wits' end. The counsellor had to stop this worker from talking and directed his attention at Beth, but there was no response. The key worker talked as if her own feelings were what mattered, leaving no room for Beth's feelings. Beth was asked if she would find it easier to talk without the key worker. Again there was no response, but the key worker was asked to leave as, usually, people do feel able to communicate more easily one to one. Beth continued to sit in silence for half an hour. The counsellor felt useless, inadequate, persecuted; every kind of intervention seemed pointless. Beth closed her eyes and seemed to be in a trance except that her eyes moved fractionally under her eyelids, when the counsellor spoke. The counsellor was made to experience Beth's power in not speaking. He also understood that this was one of the few ways she could let others know her own sense of impotence, that she had no control over events in her life. Beth's silence invoked the intense frustration that she felt which was experienced by the counsellor. Eventually when the counsellor ended the session she hoarsely whispered, 'leave me alone can't you', and then refused to leave. Her key worker had literally to eject Beth from the counselling room.

The pregnancy counsellor felt that this session was a failure at the time and was surprised to be rung up later, by the home, to find that she wanted to come back to 'talk'. Beth was able to say that she wanted to have a baby but that her last baby had been 'took away'. Beth then started simply and painfully to say, 'I want a baby but will the home let me?' Beth was then able to begin to express pent up feelings that involved a previous pregnancy.

WORKING THROUGH INTERPRETERS

The client should be able to understand the counsellor, and it is the counsellor who must be aware of any problems in this area. When the counsellor does not speak the same language as the client every effort must be made to find an interpreter. If she works in an area where the Family Health Services' Authority provides free translators then help can be arranged (though it will take some time to do so). Women often come with a friend or partner to translate. This can be useful, but the counsellor has to bear in mind that she will have no way of knowing if her words are being slanted or edited, especially if the friend or partner is in opposition to the woman's wishes. The session will take double the time, and this can have the effect of limiting the session to a discussion of the basic course to take, leaving no time to explore the client's feelings and thoughts in more depth. There are specialist support groups for minority groups, for example, the Turkish community, and these can be asked in an emergency to translate the counsellor's and client's words on the telephone and relay them backwards and forwards in small chunks. A professional translator is needed as such a person is more likely to have the depth and accuracy of another language which is required. A friend may not have the experience or language skills to translate medical information or answer the client's questions. Clients who speak a different language benefit if hospital staff are forewarned that there may be communication difficulties.

Patience is needed if no translator is available but often, after the initial panic on both sides, the counsellor will find that it is possible to understand each other and learn to make effective and creative use of gestures and signs, becoming attuned to mutually different verbal cadences and inflexions.

WORKING THROUGH AMBIVALENT FEELINGS

Once a working relationship has been established then the counsellor aims to explore what the client needs. This can be straightforward help with an abortion but often involves working with the client's ambivalent feelings.

This ambivalence can be clearly seen in the woman who comes to a counselling session totally undecided whether to continue or abort her pregnancy. Such women are often under extreme stress and can be incoherent and confused. They are also confusing to listen to. It is important for the counsellor to let the shape of their mess and chaos be fully experienced. Clients can be in a state of panic and all these feelings will flow and intermingle so that boundaries between counsellor and client become blurred. The counsellor needs to recognize the panic and focus on the feeling behind the client's words. When the client is more aware of the source or cause of her indecision then she is better able to reject or accept complex feelings, thoughts and ideas around her pregnancy.

Most pregnant women will experience some conflicting feelings – certainty and ambivalence, loss and relief, depression and euphoria – in anticipation of an abortion and about the state of being pregnant. Some women may even have feelings of love and hate toward their foetus, and about themselves as future mothers.

Psychological literature tends to focus on the ambivalent feelings a baby experiences toward its mother, who can provide a blissful plentitude or a life-threatening absence of nourishment. The baby, it is said, splits the providing from the withholding mother to protect and leave uncontaminated the 'good mother'. Rozsika Parker has turned this about and written extensively about a mother's ambivalence towards her child. She finds that this loving and hating can stimulate the mother into thinking about her baby and be creative and resourceful, or that the ambivalence can become unmanageable (Parker 1995).

There is also a tendency for pregnant clients to exhibit idealization and its opposite, denigration, presenting one option, belief or person as all good or alternatively all bad. Clients report that they 'must' have an abortion. Their strong feelings toward the pregnancy, are often so painful that they try to defend themselves against them. However, clients who are able to voice these contradictory feelings can use them constructively. The client may be more able to forgive herself an abortion if she is aware of these conflicts and becomes more compassionate towards herself. It can be more difficult when the woman can only hate and fear the alien pregnancy or feels deeply persecuted by the changes that a pregnancy inevitably brings and wants to be 'rid of it'. Some women may speak harshly of eliminating the pregnancy and their tone may indicate that there is little compassion for themselves. It can be that the 'baby' part of the woman is evoked by the dependent pregnancy and it is this reminder of her vulnerable, needy part that she wants to obliterate. This is a warning that the client could benefit from more counselling rather than signalling that she is feckless or unfeeling.

Alternatively the client may focus on the 'baby' and exclude her own separate needs and thus be unable to face ambivalence. The most effective help the counsellor can offer is gently to get the client to check if this really is their only option and see if the client can find any middle ground.

The counsellor needs to be wary if strong feelings are stirred up in herself in relation to whether the client should have or not have her pregnancy. There will be sessions where these feelings need to be unravelled with an experienced supervisor. The supervisor is not involved in the session and is able to see where and how the counsellor stopped being able to work alongside the client, and became enmeshed.

The role of the pregnancy counsellor is to offer uninterrupted time to look at the various and varied strands that are preventing the client from being able to choose to make a decision. There can be unconscious preoccupations of which the client is unaware that an opportunity to talk may bring into the open.

INTERVENTIONS

Women can feel that choosing to have an abortion is tantamount to putting themselves first and that this is deeply selfish and unacceptable. The counsellor has to choose or weigh up if this is the moment to communicate any thoughts or observations. This has to be based on a judgement of how helpful any intervention or lack of intervention would be at that precise time. For example, Esme was furious that she would have to wait to have her pregnancy ended, and behaved as if this was a cruel and deliberate persecution. To respond to Esme in a placatory way that this wait is to be expected (rationalizing), is not long (minimizing) or not the counsellor's fault (blaming) is obviously not helpful, true though all of this may be. Simple acknowledgement that this wait is torturous for Esme and reflecting back the precise way this is experienced is what is required.

Some women will reveal deeper anxieties or project judgements or myths and reflect society's own ambivalence about sexuality. Clients can make revealing statements such as:

Do you see many women who want an abortion?

I don't believe in abortion, but I'm a special case.

This must be very depressing work.

Would you (the counsellor) have an abortion?

You must think I'm stupid/feckless/immoral.

When clients are highly anxious the counsellor needs to resist the pressure to join in and rush to alleviate anxiety, as this is often not what is needed. For example, a counsellor may set up an urgent gynaecological appointment which the client then fails to keep. It is more effective to stay calm and be patient. It is often an illusion that going for an abortion tomorrow will solve the client's pain.

The anxious client can literally follow every word, continue to talk to the counsellor when she is writing a report or ring the counsellor many times for reassurance (often under the guise of checking facts, where the hospital is, etc.)

The counsellor tries to contain this anxiety, and the conflicting tensions that arise, by 'handing them back' in a more manageable form.

Clients will sometimes hold on to what can appear to be deeply illogical notions as these help them accept an abortion and extricate them from their own conscience. The counsellor needs to let them do this without colluding.

> Iysha stated that she wished she could miscarry as she did not want a proper abortion. She was Catholic and this would be a cardinal sin. If only, she pleaded, she could take a pill to bring about an abortion.

The counsellor was presented with the dilemma of whether or not to point out that a medical abortion existed or if this was colluding with Iysha's desire to have her pregnancy ended without taking responsibility for her action. Withholding this factual information seemed punitive but should the counsellor allow Iysha this salve for her conscience? The best check is for the counsellor herself to ask what would be the purpose of her intervention, and keep silent if it is not of benefit to the client. The purpose of the session with Iysha was to help her look at how difficult it was for her to face the reality of requesting an abortion and her own part in ending the pregnancy, at the same time as organizing a medical termination. Iysha went on to accept the idea of a medical abortion, where mifepristone causes a more 'natural' miscarriage.

DENIAL OF LOSS

Women can wish for an impossible solution; that they could suspend a pregnancy and 'come back when they are ready'. Clients can so fervently believe that the pregnancy should not have happened that they deny that a conception has happened or present their family planning doctor as refusing to give them a satisfactory method of contraception. The client is finding it too painful to accept some responsibility for what has happened and tries to escape, placing or displacing her feelings onto a powerful figure such as the doctor. In fact, the doctor may have been suggesting that a certain method was contra-indicated.

Clients can simply be unable to begin to deal with their feelings and make a decision because they cannot acknowledge emotionally that they are pregnant: this is separate from understanding intellectually that a pregnancy has begun. This typifies the type of primary process thinking we have already spoken of (Chapter 2) as occuring in early childhood and the logic of dreams, fantasies and the unconscious. In this world there are no time constraints and everything is possible; this is a seductive way of thinking and the unconscious mind cannot be influenced by ideas of rationality or logic. This mirrors the more complicated grieving that can occur when an individual cannot emotionally accept or allow their loved one to be dead. The temptation or need is to hold on to the thought that the person is absent, not permanently missing never to be seen again. The dead are unchanging even in memory, they do not age or grow or change (Lewis 1979). In the same way, women mourning an anticipated abortion are in limbo with a pregnancy that cannot become fully formed into a separate being by birth. Their pregnancy is mummified and in the counselling session there is a marked degree of 'stuckness'. The counsellor may observe physical agitation, with a client wringing tissues or moving around in their chair; more often agitation is shown in flushes that come and go on the upper chest and irregular breathing.

Pregnant women are faced with an inevitable decision: to continue or terminate their pregnancy. This dramatic choice involves change, and change inevitably means loss. In choosing one option the other option has to be abandoned. There could be gains and losses attached to either option and these can be explored. Loss can be particularly painful to acknowledge. The gains may be unimaginable. Can any woman know what actually going through labour, birth and caring for a baby will be like?

At a deeper level anxiety around abandonment can be stirred up by being in a situation where making a choice cannot be avoided. This anxiety can heighten a need for attachment, and some behaviours where distressed clients sound very young or fasten on every word can be seen as behaviour designed unconsciously to escape abandonment and procure by this behaviour the protection of the counsellor.

OTHER PEOPLE'S VIEWS

The client may tell you that 'abortion is wicked'. This could indicate her own views or that she is expressing the views of other people who are important to her, for example, her mother or boyfriend. Powerful dynamics between other people can result in the client's feelings being a reaction to, or distorted by, trying to balance pressure from a different direction.

Women especially can feel pulled in different directions by others' needs and expectations. The counsellor can help by bringing these conflicting feelings into awareness and making them explicit. She might ask, 'Who feels abortions are wrong?' This encourages the client to look at the source of this influence so they can challenge being pulled in various directions, or 'going round in circles'.

Julie came with an older boyfriend. He was 21 and she 17 years old. She was agitated, and her face crumbled as soon as the counsellor looked at her and acknowledged her distress. Julie spoke haltingly of a web of conflicting feelings and apparently unresolvable problems. She knew she could not cope with the pregnancy. Julie told how her mother had discovered her hidden pill packet, brandished it and then dumped it in the waste bin – a symbolic act not lost on Julie. Her mother forbade her to see her boyfriend again, an injunction that Julie ignored, and that added to the lies she told and the widening gap between herself and her mother. The boyfriend was seen by her parents as 'hopeless', with no money or job prospects. He sat impassive and looked somewhat sheepish. He took no responsibility for Julie's pregnancy. Her mother knew she hadn't had a period and Julie confirmed this, but bought time by saying she would go back to the Brook centre to sort out what had 'gone wrong', as this centre had given her the pill. Her mother was waiting at home to hear the outcome of her visit and Julie thought her mother would force her have a home test if she said she wasn't pregnant. She couldn't tell her mother as she feared losing her relationship with her father who so far had not been told about the pill packet. She felt trapped.

Julie was aware that she did not need her parents' consent for an abortion but she could not look beyond the immediate problem and this obscured her feelings about her pregnancy. There also seemed to be a battle for ownership of her body and what she could do with it. The counsellor could only point out how her mother kept intruding into her thoughts and feelings and into their session.

PARTNERS

For some women the situation is further complicated by conceiving and then 'getting rid' of their pregnancy forming a collective experience. A woman can thus exercise control over the ability to create life by ending the pregnancy. This is an awesome power and responsibility (Dana 1987).

Although it is impossible to generalize, other women act as if they cannot bear a whole, perfect child and are at a deep level fearful of seeing what is inside, hidden from view, being uncertain that it could be wholesome. Women with such feelings may hope an abortion will extinguish the pain they feel, that this act will mop up their feelings and leave them unchanged and as they were before the pregnancy was discovered. This can be underscored if whoever they have a close relationship with is behaving as if they do not want their shared pregnancy. Women can view a mutually desired pregnancy as precious and will not continue if they feel a partner does not actively want them to be pregnant. A woman may want her partner to be strong enough to look after *both* the client and their baby, but the partner may be unable through choice or circumstances to provide a protective boundary from the pressures of the everyday 'outside world'.

MAKING A DECISION

At some point a decision will have to be made, and may be made rapidly to avoid the insecurity and dysphoria of not knowing what is 'best' or is 'right', or to escape clashes with the client's personal value system. Young clients particularly cannot easily explain their moral code yet are often operating on the basis of a complicated system of rights and wrongs, morals and ethics.

When the client is faced with making a decision it will help her to feel that the counsellor is 'not ruling anything out or in', and that she is not being 'steered' in any one direction.

The pregnant woman or her partner is in a situation that is totally new, and this often represents a crisis.

It is rare, for most of us to have to take a decision of this magnitude and often counsellors see those who have had very little practice in any sort of decision-making. Clients may have decisons made for them by protective parents or perhaps have been 'in care' and had little chance to execute any decisions.

The counsellor cannot know what would be the 'right' decision for someone else and this is vital to accept emotionally as well as intellectually. There seem to be basic ways in which people make a decision, but each has its positive and negative aspects. For instance, an impulsive way to make a decision is to 'jump in' which affords immediate relief but leaves little time for reflection or acceptance.

Weighing up the advantages and disadvantages can be helpful for clients. However, those who are unable to trust their own judgement may avoid making a decision. They achieve this by constantly balancing up their negative and positive lists so that a rational list proves useless.

Some clients allow time to slip past without being able to make a decision, so that it gets made by default. This procrastination can mean that they are too late for an abortion, and their options are reduced. This way of avoiding conflict or confrontation can be gently pointed out.

Other clients can present their decision as made for them by other people, avoiding personal responsibility. The advantage for the client is that she cannot be held responsible, but the disadvantage is that she has lost control of the outcome.

When a client does not 'know what to do' this may indicate that she hopes or expects that the counsellor will tell her what to do. The counsellor needs to avoid getting drawn into coming up with increasingly inventive and clever suggestions that are inevitably rejected. They need to recognize and avoid rescuing the client and allow them 'not to know'. The counsellor also needs to remain 'not knowing' and not having 'all the answers'. Sometimes people will seduce or flatter the counsellor by implying that you are the expert and should know what to do. This is a double-edged compliment, as the implication is that the client expects the counsellor to come up with a way out of their impasse and yet the client can feel better if she can flummox the counsellor. The client is feeling defeated and wants the counsellor to feel the same way, this is usually unconscious so they are not aware of this motive.

People can see the counsellor suffering from shock and may literally not 'know what to do'. Faced with this uncharted territory they can sound like a small child, whining and whimpering.

It can be useful for clients to look at how they make a difficult choice and at the loss involved. The feelings and fantasies about what would happen if they followed either pathway can be explored. When clients see both pathways negatively, then reframing them so they can concentrate on the positives of either choice can be helpful. This can free the client to plump for one pathway, rather

Anger = Around the unfairness and threat of a pregnancy, 'Why did this happen to me?

Sadness = Of anticipated loss and emptiness.

Fear = Of primal forces beyond knowledge and human control.

Joy = Of creativity, power, a new beginning.

Figure 5.1 Four basic emotions

than being paralysed by the gloom of two negative choices. Strong feelings can be expressed which vary from individual to individual but are often a mixture of four basic emotions:

Drawing a family tree, can help illuminate the origin of feelings that are preventing a client reaching a decision. For example, Figure 5.2 shows family ages when Jill was born.

This way of laying out a history provides concise information in a quick and structured way. The woman herself can draw her own. This will often have been the only time anyone has taken the trouble to notice what are often very complicated family histories today with many half- or step-siblings.

In the example, Jill was born a year after her sister and this was important. It could indicate that her conception was unwanted, or a source of ambivalence, or a happy surprise or many other possibilities. The counsellor could ask what Jill herself thought. Even if Jill was wrong, for example, in thinking she was the result of a contraceptive failure, this idea will obviously have influenced her and be involved in her current dilemmas. In fact, her father was absent from her birth and was always a source of fantasy, mystery and speculation. She felt unwelcome, that more fuss had been made of her elder sister because she was the first baby girl, and that her brother had been the 'right' sex and therefore wanted. Jill could not compete. When Jill had more of an idea of what her own imaginings were she was able to choose to override them or to look at what this meant for her in her current context.

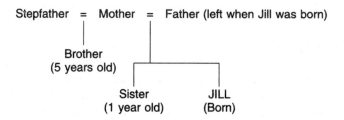

Figure 5.2 Family tree

It can be that a client wants to 'please everyone' by placating others by giving them what she assumes they want and and thereby deflecting anticipated or real hostility. The client is in a situation where the alternatives are stark, making a decision often impossible. When a client wants to please her boyfriend, her mother, herself and the pregnancy she has an impossible task. These conflicting interests can make her feel 'stuck'. A client who identifies strongly with the pregnancy can find that she cannot 'reject' herself. This is especially painful if she has felt the extreme crisis of abandonment or come to the conclusion that as a child she must have been unloveable for a parent to leave or abuse her.

Sara (17 years old) had a late abortion a year ago by induced labour. Sara had come early for help when she realized she could be pregnant again, following a contraceptive mix-up. She wanted an abortion and was now old enough to sign a consent form. Sara had decided not to anger or upset her seriously ill mother and had not told her she was pregnant. She returned twice for counselling as she was undecided, and had not turned up on the appointed day for her abortion.

Sara smiled constantly. The discrepancy between her confusion and her smiles gave the counsellor the dilemma of responding to her anxiety or the smiles. This was tentatively commented on, Sara laughed and suddenly stopped smiling, and looked briefly grief stricken. Sara said that her smiles were habitual. Her family only paid attention if she was smiling or not making any demands. Otherwise her mother quizzed her about 'what the matter was' in a way that expressed irritation and tension. Her mother was a single parent often working nights to support Sara and her siblings. Sara had little privacy at home, her relationship with her 20-year-old boyfriend was an area where she could have an inner life that was secret and hidden. She had promised herself that she would not have another abortion, yet she did not want a child now either. Taking any action was excruciating. Sara was scared of accepting the responsibility for stopping the pregnancy. Last time she had been carried along by her mother's shame and anxiety. She had grieved over the last pregnancy and for her this pregnancy did not seem separate either from her body or from her last pregnancy. She saw the pregnancy as a 'precious gift' and also as a part of herself that was 'baby-like and innocent'. She saw rejecting this helpless part of herself as deeply selfish, uncaring and harsh; yet at the same time she had no wish to have a child who would grow, change and separate from her.

Sara did not return for a booked counselling session and the counsellor was left in limbo as to her final decision. Women can need several sessions to work out what is best for them. If a woman does not return, the counsellor may want to write to her but she should honestly weigh up whether she feels this would genuinely be seen as a helpful reminder by the client or whether she is simply relieving her own conscience.

POST-ABORTION SESSION

It can be especially painful for the counsellor and client when women return following a termination with negative emotions: angry, bitter, resentful and 'hurting'. Clients can have shifted in the counselling session and have stated that they wanted to continue and then have been unable to sustain this decision outside the session. Other clients will have sounded 'certain' and their distress can be unexpected by both the client and counsellor. Some will openly blame the counsellor, 'Why didn't you stop me?' Others will bring gifts or come back to thank you when they also feel compelled to project their own anguish and hostility but cannot be openly hostile. Cards etc. , can be warmly given, but there is another type of gift giving, reminiscent of the 'poisoned apple' in the fairy tale *Snow White*. The recipient of the gift may notice that they feel immediately uncomfortable. Colleagues have 'forgotten' to take these gifts home or more consciously feel contaminated by these offerings. When the counsellor is able to reflect on the purpose of the gift for the client then she can be of more help to the client.

RELATED AND OTHER ISSUES

A pregnancy counselling session may represent a fresh opportunity for some individuals to raise other concerns woven around a request for abortion. These may include: domestic violence (male and female), low self-esteem, depression or eating disorders, and help can be sought for these often hidden areas.

Women and men also have the opportunity in the counselling session to look at how they conceived, and this gives them a better chance of protecting themselves in the future. Accurate information about risks and when they are most fertile can help women alter behaviour or switch to a method of contraception more suitable for their own life-style.

Pregnancy counselling can allow a woman to talk about the quality of her emotional and sexual life. Women may need to discharge their frustration, anger and envy after having, for example, non-enjoyable sex or getting pregnant from one isolated intercourse.

ENDINGS

Some clients are sensitive to endings and want to explore feelings around loss and any resonances to other endings which all clients will have experienced to some degree. For other people endings can be a source of pain and anxiety, and each client will have their own way of handling these feelings. The nature of pregnancy counselling, which is predominately limited to 'one-off' sessions, means that the counsellor will be faced with continual endings.

There can also be a tendency on the part of the client to ignore, forget or truncate endings. Perhaps the sensitivity of this aspect of the counselling session is not surprising as clients are seeking to impose an ending on their own pregnancy. Each ending is unique and the counsellor can 'model' how to use endings. This may be by getting the client to summarize where she is, what has helped and what is her next step. The counsellor publicly acknowledges endings by talking about them with the client. When this opportunity is missed it may mean that the client, and indeed the counsellor, loses the chance to reflect, pause and allow herself to take in the positive feelings or thoughts that have happened in the session.

The rest of this chapter deals with the particular concerns of women who have made a decision and choose an abortion, or choose to continue with their pregnancy with a view to adoption or keeping their baby.

WANTING AN ABORTION

Information

The majority of women (with or without a partner) who seek an abortion will be dismayed to be pregnant, but already know what they want and have made a decision. A woman who has been to a doctor and had her request for an abortion agreed, has completed half the required procedure and can therefore feel more relaxed as she knows that her request has been sanctioned. There will still be some women who think an abortion is illegal or that they cannot get free help within the NHS. Wendy Savage, obstetrician and gynaecologist, has written that 'some women have to know whether they can have an abortion before they can fully grasp their situation and be quite sure it is what they want' (Savage 1986: 16).

In order to allow the woman and/or partner to explore the situation fully, the following areas need to be covered:

1 The woman's social circumstances: age, status, family, housing, means of support (which may be work or benefits), family, friends or partner.
2 How the pregnancy has happened: contraceptive use or misuse, non-use, any failures and any of the woman's factual misunderstandings. Reason for any delays in getting help so far.
3 How she feels about being pregnant, also how she feels about abortion and adoption. How significant others feel. Any conflicts or pressure internally or externally.
4 Why abortion has been chosen and the reasons against other options.
5 Future contraception and fertility.
6 How she anticipates feeling afterwards and the possible reactions of partners, parents, etc. if told (imagined and real).
7 Any needs: e.g., child care, fear of needles, mental health, etc.
8 Where the client is being referred and where to return for a check-up and counselling if wanted.

9 The possibility of post-abortion counselling and practical help if unwell after an abortion.
10 GP's name and details, and the reasons if the client does not want contact with their GP, or is not registered.

If this information is needed as a report for the hospital gynaecologist it should be written in the role of an advocate for the woman, reflecting her dilemmas, feelings and wishes, and be read back for any corrections.

Simple questions such as 'What do you need to know now?' are effective. Most women will want to know:

1 How an abortion is performed.
2 Risks, short- and long-term; complications and information about any effects on future fertility.
3 How they might be expected to feel emotionally afterwards.
4 How quickly help can be arranged.
5 Which hospital, and the reception they will receive.

Information requested by the client needs to be clearly stated so that a woman knows what method of abortion is appropriate at her stage of pregnancy and what risks or complications are expected. As hospital practice varies, it is possible for a woman at fourteen weeks gestation to be offered a day-care procedure, induced labour or even to be refused an abortion at different hospitals or clinics. Counsellors need to be sure they keep up-to-date and have all relevant information about abortion provision in their area.

Safety

Safety is a complex question as it involves looking at abortion in general and the woman's particular medical history and circumstances. Often there will be questions that only an experienced gynaecologist could answer and then they are always open to interpretation. Obviously the individual surgeon's answers are going to be shaped by his or her clinical experience, research knowledge and personal attitude to abortion.

No one can know if an individual woman will conceive again and the woman needs to decide for herself if she can accept the very low risk of infertility and morbidity. Does she find this risk acceptable? How would she feel if she had problems conceiving again?

The waiting time to have an abortion performed can vary considerably from a few days to 4 to 6 weeks. The waiting time is usually only a couple of days if the woman goes to a charity pregnancy advisory service and pays (approximately £300 if she is under twelve weeks gestation). The ideal would be a total wait from initial counselling to abortion of between seven and ten days. This allows time for a woman to reflect and make the necessary arrangements for a hospital stay. However, delay can occur for any reason, such as denial by the woman herself that she could be pregnant, or failure to diagnose a pregnancy. A late, mid-trimester abortion is more expensive, the pregnancy further developed and medically more risky. The International Medical Advisory Committee statement on abortion states that 'beyond 10 weeks the health risks of abortion rise with each week of pregnancy, the risks of late second-trimester abortion being three to four times greater than those of the first trimester' (International Planned Parenthood Federation Medical Bulletin 1992).

Although this has been recognized by the Government of the day, Virginia Bottomley, the then Minister for Health, stated in the House of Commons that: 'Delay can occur at various stages in considering a woman's request of termination, those terminations over twelve weeks are much more likely to lead to complications, quite apart from the additional stress to the woman' (Hansard 21 June 1990, Vol.17, Col.1158). There has never been a systematic nation-wide campaign to facilitate early first trimester referrals. How long a referral takes varies from regional health authority to authority and from hospital to hospital and even from gynaecologist to gynaecologist. The reality can be a six-week wait. This is unacceptable as only women who are referred before they are six weeks from their last menstrual period have any hope of being seen before the common cut-off point for clause C abortions.

Reception and complaints

The quality of her reception cannot be guaranteed when a woman is referred on for help. However, complaints can be made via the woman's local Community Health Council if more direct methods have failed and there is documented evidence of a persistent poor service or breach of confidentiality. Women can be very vulnerable. A woman complained bitterly of the treatment she had received at a pregnancy charity that had a good record for sympathetic and skilled help. The client reported that a nurse had strutted around her bed in high heels preventing her resting after her abortion. After some unravelling, she identified that the sound of the nurse's shoes had for her symbolized the high heels of a prostitute touting for custom. She was condemning herself for the abortion which deep down she thought of as morally repulsive like prostitution. The nurse was probably just walking around the bed.

Other women have found their own trauma deepened by the cavalier treatment meted out by some hospital staff, whether or not this was consciously intended. A client who reported having to explain her reasons for wanting abortion whilst she was having an internal examination, was so outraged at this treatment and the attitude it implied, that she showed him how she felt. She retaliated by chasing the doctor down the hospital corridor without pausing to replace her clothes.

Clients fears and expectations

All surgeries, clinics and centres will experience women: ringing to cancel appointments at the last minute, failing to turn up at all or arriving at the hospital in distress. It can be difficult for even sympathetic staff to tell if this distress is anticipatory grief or that a woman has changed her mind and hopes to be rescued.

False reassurance, such as telling a woman she will be 'all right' or over-stressing possible problems can be unhelpful. The helper needs to be factually accurate. Some staff, for example, emphasize the possible risks of incomplete abortion without saying this occurs in 1 per cent of abortions under twelve weeks, thus putting the information in context. When a client is scared of having an anaesthetic, then the most helpful intervention is to find out what it is about having an anaesthetic that is frightening for the client. Once the source of fear has been identified or named – perhaps that of being unconscious and at the mercy of others, or that the client 'will not wake up' or die – this helps the client accept and maybe understand the fear. Although the risk of death or serious morbidity is slight, being told that this is silly or impossible belittles natural anxieties. This can also give the impression that the counsellor cannot cope with the risk and wants to jolly the client along or minimize her own fears.

Occasionally a client will ask a direct and difficult question, for example:

What do they do with it [the foetus] after an abortion?

I don't want this child if it's a boy/girl/twins.

How exactly do they abort now I'm this late? [twenty-three weeks].

How do they get rid of it, is it burnt?

Will the abortion hurt it?

Do they use foetuses for experiments?

These questions force counsellors to examine their own feelings and attitudes to emotive work that deals on a daily basis with life and death issues. The counsellor can help the client by asking both what has prompted the question or statement and how it would help the client if they did 'know'. It is more important for her to explore and answer her own question than jump in with an answer. However, the client may not be able to explore the feelings behind her question unless a straightforward factual answer is given.

Great care has to be taken as whatever words are used will have many different subjective meanings to the client, and time needs to be allowed so the client can expand these thoughts and feelings.

How women expect to feel after an abortion is important; often the answer is neutral or delivered in an off-hand way. They either 'don't know' how they will feel or can't imagine or describe their feelings. Their answers are usually along a spectrum beginning with 'I don't know', to relief, sadness, anger, envy, guilt, regret and remorse. Women need to know that all these reactions are possible, many at the same time, and that counselling after an abortion is available. A client can return in the future days, weeks, months or even years later.

A woman may need to be able to justify and explain her need for an abortion to herself; to feel she had the time and space to decide what to do. Very few women have an abortion lightly or instead of using contraception, unless they effectively cannot use contraception or no contraception is available. In the 1970s and 1980s when contraception was virtually unavailable, there was a staggeringly high abortion rate in Bulgaria and Hungary, 98.5 per 1,000 live births and 122.8 respectively (Ghetau 1978).

It is only when the woman allows an abortion to begin that she finally consents and voluntarily ends her pregnancy. Women need to be aware of who to tell if they need more time for counselling, or simply want to stop the procedure. Those hospitals which do not provide a counselling service cannot rely on general practitioners to provide the detailed counselling help some women will need. Sadly, these can be the very women who return and state how they had no counselling and no one else to talk to.

It is also useful to remind clients when they are almost at the end of the session, that they have five minutes left so that both the counsellor and the client can adjust to this intimate time being over.

The counsellor may need to check if the client is clear about any practical actions they need to take. Does she know exactly what is expected of her and where to go? Has she remembered all her papers and any written information you have provided?

DECIDING TO CONTINUE A PREGNANCY

When a woman has decided to continue her pregnancy there may be many concerns, but there is a breathing space. The adaptation to pregnancy involves women having to lose some of the certainty and mastery that they have gained from being an adult. This mastery may be tenuous, to move on and become a parent and have a dependent baby is a major new role. Women start on an unknown journey for which it is impossible to be completely prepared. Experience literally teaches the pregnant woman as she proceeds. The counsellor's position as an outsider can be invaluable as an uninvolved adult who does not judge and has the time and space to look at what the client's problems are, and which are most pressing. The client can be helped to identify the main area in which she needs help, by asking her to rank her concerns. Whatever the answer is, this is a good place to begin.

Benefits and practical considerations

Some people will want practical information on benefits, this can be given or referral made to the appropriate agencies. It is now possible to qualify for maternity benefits if you have worked for the same employer for six months from fifteen weeks before the expected delivery date. Formerly the period was two years for full-time staff and five years for those doing less than sixteen hours per week. Depression and swingeing poverty can mean that a woman fails to volunteer that she has a broken cooker that she cannot afford to mend, or only one habitable room as a result of infestations or fungal growths. To discover this sort of information a counsellor needs to ask tentatively about problems with repairs or arrears, and direct the client to where help is available.

Young single parents (16 and 17 years) are entitled to some benefits (though their non-pregnant peers had their entitlement to income support withdrawn in 1988). Short-term emergency payments, called 'severe hardship payments' can be claimed but this is a discretionary award and is prioritized according to need (£36 for those living away from home).

The counsellor will need to check that the client has secure accommodation. Women may give as many as three different addresses, eking out benefits by staying with a boyfriend at the weekend and their mother during the week, and shunning the paralysing isolation of a tower block council flat in an inner-city estate. Those young people who are are homeless and pregnant may be able to live at home or have to await eventual rehousing. They can be offered dismal 'bed and breakfast' accommodation with inadequate cooking facilities in a tiny, cramped room. The evidence of women getting pregnant to 'jump the housing queues' is not compelling. Research has been undertaken in the Tayside area of Scotland that shows that young women from affluent areas chose to have abortions and those from the least advantaged areas of Tayside continued with their pregnancies (Smith 1993). Women often state that at least a baby is something of their own that they can love and which will respect and love them. When you have very little, then a baby is more than nothing. For example, one client said: 'one of the few times I feel good is when I'm pregnant, at least I'm making something grow, and I can feel hopeful'. A client may smoke heavily, or owe money to catalogues or use her meagre finances on drugs or alcohol. These small extravagances balance up for an overwhelming feeling of deprivation. If the extras are for the baby, then she may say to herself, 'Why should my baby suffer?'

Checklist

It is useful to have a mental checklist of the essential support a woman continuing with a pregnancy will need so that you are able to refer on appropriately, for example, to a debt counsellor or local citizens Advice Bureau/ Social Service (Table 5.1).

Issues such as drugs (illegal) and (legal) alcohol, tobacco, and the risk of HIV infection can be raised, bearing in mind the individual's receptivity at the time. Some health workers feel they always have to state, for example, how dangerous smoking is. Many clients 'glaze over' or agree to stop smoking simply to get the counsellor to quit 'ticking them off', as they perceive it. The aim is to get them

Table 5.1 Checklist

Immediate needs	Longer-term needs
Shelter – tonight? This week?	Quality of support
Money – Emergency claims	Adequate housing now and when baby is
Physical and mental health	born
Are they safe? Abuse, exploitation	Antenatal care arranged
How young (age and maturity)	GP support

to alter their behaviour, but changing the attitudes which inform this behaviour is much longer-term work.

Feelings

Clients may want to talk about how other people in their lives will feel about their pregnancy and either how to break this news or how to cope with others' reactions. It may be that the pregnancy has had to remain a secret, and in extreme situations a young woman may need a 'safe house'. This is accommodation for those unable to live at home due to domestic violence or abuse. Clients can be referred to Women's Aid Refuges or similar provision, but this is unfortunately scarce.

Some individuals or couples will come stating that they want to continue a pregnancy but want to talk through emotional conflicts they are having as a couple. Often this will be appropriate as they are debating what it means to have a child and be parents. Women can rage, quietly or loudly, that their partner is unable to spontaneously understand their needs: 'He should know what to do without being asked'. Women are trained by daily socialization at home and school to put themselves in others' shoes. This need can be strongly felt by pregnant women, who are being asked to give care and undivided attention to a baby. A woman may want to be unconditionally mothered herself and feel angry and resentful that these needs are not met by her partner. In addition, there is the idea that if these needs are not acknowledged then they are 'too much' for others, and are thus shameful and should be suppressed.

Women who are continuing often want additional support which may be able to be provided by a counselling agency or midwives during their pregnancy. Those women who are either blasé about their pregnancy and unrealistically optimistic or those who show a high degree of anxiety are often those who need the most support. Women who are aware that being pregnant and caring for children will be bound to bring up positive and negative feelings seem to use this balance to be more effective and cope well.

ADOPTION

Statistics

It is good practice and is recommended by the International Planned Parenthood Federation to mention the options of adoption and fostering in your pregnancy counselling session. Rarely a woman will feel unable to choose an abortion or take on responsibility for a child, and will want to consider adoption.

The number of adoptions has fallen dramatically in the last two decades, in the USA only 3 per cent of women chose this option. The highest number of adoptions in the United Kingdom (27,000) occurred in 1968, when the Abortion Act had just come in but was not fully operational. By 1991 the numbers had fallen to under 8,000 per year. The number of babies available for adoption has fallen to fewer than 900 a year. The recent white paper on adoption has emphasised the child's welfare and called for more openness surrounding adoption. John Bowis, junior health minister was quoted in Community Care (April 1996) as saying 'we are trying to promote adoption as an acceptable alternative to abortion and the burden of bringing up an unwanted child'. There is little evidence in our experience of women wanting to continue a pregnancy to give a baby up for adoption.

Compared to the roughly 180, 000 abortions a year the number of babies who are put up for adoption is very small and it is the lack of babies to adopt that is most noticeable. There are now fewer children in the UK, 11.8 million in 1994, 17 per cent fewer than in the 1970's, and they form 20 per cent of the population. The estimated numbers of children looked after by local authorities (March 1992) is 58 per cent fostered (32,100), community homes 16 per cent (8,700), private homes 12 per cent (6,600) and other accommodation 14 per cent (7,600). The total number of children in local authority care in England and Wales is 55,000 (1992) and in Scotland is 12,665 (1991) (Children Act Report 1992; The Statistical Bulletin 1991).

Table 5.2 Adoption (by age) in England and Wales in 1977 and 1991

Age	1977	1991
Under 1 year	2,945 (23%)	895 (12%)
1–4 years	3,002 (24%)	2,071 (29%)
5–9 years	4,185 (33%)	2,049 (34%)
10–14 years	2,192 (17%)	1,381 (19%)
15–17 years	424 (3%)	415 (6%)
Total	12,748	7,171

Source: Marriage and Divorce Statistics Series, FM2 (OPCS 1992)

Women rarely choose adoption again after having gone through the process once and can suffer deep sadness and loss afterwards, exacerbated by a lack of open grieving. This is true however dire the circumstances were that caused them to have to give up their child for adoption, even after rape or sexual abuse. For some women, however, who are too late for abortion, adoption is the only other option and needs careful examination.

Information

Women need to know that adoption is a permanent decision which means giving up all rights and connection with their child.

Check your own local information and state that they can go to any of the agencies below:

1 Social Service, Adoptions Officer;
2 Obstetric and Gynaecological Social Worker of local hospital;
3 British Agencies for Adoption and Fostering, Skyline House, 200 Union Street, London, SE1 OIY;
4 independent/private adoption agencies;
5 possibility of family members adopting (over 18);
6 The National Organization for the Counselling of Adoptees and Parents, (NORCAP), 3 New High Street, Headington, Oxford, OX3 7AJ, Tel.: 01865 750554.

Feelings

Women who have an unplanned pregnancy may well have been adopted themselves. The counsellor may broach with the client if they were adopted as this can help the client gain more understanding of the dilemmas their birth mother faced, which can foster compassion and empathy and also bring up intense sadness.

The estimated half a million birth mothers who have given up children for adoption are a group of women rarely talked about, and it is generally agreed that there are around 750, 000 adopted people ranging from babies to the elderly.

If someone is faced with this difficult decision there is more time available and this can be effectively used. As there are so few babies available for adoption, they are much in demand and a woman can request the sort of parents she would like to parent the child with regard to race, culture and religion.

Hospitals vary a great deal as to how they handle a woman antenatally and at birth who has stated that she wants her baby adopted. Few nursing staff will not have strong feelings, and women have been faced with staff who avoid and distance themselves from the pain these women stir up, and are unable to support them. It is therefore helpful for the counsellor to act as an advocate for the woman and write a letter for the other staff she may meet.

Chapter 6

Special situations

This chapter focuses on particular issues that pregnancy counsellors will encounter that require special attention. We have had to be selective and realize that there are other situations that we have excluded.

We start with a section devoted to the young and then look at clients coping with the additional stress and trauma that can occur if they were adopted, are HIV positive, depressed or suicidal, or have experienced rape and abuse.

Clients who have a physical disability or learning difficulties need further care and consideration, as do clients who have been 'in care', and we have finally concentrated on the needs of women who have repeated terminations.

THE YOUNG

The young are a vulnerable group who merit careful attention for many reasons. Issues concerning young people are discussed throughout this book. In this chapter we will look at their specific needs and concerns in more detail. There will be some unavoidable repetition so that this section can be read in isolation.

The high pregnancy rate of our teenage population is a major source of concern. In 1991 in the UK the conception rate for teenagers over 15 years old was 65.6 1/1,000 and for under 16-year-olds 9.3/1,000. At present Holland boasts the lowest teenage conception rate in the West of about 10/1,000 and pregnancies in the under 16 age group are almost non-existent. The USA has the highest teenage conception rate of about 100/1,000. It was the target of 'The Health of the Nation' (1992) 'To reduce the rate of conceptions amongst the under 16s by at least 50 per cent (from 9.5 per 1,000 girls aged 13–15 in 1989 to no more than 4.8)' (Department of Health 1992).

There are known links between poverty, poor social conditions, poor educational attainment and early sexual activity with consequent risk of pregnancy. Many young people are trapped with little expectation of realizing their hopes. It cannot be suprising then, that some young people see increased sexual activity as a way of achieving immediate pleasure with little concern over the foreseeable risks. This chapter thus starts with a plea for the enormous investment that is needed financially, socially and in education so that young people can have the chance to live life to the full while enriching other aspects of their lives.

Apart from these basic social improvements, the priorities for this age group should be initially to give young people a sense of ownership and pride in their bodies. Young people need to learn about relationships generally, assertiveness and negotiating skills. They need the ability to know what they want so that they can withstand peer pressure and say 'no'.

This obviously needs to be combined with knowledge and information about reproduction and contraception and should be delivered in a way that is relevant and enjoyable for young people.

The lack of basic knowledge many young people have is dire; a survey in Australia showed that six out of ten teenage women had no idea when ovulation occurred and the same number did not know that pregnancy was more likely to occur if intercourse took place around the time of ovulation.

Twenty-five per cent of young people do not use contraception for the first few months they have intercourse and the younger they are the less likely they are to use anything. This, coupled with lack of biological knowledge, increases the risk of teenage pregnancy.

Many factors are required for a young person to consistently use birth control. This is well analysed by Urberg (1982), who describes five major steps in the decision to contracept and is summarized in *Sexuality in Adolescence*.

The individual must first recognise that pregnancy is a likely outcome of unprotected sex. Next she must be motivated to do something about it. This step involves the belief that one needs to, and can do, something effective, as well as the belief that the possible outcome is undesirable. Third, the individual must be able to generate possible solutions to the problem. Fourth, these solutions must be evaluated and one chosen; and finally, the chosen solution must be implemented. Each of these steps in the decision-making process is a necessary but not sufficient condition for effective contraceptive use.

(Moore and Rosenthal 1993: 17)

As can be expected with young people, many factors could lead to breakdown of these steps and subsequent unprotected intercourse. These include lack of knowledge and the 'personal fable' of many young people that causes them to believe nothing bad will happen to them, only to others, so that they do not acknowledge any risk.

A young person needs to have the confidence and ability to set about arranging contraception. This may be too hard for some or may be too much of an unwelcome intrusion into their private lives. Young women can also find the psychological cost of owning their sexuality too high to consider being prepared for sex.

Another mitigating factor is the often unplanned and sporadic nature of teenage sex which leads to difficulty in preparation and the urgent forceful nature of sex when it does happen. In heat of the moment, contraception can get 'forgotten' and it is also difficult for a girl to be assertive and negotiate under sexual pressure.

Young people often have enormous difficulty in talking about sex to their partner and lack the necessary communication skills that would enable them to discuss their concerns. They may carry on having unprotected intercourse with their anxiety unresolved or equally may cope by denying any risks. Many young people find the cost of using condoms outweighs the benefits, until of course a pregnancy results.

One way of reducing the number of contraceptive hurdles is to improve services for young people. Young people need confidentiality. This is paramount. Surveys show that many young people would prefer to risk pregnancy than run the risks of their parents finding out that they were having sex. Brook had a drop of 43 per cent of under 16-year-olds attending the clinic and an intriguing rise in the number of 16-year-olds, after the Court of Appeal ruling in December 1984 made it illegal for doctors to offer medical treatment (including contraception) to under 16-year-olds without parental consent. Despite the ruling by the Law Lords the following October, many young people remain anxious about confidentiality.

A survey in Camden and Islington (Turner 1994) showed that young people want to be able to go to a clinic that is anonymous and run by health workers who they are least likely to know. They want services not to be obvious from the outside. They want to be met by friendly and uncritical staff. They want flexibility with appointments after school and Saturday afternoons as well as a drop-in facility.

They want sexual health services designed specifically for young people, as they find the presence of older people inhibiting. Many young people do not know where services are and many do not even believe they exist. Clinics need to be advertised widely but paradoxically services should also be discrete or there may be concern that confidentiality can be compromised. The name of the service is also important and needs to be relevant to young people; 'family planning'; can easily be misconstrued as being just for those people who want children!

Young and pregnant

Moving on now to the young woman who does get pregnant. Pregnancy, as we have outlined, is a time of enormous emotional upheaval even in the most favourable of circumstances. This is even more the case for a pregnant adolescent who is already emotionally loaded with the turmoil of negotiating their way through adolescence.

Adolescents are particularly vulnerable as they face the changes young adulthood brings and face the loss of their childhood. They have to make renewed relationships with their parents and friends as well as forging their new identity. As mentioned in Chapter 1 pregnancy can be the means through which these tasks are completed.

A young person will need to make an irreversible life decision at a time when she may well be cognitively unprepared. Adolescence is a time of idealism and extremes, and the subject of abortion can stir up strong negative feelings. A British study quoted in *Sexuality in Adolescence* showed that only 38 per cent of boys and girls approved of abortion, 49 per cent disapproved and the remainder had mixed feelings. (Moore and Rosenthal 1993: 152). In adolescence, therefore, the decision to abort an unwanted foetus may be harder and associated with more guilt and anxiety. There are opposing views on this.

Two studies are noted:

> one view is that, while abortion may be seen as a quick and easy solution, the consequences of abortion may be distressing and long-term (Hudson and Ineichen 1991). Sharpe (1987) is one who argues that teenagers cope well with abortion and that long-term psychological stress is uncommon, although there may be short-term, transient episodes of guilt or depression.
>
> (Moore and Rosenthal: 152)

Young girls are often terrified that they are pregnant and this in turn leads to increasing likelihood that they attend late in the pregnancy. They may well deny the fact they are pregnant until it becomes physically obvious. They can also seem to lose touch with any sense of involvement in 'getting pregnant', sometimes it can seem that they really were not present at the conception. In a similar way the girl may try and make the counsellor or doctor make the decision for her, as though in abdicating responsibility she really has nothing to do with it. It needs ownership of the pregnancy before a girl can make her own decision about whether to continue the pregnancy or have a termination.

Other girls need to put the 'blame' anywhere but themselves, so that they say that they were forced to have sex, or told that their boyfriend was infertile or the doctor told her it would be best for her to have an abortion as she obviously could not cope. In this way guilt is put elsewhere and an abortion forced on the girl as though against her will. This can be effective as a temporary defence, and for some may be the only way they can make such a decision but it diminishes their own person and may need working through later. Maturer girls may be able to acknowledge their part but then make themselves open to these difficult feelings.

The pregnant girl's relationship with her parents

When a young girl is still living at home there is often the dilemma over whether or not she should tell her parents that she is pregnant. This can put the girl in a trap: she wants support from her parents but must also make her own decision. When she is able to tell her mother she then has to be able to separate from her in order to make up her own mind. She may be put under tremendous pressure to have an abortion or equally to keep the baby. Her future emotional life may depend on whether she feels she is allowed autonomy in this.

Parents and doctors may feel they know what is best for the young woman and need to wrestle with the dilemma of how far to allow an extremely young and immature girl to make a decision that will affect the rest of her life. There often tends to be a panic reaction as though by getting rid of it, all traces of the pregnancy is destroyed. A young girl may be swept into an abortion without having a chance to think of its meaning to her. Everyone else has been swept into activity leaving the girl confused with her painful feelings ignored or denied. The abortion may be seen by the concerned carers as an end of the problem and an excuse for not paying attention to the girl's emotional needs.

The reality is that very young women need time and extremely careful, sensitive counselling in order to make a decision that they own and can live with. Many value the opportunity for reflection with an empathic person who tries to understand their predicament.

Gale came to the centre for a pregnancy test and was happy to find that she was pregnant. She was now 19 and she and her boyfriend had been trying for a baby for several months. During the consultation she talked of the termination she had had when she was 15. She said her mother had arranged the termination immediately she heard about the pregnancy. Gale had not known what to do, she had gone to a clinic but had withdrawn more and more from the proceedings, just agreeing that a termination was for the best.

Immediately afterwards her mum took her on holiday to forget about the whole thing, including her boyfriend. The pregnancy was never talked of again. As Gale talked she started crying about her lost baby, her feelings about the termination that had never been honoured before. It seemed to the doctor that she had been in arrested mourning all this time. She could finally let go of her experience as a terrified 15-year-old and look forward to what this new pregnancy in fact meant to her.

A young woman may feel unable to tell her mum about the pregnancy as she is too frightened. This can lead to pratical (but surmountable) problems regarding consent for the under 16 age group. She will also experience the pain of needing to keep the pregnancy secret at a time when she is distressed and may long for the support of an imagined ideal mother.

Amy came to the centre with a friend, she was pregnant and said she just wanted an abortion. The doctor was already stirred as she had seen her a few weeks ago for contraception. The doctor had been rather inexperienced and had not queried, even internally, the girl's stated 16-year-old status. She now gave a different name and said she was 13 and the doctor heard that the condoms she had given her were a great party success as balloons. Amy had a 14-year-old boyfriend with whom she had been having unprotected sex. Amy's father was dead and her mother was ill, both physically and with depression. Amy insisted that her mother must not hear about the pregnancy. She had an older sister who came with her to the next appointment and would be willing to sign the consent form and give her support. She agreed with Amy that her mother could not tolerate such news. Amy came back for a follow-up two weeks later. She said everything was fine and she had no problems at all. It was as though nothing had happened. The doctor who had been incredibly concerned and involved was suprised as she herself had been feeling so bad. Later, she decided that Amy was cognitively too young to really have assimilated this experience and maybe it was really 'nothing' compared with all the awful other things that had happened to her.

Mothers may be allowed to know about the pregnancy but fathers often need to be protected or, alternatively, all the feared blame is thought to reside in him. A common response to an unwanted pregnancy in a young adolescent is that 'my mum must not know it – would kill her or she would kill me'. These statements are said often after an unwanted pregnancy has been accepted in a very matter of fact way, as though all the negative muderous feelings now reside in the parents. When a high proportion of these girls are enabled to turn to their parents they are usually supportive, allowing the girl to acknowledge her own distress.

It can seem cruel to disturb the smooth surface of a young girl who is superficially unperturbed about her pregnancy. This needs to be handled sensitively and is one of the greatest challenges of pregnancy counselling. The dilemma is whether careful exploration could make things worse by opening up areas that are painful and cannot be resolved or whether doing so it could in fact prevent long-term emotional sequelae developing.

Sonia, aged 19, came back to the clinic from which she had been referred for a termination two years earlier. She had never come back for a follow-up and now thought she could be pregnant again because of contraceptive failure. She told the doctor she would continue with the pregnancy this time as she could not go through that experience again. When asked how she had felt then, Sonia said she had been fine initially but she was now feeling worse and worse. At the time she hadn't wanted to think about it at all, she did not really believe it was happening and just wanted it over and done with. It only became real on the operating table and then it was too late to change her mind as people were doing things to her and she didn't have control. They made her have the abortion against her will. Two years later she seemed more accessible to looking at her part in this so that she could grieve and move on. She was delighted to find she was not pregnant.

Parents may also be struggling with difficult feelings about their daughter's pregnancy. These could involve anger, grief, guilt and jealousy of their daughter's sexuality. These need to be acknowledged as they will have a powerful effect and influence over the young girl.

The pregnant girl's relationship with her boyfriend

Little has been said about the boyfriend's involvement with the pregnancy – at our centre very few boyfriends come into the consulting room to share the process. Some girls get the support they need from their boyfriends while for others an unwanted pregnancy heralds the end of a relationship and quite frequently the boy is not told.

In other cases it becomes the turning point for when things start to go wrong. The girl's resentment for being the one who had to go through the abortion is never acknowledged enough to be dealt with. Other young couples can use this crisis as a starting point for renewed closeness. We also meet girls for whom their relationship meant little and they have active reasons for not wanting the boy to know that they are pregnant.

When a girl is young the possibility of incest or that she is involved in an abusive relationship must also be considered.

Common fears and anxieties

The actual operation may well be greatly feared by the adolescent with concern about the procedure as well as future fertility. These fears must be addressed and the anxiety faced. It is unfortunate that the young in fact account for a high proportion of late abortions due to delay in presenting and therefore have to face a more complicated procedure with higher attendant risks (see Chapter 3).

It is extremely important to discuss future contraception and this should be done as sensitively as possible. It can sometimes feel intrusive to be discussing prevention of the next pregnancy when a girl is facing a termination. However, this challenge must not be wasted, sometimes it is the only opportunity to sort out contraception and the young woman may also be able to use this experience to look after herself in the future.

Approximately half of all conceptions in under 16-year-olds are aborted. Older teenagers are more likely to continue the pregnancy. Altogether two-thirds of the teenagers who conceived have the baby (Central Statistical Service 1995: 41). Young women decide to keep their babies for many and varied reasons which are discussed in Chapter 5. Issues that are particularly relevant to the young include ignorance, fear and denial of the pregnancy until it is too late to arrange an abortion, or strong anti-abortion views. For some young women a baby confers adult status, a purpose in life and something to love. Teenage rebellion may also be a factor that makes a young woman continue a pregnancy against all the odds.

When a young woman does decide to continue her pregnancy and to keep her baby, it is of the utmost importance that she receives careful support from the health care team so that she can make the transition to motherhood in as favourable circumstances as possible.

ADOPTED WOMEN

Women who have themselves been adopted often have strong feelings about being pregnant, especially when their pregnancy is unwelcome. There is an infinite variety of ways in which the experience of knowing that their birth mother 'gave them up' for adoption can be perceived by a client. Women can have always been informed by their adoptive parents that they were adopted and as such were special, chosen or wanted. Others will have found out about their adoption much later, perhaps only when they are adult, and can feel that they are a secret.

Adopted women are often acutely aware of and sensitive to rejection. Faced with an unplanned pregnancy they can find the idea of abandoning their own pregnancy excruciating. This is an acutely painful situation for them. They may strongly identify with their pregnancy as a representation of themselves. Their potential baby is in the same imagined predicament as themselves when their birth mother patently could not, or did not want to look after them. Women can passionately want to look after a child and 'make up for the past'. It is almost as if continuing with their unwanted or unwelcome pregnancy would lessen this pain, and give them an opportunity to repair the past.

At the same time, and often for the first time, the pregnant woman who is adopted can be aware of the range of feelings and dilemmas that her own birth mother might have been facing. Women can question their own 'right to be here'. A pregnant adopted woman can thus be dealing with an often unresolvable conflict. Adopted women can feel ashamed that they were not wanted and different from other women.

When a woman is finding the decision about a pregnancy unusually intense and difficult it is worth considering that she may have been adopted. Some women will have given this information as part of their medical history but many will not.

Once the subject comes up a client can have a chance to air their feelings which can bring up intense sadness, anger and also hope.

HIV

The diagnosis of HIV adds yet further complications to any decision a woman makes as to whether to continue a pregnancy. A woman infected with HIV has the knowledge that her own life may be curtailed or marred by ill health during the baby's childhood. Also, a baby born to her runs a 14.4 per cent risk of being born with HIV infection. (European Collaborative Study 1992). As so starkly stated by Sunderland, 'The scope of the paediatric HIV epidemic will be determined by the reproductive decisions of these women' (Sunderland *et al.* 1992: 1027).

Globally the problem of HIV infection is awesome. By the end of January 1993 there were an estimated 8 million women infected with HIV and the vast majority of these women were infected through heterosexual sex (Murphy 1994: 31).

It is predicted that 3 million women will die of AIDS in the 1990s and by 1996 the number of children orphaned by AIDS will rise to 3.7 milllion (Keenlyside 1994: 44).

In Britain HIV infection in women is rising. Out of the total 8,669 AIDS cases notified since 1982, 696 have been female and of these nearly one-third were reported in the single year from February 1993 to January 1994. By June 1993 there were 2,586 women in the UK who had positive blood tests for HIV (Murphy 1994: 31). In June 1995 Barnado's estimated that more than 3,000 children have mothers who have tested positive (Imrie 1995). These figures are likely to be gross underestimates, as for every one woman who knows of her seropositive status there will be others as yet unaware of their infection.

In London the prevalence of HIV in pregnant women who attended antenatal clinics between January 1990 and June 1993 was 0.23 per cent. This level fell to 0.011 per cent in cities outside London and to 0.007 per cent in non-metropolitan areas. (Nicoll et al. 1994: 376).

In another study carried out in Dundee the prevalence of HIV infection was found to be significantly higher, at 0.85 per cent, in women who attended for termination of pregnancy, compared to those seen in antenatal clinics where it was 0.13 per cent (Goldberg et al. 1992: 1082).

The diagnosis of HIV infection in women during early pregnancy throws open a wider debate, which cannot be pursued here, as to whether named testing for HIV should be introduced at antenatal booking. In 1991 a study using anonymous testing showed that obstetricians were only aware of 20 per cent of the cases of HIV infection (Ades et al. 1991). Named testing would supposedly give seropositive women the opportunity to receive more care during their pregnancy and in particular more choice over the option of termination.

For the purposes of this chapter we will concentrate purely on the effect that an HIV positive diagnosis will have on a woman in early pregnancy. As a society we are apt to make moral judgements, no doubt further kindled by the fear surrounding AIDS, that a woman with HIV should not have a baby and would probably want a termination anyway. Harsh economic reality also adds its powerful voice to this reasoning, with estimates that each infected child in the United States would eventually require $90, 000 in health care costs (Sunderland et al. 1992: 1030).

In fact, research, though limited, indicates that the supposed automatic choice of termination is an unfounded simplistic assumption. It does not allow for or understand the huge complexity of this decision (Sunderland et al. 1992; Johnstone et al. 1990; Selwyn et al. 1989).

The Edinburgh study showed that the abortion rate was high in the group of women that they were studying. The women were either intravenous drug users or the sexual partner of an infected drug user. However, finding out that they were HIV positive did not alter the woman's original intention. 'When the pregnancy was wanted the desire to have the baby overrode all other considerations' (Johnstone *et al.* 1990: 24).

The three papers suggest that the reasons which led to the increased abortion rate related to issues surrounding the pregnancy and not the HIV diagnosis. Some women cited their concern over their health and the risk of perinatal transmission as an important factor in their decision to have a termination. However, they found that the most important indicators for choosing a termination were if there had been a prior elective termination, or a negative emotional reaction to the pregnancy and if it was unplanned. The women who opted for termination reported the most difficulty with their decision, compared to those women who continued their pregnancies.

They found that many women had strong anti-abortion feelings and were also under presure from the family to continue the pregnancy. Some women were descibed as having an overwhelming need to have a baby. Various reasons were cited:

> Pregnancy and child bearing may be seen by both addicted women and treatment professionals as a symbolic process that signifies affirmative life-style changes. Having a child can be an important expression of love for a partner or symbolic of a commitment to a relationship. Further, there may be other compelling issues involving pregnancy in HIV infected women, such as denial of illness or the hope of having an uninfected child in the face of a potentially fatal disease. The latter hope has at times been expressed by seropositive women in our patient population whose husbands already have been diagnosed with AIDS, cases in which having a child is perceived as the final legacy of that relationship . . . the dilemmas regarding pregnancy and child bearing for HIV infected women are among the most difficult faced by any persons with HIV infection.
>
> (Selwyn *et al.* 1989)

In order to illustrate these points we share two examples:

> Jane attended the clinic one week after missing a period. She had been diagnosed as having HIV infection the previous year and was symptom free. She had rejected the offer of counselling in the past. The pregnancy was the result of a condom accident.
>
> When Jane was told that her pregnancy test was positive, she remained impassive and just said, 'Get rid of it'. She was adamant that she would not continue with the pregnancy. It was as though all vestiges of the pregnancy had to go immediately like there was 'no tomorrow'. The counsellor's sensitivity to the lack of time and space was indeed an accurate reflection of how Jane was feeling about her own illness. The counsellor was able to share her own sense of how rushed it all seemed to Jane in a way she could use. Jane talked about her belief that she might 'die tomorrow'. She spoke of her own mother who had left suddenly when she was 5 to go and live with another

man. She had since sworn that she would never have a baby whose mother let it down. By allowing herself a little time, Jane made links between how her own early experience had violently connected with the difficult reality of her present predicament. She still decided she wanted a termination, but was able to do this from a different position armed with more resources. She was able to let go of some of her wilder fantasies about HIV and decided to continue counselling at a specialist agency and get the support she craved but had been unable to accept in the past.

Caroline was delighted to discover that she was pregnant. In contrast to Jane she could not see the baby as separate from her, and could not envisage the baby without a mother. She seemed quite 'manic' as she went through the first weeks of her pregnancy and was unable ever to acknowledge any difficulties. It was as though Caroline herself was going to be reborn within the baby and in fantasy continue to live on through her.

DEPRESSED AND SUICIDAL

More attention recently has been paid to young people who attempt or succeed as suicides. The Samaritans have provided figures showing an increase of 70 per cent for young male suicides (15–24 years) and a corresponding increase in the rate of attempted suicides in young women (Samaritans 1995: 5).

The counsellor will be aware if a client has an apathetic, flat voice, but the client's sense of futility and hopelessness may not be so obvious. There is still a stigma surrounding depression and it is not easy to work with as it saps a counsellor's energies. It is hard to concentrate if the room is filled with an overriding feeling that nothing can or ever will improve and that there is fundamentally no possible relief.

An assessment of the severity of the depression is needed, and an indication of how their depression affects the client physically, practically and emotionally. Can she sleep? How is she eating? Has she thought about suicide? Does anyone else know how she is feeling? (Home, school, work, friends, partner, etc.).

If she has thought of suicide, a client may feel able to talk about the appeal of this drastic solution. Obviously there are many feelings circulating about the wish to harm oneself and anger is one of the most common but often least acknowledged emotions.

Meg had been finding the decision to end her pregnancy very difficult. She came the following week and seemed more cheerful and purposeful. She thanked the counsellor for his help and left shaking his hand and then peered into his face as if studying it.

The pregnancy counsellor did not ponder on this reversal. A couple of days later Meg turned up unexpectedly. She related that she had spent the morning standing on the Northern Line platform and had made to throw herself under the train but a fellow passenger had grabbed her. This profoundly shocked the novice counsellor but he was able to talk to his team and the doctor.

It is imperative to make good use of supervision and discuss all such situations. The counsellor cannot be ultimately responsible for the actions of the client but can keep in mind how unbearable a pregnancy can be, and that clients can be suicidal. It may be necessary to have a detailed medical history and to take especial care if there is a past history of depression. If the counsellor is not sure or has doubts these must be checked out by asking pertinent questions, for example, 'You look as though you are finding this very difficult, how are you feeling?' Clients can be asked if there is anyone who is supportive at home now, and to discuss getting medical help from their GP. It is very useful to work with doctors who can help with a referral for emergency psychiatric help if necessary. Clients need to know who they can call around the clock.

RAPE

We have chosen to look at rape as it is a common experience and encapsulates so much of women's experience of helplessness. We also hope this will provide a better understanding of the especially difficult situation of a rape that leads to pregnancy.

A rape may be an attack by a complete stranger, though most clients will have met or seen the person before and therefore have a relationship of acquaintance. The rape can have been perpetrated by a sexual partner or spouse. When a client has revealed a forced intercourse, the counsellor will ask herself, 'Is the client fully protected by contraception? Could she be pregnant? What about physical damage, sexually transmitted infection, and HIV? If the client was unprotected, when would she be able to cope, for instance, with a vaginal examination? Where could she go for the most sympathetic help?'

In training, counsellors can find this area especially difficult and wish to avoid clients who have been raped by saying that the client needs to see another more experienced counsellor. This withdrawal by the counsellor can be unhelpful as the client is super-sensitive to fear, and needs a counsellor who is able to withstand and survive the client's trauma unharmed.

Rape is a betrayal on many counts, not least the slender but seductive belief that we are able to take care of ourselves and by our actions avoid rape and other totally unpredictable events. The counsellor needs to be a witness, to be empathetic but to survive the retelling of an experience which the client may find, through the process of flashbacks, to be terrifyingly real. It can be helpful to state that the client only has to tell whatever she wishes to tell and that she can stop whenever she wants. The counsellor can help by endeavouring to check that the client is in touch with current reality before she leaves the counselling room. Clients are surviving the attack as best they can, and sometimes this will involve disassociation, memory loss and other elements of shock.

Some women who have been raped often do not want to talk about what happened at all, but do want practical information and are helped by knowing that they can return to talk, should they want to. The clients desire not to 'talk' can be part of their wish not to feel powerless again or suffer the extreme shame of having been unable to stop the rape or protect themselves.

Clients, especially if young, can come and want verification that something 'bad' has happened to them but present this as being unsure about whether what happened could be classed as rape or how seriously they should take the assault or rape. It is crucial to acknowledge that whatever happened was unacceptable. The most important help the counsellor can give is to wait, especially when the client is so upset she may be unable to talk. It is important to let the individual tell you the story of her rape and how this experience has affected her.

Traumatic events can frighten the client by removing her to a world where she has been singled out. The experience can warp her sense of reality so that nothing can be trusted. This can lead to massive alienation, so strong that she may fear she is mad or must have done something to deserve an unprovoked attack and be thrown back to childlike dependence. Many feel dirty or unclean and even reduced to being, as one woman named it, 'a piece of shit'. The attacker will often have verbally abused her, and have found a way to make the client feel she does not matter and even deserves to be treated in this way. The function of this behaviour for the attacker is to control the client.

Some women will experience a situation that to the counsellor seems unbearable; perhaps a violent savage rape by several people, with accompanying violence of a sadistic, disfiguring nature, but be resilient enough to cope. Whilst others will have had an incident happen, for example, a man exposing his sexual organs with no direct touch, which for them will have been devastating.

Often women describe enduring the rape and expecting to be killed at any time. Although this can be a physical reality, this statement also holds an emotional truth. Those who have been raped can experience their emotional sense of self threatened with extinction, a woman can be trying to express an emotional death. A strategy sometimes employed by a woman to survive a rape is one in which she 'gives up' or stops protecting her body and retreats into her mind. Thus she is protected and remains inviolate. She may suffer the disadvantage once the immediate danger is over of guilt at not protecting her body or fighting the attack. The level of fear experienced can be paralysing and terrifying. When a client's wishes, and by extension their very person, have been treated as if they were of no account, this can amount to annihilation.

Those who are already living in highly violent situations are subjected to such continual wearing down of their own natural sense of outrage that they can talk in an almost disinterested, lifeless voice of occurrences that can make counsellors feel physically sick.

The most common themes that clients express when raped are: damage to the ability to trust; fear; insecurity; repulsion; anger; depression; and a sense of helplessness, hopelessness and impotence. Damaged trust can be focused on:

1 The body for having attracted the rape.
2 Feelings of responsibility for the rape.
3 Men if attacker is male (or particular age, racial group or whatever is similar to rapist).
4 Others (for not helping the client or for not preventing the rape even if they were not present).
5 Society at large.

This trust can gradually be rebuilt with the aid of the passage of time, friends and sympathetic relatives or a counsellor. There may be a kernel of trust remaining if a younger sibling or the client's children treat her normally. The client can see that some aspects of her life remain unchanged, and feels that she is respected and valued. Consistent help from the counsellor can also begin to restore trust to a level where the client can function.

Where attacks have taken place in the client's own area or street (or the worst case) in the client's home where she previously felt safe, an alternative safe place may need to be found. The client may wish to return to her parents, to friends, or have relatives stay for the first week or so after the rape.

Some women will want to explore hours, days or even weeks after a rape whether or not they should report the attack to the police. A woman has a right to report rape even if there will no longer be much or any forensic evidence.

It is important to be accurate about what will happen if a client chooses to go to the police. Police forces have improved their treatment of those who have been raped but the experience of giving a full verbatim statement is arduous, painstaking and long (often over four hours). The client would normally be interviewed by two officers, not always women, and the client's story is rigorously checked for conflicting evidence or signs that the rape was or could be seen as consensual sex. Clients can expect to be asked if they have regular sex, use contraception etc. Hopefully this is done gently but even being asked these types of question can be seen as threatening and tantamount to not being believed. The client can easily feel as if it is she who is the criminal and this can exacerbate depression. Clients need to know they can ask for a woman doctor to examine them and to have someone they trust with them. However, some women will feel unable to be assertive and find the thought of an examination or anyone else knowing intolerable.

The physical examinations by the police surgeon involves rectal and vaginal examinations and being asked to spit into a specimen jar. Clients are unable to change their clothes until these have been systematically 'bagged'. They can also expect to stand on a piece of paper and have to strip whilst the doctor is present so that any hairs etc. can be collected for forensic evidence.

If a client does not want to report rape or go for STD tests then that is her choice.

Men can be and are raped and this has thankfully begun to be recognized. In May 1995 the first Old Bailey case of male rape was tried and a successful prosecution was brought.

Many clients are often so frightened that under-reporting is commonplace. Their attacker may have had to issue threats to subdue and dehumanize the client and to boost their own justification for treating the client to this abuse, especially if the attacker is not a stranger.

Women sometimes come to talk about sexual problems with a current partner and then go on to reveal a past history of rape which their partner may or may not know about.

It is not helpful to tell those who have been raped how they are expected to feel (depressed etc.); clients tend to reject any further intrusion or suggestion of how they should think or feel having had the experience of someone ignoring their wishes and feelings.

Women who have had the misfortune to become pregnant from a rape have not only the rape or abuse to cope with but also a pregnancy. It may be that opportunities for after-sex contraception, or a confirmatory pregnancy test will have been missed if the client was too petrified to go for outside help, thus the pregnancy can be advanced. The client may have had to block out the idea that a pregnancy was possible. In cases of abuse the client may be very young and not be fully aware that a pregnancy is possible. Where abuse is incestuous, the father may have planted the idea that the client can have his baby.

No assumptions can be made. Some women will want to continue with their pregnancy whatever the circumstances of how they got pregnant. They still have a major decision to make about their pregnancy, and abortion is not the automatic choice. The foetus can be viewed by the woman as innocent. Clients can feel fiercely protective and guilty. Some will want a speedy and immediate abortion but feel unable to have the procedure done in fear of discovery and hospital examination. As with any client, patience and the ability to appear to have time are invaluable. The mental scars of rape can last a lifetime and cannot be underestimated. Confidentiality is essential.

Phong, a shy, innocent Chinese girl of 17 was raped, on her way to college, by two men, one after another, in an alleyway within hearing of passers-by. Phong was requesting an abortion. She expressed deep shame, reinforced by her culture, and felt this meant her life as a woman was finished and that nothing could exculpate her. She was not able to dwell or talk about her feelings, and pressed to have an abortion immediately. Phong had told her mother and her mother's reaction was to blame her as she had shamed all her family.

Sonia, mixed race Caribbean/Irish, was 14 years old, and had been taken by a cousin of a similar age to an older boy's house. Sonia was not allowed to have boyfriends, went to a girls' school and had little experience of a sexual situation. Her attacker had taken her hand and silently led her into a bedroom and locked the door. Such was her innocence that this had not worried her until he then threw her to the floor. Her mother had only found out by listening to a telephone conversation. Sonia's mother assumed that Sonia had simply had sex, she therefore complained that Sonia had been told that men (not boys) were dangerous, had disobeyed her injunctions and by so doing deserved just punishment.

Sonia felt there was no point in living, she looked grey with distress. She was Roman Catholic and had gone to confession, where she had been further anguished by having her sin forgiven but received no condemnation of the attacker. However, this had also angered her and this helped her be less of a victim. Nevertheless, it was a slow process of rebuilding her sense of trust. The inability of her mother to respond to Sonia was her deepest regret, especially as she presented herself as a model student and 'good girl', undertaking many domestic duties without question.

Slowly over a number of sessions her confidence returned and she went out with her friends again. She was also able to talk about her feelings of resentment, reveal hatred and a strong wish to be revenged. She was also able to express anger and disappointment towards her mother for being unable to cope with her rape, her attacker, her elder brother 'who got away with things at home' and towards the priest who forgave her rather than condemning the rape.

ABUSE

Our definition of abuse is where the client has been systematically manoeuvred into a position where she is unable to protect herself from harm. She may have had to deny her own feelings, or be cut off from these feelings to continue to live and survive. The abuse has led to the client being treated as an object that can be used to gratify the other person's wishes. Abuse covers emotional cruelty, neglect and sexual and physical attacks, all of which are often combined. Most people will have suffered some form of abuse, if widely defined from the minor to the more extreme, but may have been able to protect themselves or have had other people who were reliable and listened to them which has offset the effects of this abuse.

The abuser may have carefully constructed a web, designed to sap the client's sense of self and esteem over time. The effects can be long lasting and long-term therapy may be needed. Unfortunately, high-quality psychotherapy is in short supply. It is often the case that projects set up to deal with 'disturbed adolescents' find at least 50–75 per cent of the children have suffered abuse. However, sufficient psychotherapeutic help and financial resources have rarely been built in to meet their needs.

It is often the pregnancy counsellor, working directly with the results of sex and sexuality, who is in a position to have abuse revealed to her and who can provide a bridge to further help.

In recent times it has been acknowledged that the policy of concentrating on investigations and proving abuse (which often does not lead to convictions) damages clients if their needs go unattended. The Department of Health has published twenty separate studies into child protection, since 'Working Together' guidelines were drawn up after the 1987 Cleveland controversy and admits that financial resources have been poorly focused and insufficient help provided for those who have reported abuse.

The numbers of children on the Social Services 'at risk' register in the UK had risen to 28, 500 in 1994, a reversal of the downward trend since the Children Act became law in 1991.

For clients this may be the first time that they have been able to 'tell'. They may have tried to tell others but have found that people do not want to be aware of such unbearable facts and can become psychologically deaf. This is even more likely if the client can be seen as vulnerable, mentally or physically handicapped or very young.

The counsellor needs to be aware of, and at the same time avoid being drawn into, the abused client's world which is bounded by lies, mistrust and delusions. Clients can disclose abuse with no preamble, but at other times there is only an air of something too awful to be mentioned or named: the client hestitates, pauses and there can be an acute atmosphere of shame and anxiety. The thought, 'Is this abuse?' may occur to the counsellor. It is possible for those in the helping professions to push away this idea and not ask. Counsellors can worry that any suggestion of abuse that does not come from the client could be construed as implanting the idea of abuse and be encouraging a 'false memory syndrome'. There will most probably be others in the client's life who have wondered also about abuse but not asked. If the client has denied the possibility of abuse, the counsellor may be aware of her own immense relief. Disclosure is highly sensitive and needs experience and skill. The counsellor will need to work so that the client can be referred on for this help.

More commonly clients will talk about abuse that has occurred in the past, when they were children. Clients can feel they have coped with this situation and do not want further help at this time. Some clients will want further counselling and a comprehensive, up-to-date list of the different types of help in the counsellor's area is essential. It may be that a survivors' group is appropriate or long-term pychotherapy.

It can be helpful for the counsellor to define abuse and clearly state who a client could be referred to, in such a way that a client can understand when and where help would be available.

When clients have been abused by a close family member, they feel betrayed, perhaps by their body that enjoyed and may have responded sexually to the abuse, and this adds to the immense guilt. This can be very difficult for a client to admit. When the abuse is brought to light often all contact with the abuser will abruptly stop, thus depriving the client of the good parts of the relationship and leaving her with further guilt and confusion. This separation can seem further punishment. The counsellor can be aware of the struggle or immense effort that is going on inside the client to maintain the secret of the abuse. The client has often been instructed repeatedly 'to reveal nothing', and has been told whatever is most likely to be obeyed (for example, that mummy will die, that the client will be put in prison). The client can, at the same time, be aching to have someone know how to stop the abuse. Often the stopping of abuse is a magic wish for the abuse to have never happened and be non-existent. Clients can return many years later to tell the counsellor that they could not cope with saying anything at the time and were unable to ask for help.

> Becky, 24 years old, came to see the pregnancy counsellor shaking and obviously distraught. She appeared deeply ashamed and hid her face in her hands or so that only the top of her head could be seen. After a long time she said the pregnancy was the result of incest and that she wanted an abortion as being pregnant was emotionally and physically unbearable. Becky was booked into a hospital that day and would have seen a social worker. However, she failed to arrive and over the next month rang and was told that she could just turn up at her local hospital for treatment. The centre had no phone number for her, she had not given a real surname and letters sent to her were returned undelivered. She would ring and put the phone down as soon as it was answered. She then stopped phoning altogether. The centre's counsellor supervisor and senior maangers were consulted, but had no information on which to act.

The effects of abuse on women's sexual health, as outlined in the following summary that appeared in an American journal, gives an indication of the havoc that can be wrought: 'Survivors of abuse have longer labours, pregnancies, low birth weight babies, more abortions, earlier age at first pregnancy, more medical problems and greater stresses' (Jacobs 1992: 112).

PROSTITUTION

As with the prison population, and those who are homeless, a high proportion of prostitutes will have abuse as part of their background.

Clients may work in the sex industry as prostitutes, and it is not possible to give figures as to how many women this may affect. A Children's Society Report noted that there were 1, 500 convictions for under 18-year-olds involved in prostitution related offences in 1989–93 and that cautions for those girls of 10–16 had risen by 50 per cent and convictions by 10 per cent (*Guardian* 17 October 1995). Rarely, in our experience, will women talk about their prostitution, and most are extremely careful with contraception and protection against infection, as this is seen as an occupational hazard. Women do not feel able to talk openly about their trade and life, expecting prejudice, and therefore choose not to reveal their true circumstances. We mention this because so often women in this situation are ignored or treated as special cases.

THOSE IN CARE

The British Youth Council noted in 1994 that 57 per cent of the homeless at the Centrepoint homeless shelter in London had been in care, and that nationally 75 per cent of those in care leave school without any qualifications. Government research (MORI 1991) revealed that one in ten young people who have been 'in care' qualified for 'severe hardship' payments (a discretionary temporary payment for 16–17 year olds in desperate need since statutory entitlement to income support was removed in 1988).

Those in care can have many individual problems as well as suffering from the effects of a lack of intimacy and consistent attention from adults and other young people. On-going support for those leaving care is at best patchy as the limited resources available have to go into providing for those still in official care and under the protection of the state.

For some, the experience of being in care has been unhappy. They are not able to form sustained relationships with either peers or workers as they are continually leaving and moving on. Young people in care (often damaged in any case by difficulties their parents have had in providing consistency and being reliable) can find their ability to make attachments severely impaired. Trust is both longed for and feared, for relying on someone restimulates the pain of earlier rejections. Hurt is often avoided by the client deciding not to trust anyone or to assume that all relationships will fail. Such clients often present as hostile, flippant and derogatory and thus gain less compassionate help as professional staff who find the client difficult to deal with can distance themselves.

Crucial to helping is to establish what the client wants to happen and if the client is reluctant to come for counselling. Once it is established that they are free to leave or stay, most clients chose to stay and the atmosphere lightens. Clients need to know at the same time that the counsellor is prepared to listen to them without requiring compliance. A beginning can be made, although this help may well be rejected and will certainly be tested.

PHYSICAL HANDICAP

A minority of clients will come to see the pregnancy counsellor with physical handicaps. Many people who have disabilities would not see themselves as handicapped, and in any case need to be treated as other clients would be. The counsellor needs to try to ensure that people who could be prevented from using the service are seen. For instance, it is good practice to pay attention to access, and if the counselling room can only be reached by a flight of stairs this needs to be stated in the literature about the service. When access is prohibitive, appeals can be made to move the counsellor to more suitable accommodation.

Greater London Association of Disability has simple pamphlets that outline how to make a premises accessible, for example, giving door measurements for wheelchair access, a checklist of the needs of disabled people and where to go for information and services.

When working, for example, with a client with hearing loss, a variety of ways of communicating can be used; writing, drawing and speaking with a clear enunciation whilst maintaining eye contact so the client can lip read. The counsellor may feel inadequate if unable to sign or lip read, but it is helpful to remember that those who have a hearing impairment are often adept at dealing with the hearing world. Those with impaired sight will obviously not be able to benefit from visual aids but can be given condoms etc. to feel, or feel the counsellor's hands if she is illustrating size or shape.

Confidentiality is just as important for these clients, as for any others.

Saheeda came confused and hurt that her relationship with her boyfriend had fallen apart after she had a termination. She struggled in the first session to understand the counsellor and several times stood up and made a move to go but then sat down again. The counsellor was also struggling to decipher what at first seemed to be guttural and incomprehensible sounds. Once the counsellor had stated how difficult it was and that, although Saheeda was clearly deeply frustrated by their mutually slow progress, the counsellor was prepared to keep trying, then both could relax. But checking had to occur, with many single words written down and the judicious use of gestures.

LEARNING DIFFICULTIES

People with learning difficulties can also be seen as having 'special needs', more care needs to be taken, but the emotional needs of such clients are not different from those of other clients.

The range of understanding under this heading is vast and there is not a clear-cut delineation between those with 'learning difficulties' and the rest of us, though there is a matter of degree. It is only by listening that the counsellor can gauge what the individual can understand. It is especially important to dispense with any abstract statements, idioms, or other figures of speech that can obscure meaning, and keep the focus on the client's needs. The video *My Choice – My Own Choice* (First Field Production 1993) is an excellent example of a resource about safer sex for people with learning difficulties where the principal actors play themselves.

Often clients will have pieced together bits and pieces of information about sex and sexuality from many sources into a 'hotchpotch' by which they are both frightened and fascinated. On occasion a person with severe learning difficulties can only show by their behaviour something of their own discomfort and agitation. More checking, and re-stating what the client says and what the client has understood is needed so that the counsellor is clear that there is a mutual understanding. Such clients can be refreshing to work with as they can be direct and open, and this aids communication.

Michelle was sent along by a centre for those with moderate learning difficulties. She was nervous and stumbled over her words. Michelle told the counsellor that the centre thought she should come. Haltingly she said that she had a boyfriend and a doctor had suggested she have a sterilization. She had understood what this meant but had not felt able 'to talk' about what this meant for her and whether she could refuse, or wanted children. She needed to look at other less drastic contraceptive options and help with answering all her questions.

Those with learning difficulties may assume that the counsellor could not understand them and more poignantly that they would not be able to make themselves understood. Often people come accompanied by an experienced worker who can help put the client at ease and also help the counsellor gain an idea of how the client functions and generally fill the counsellor in with the background to the concern or problem that the client is having. Clients may also have been helped by staff to begin to ask questions. A referral can be made by the manager at the centre or hostel, because staff have been disturbed by the client's behaviour, feelings or verbal communications that were seen as inappropriately sexual (for instance, masturbating in public). The client may never have been told what behaviour is socially acceptable and what is not, and why. Beth (see p. 98) was a client who staff felt unable to help as she refused to discuss her feelings about her pregnancy and clung to silence as a way of communicating her distress.

It is possible those with learning difficulties can have had less chance to protect themselves from abuse. They may also have had little chance to think about what happened and even less chance to talk about what happened to them.

REPEAT ABORTION

Repeat abortion accounts for about 10 per cent of abortions (Davies 1991: 200). This figure indicates that many women need to make this difficult decision for a second or even third or more time.

The decision may be much harder to make a second time round with many women feeling unable to go through with another abortion. If they do decide to go ahead with a termination, they may take on more blame, and be less forgiving of themselves for their second 'mistake'. They may become more anxious about their out of control bodies, and have the added fear that repeated abortions may effect their future fertility. They also have to cope with the undeniably judgemental attitudes of others who feel they should have learnt lessons from their first experience.

Other women find the decision to repeat their termination less fraught. The decision to have their first abortion was their ethical watershed, they are aware of the emotional impact the first abortion had on them and they also know what will happen to them and need not fear the unknown.

Research in Denmark on fifty women undergoing second-time abortion suggests that 'repeat aborters' cannot be characterized as a special group of women with complex psychological problems (Osler *et al.* 1992). Their suggestion for possible intervention is thorough post-abortion contraceptive counselling and follow up of women who undergo initial induced abortion.

Women get pregnant again for all the multiple reasons mentioned in the first chapter. Lack of knowledge about the consequences of unprotected sex is less likely but still occurs. We believe it is of the utmost importance that women attending for a repeat abortion should not be persecuted by the negative assumptions of medical staff. The reality remains that as contraception is not perfect a large number of sexually active women can be expected to need a repeat abortion.

Nevertheless we also believe the request for a second abortion warrants our antennae to be finely tuned as to the possibility of a deeper meaning to the pregnancy. The causes that are particularly important and will be discussed now are those that are hidden and cannot be explained away by bad luck or poor contraceptive counselling.

It seems to us that one of the most vital predisposing factors to multiple unwanted pregnancies that counselling can address is esteem. When a woman feels worthless, and cares little about what happens to her, it is not suprising that this also involves her sexual health. In some cases this acts as the only window to her true feelings about herself, particularly when these are protected by layers of aggression. At other times it is all too apparent what little regard the woman holds herself in and how the abortions and unsympathetic treatment, often invited by her seeming uncaring attitude, work only to confirm her sense of worthlessness.

It can be immensely rewarding to be with a young woman as she begins to understand how the unwanted pregnancies link in to some of her saddest feelings about herself. Through enabling her to become aware of this pain there is less likelihood of further unwanted pregnancy and there is also the hope of change.

Gemma was unhappily pregnant for the second time in six months. She asked for a second termination. During her session with the counsellor she cried broken-heartedly about the first termination. She also spoke about her own early years which were desparately unhappy, and how she had come to London to get away from everything. London had not given her the haven she was hoping for. She had attempted half-heartedly to get a job but soon gave up and entered a world of drugs and occasional prostitution. She looked suprised when the counsellor asked her whether she had been using any contraception as though she had never considered that looking after herself may be important. At the end of her story, she broke down again as though she had acknowledged her own part in her misery for the first time. She requested further counselling after the termination so that she could begin to believe a little more in herself so as not to put herself at such risk in the future.

Another important underlying factor that counselling can address is when a second pregnancy seems to evolve out of a sense of loss and the need to repair the damage from the first termination. This may be the woman's unconscious wish but the external reality may not have changed. This makes the impulse treacherous and leads either to a pregnancy and baby that is not wanted in its own right, or a second termination that just compounds the loss even more.

For some women it was being pregnant that was important, it made them feel good and full, they may want to repeat this experience but not consider having a baby. This type of woman may certainly expect a hostile reaction if she is honest with health care professionals. More often her own motivation is hidden even from herself so it is helpful to explore a woman's feelings about being pregnant. When it is apparent how much the pregnancy is enjoyed, it may be possible to discover what the woman feels is lacking in her and therefore what the pregnancy is carrying. This gentle discovery may be the means of preventing a reccurence.

A termination may evoke anxiety and fantasy about its effect on a woman's femininity and fertility, paradoxically getting pregnant again may be the only way a woman can prove she is still fertile. This fear obviously will only be fuelled by the next pregnancy that also ends in a termination and will grow unless explored.

Women attending for repeat abortions do evoke powerful primitive feelings in us. We both have experience of women attending up to their fifth termination. It is hard to remain open to a woman and not to fall into the easier position of being judgemental of her (or other health professionals).

A new partner in the practice came storming into the partners' meeting. She had just been with a woman who was requesting her fourth termination. She ranted that no one had told the woman about contraception. It needed one of the other partners to take her aside to ask if she honestly believed that no other doctor in the practice would have discussed future birth control with her.

When you have also been involved in previous counselling it can bring up insecurity in the helper, and lead to defensive blaming and labelling of the woman. While it remains important to wonder whether any intervention could have prevented this situation, it is also necessary to disentangle oneself. There may be no better example of the need for self-awareness and supervision than when working with women who have had multiple abortions.

Chapter 7

Termination for foetal abnormality

In this chapter the term 'medical terminations' is used to describe terminations performed for very serious medical reasons. This is not to be confused with the other use of the term, which describes a medical method (using drugs) rather than a surgical procedure for terminating a pregnancy. Terminations other than for medical reasons, mainly those covered by clause C, will be called 'social terminations' to differentiate between the two.

Although abortion remains the common theme, the circumstances surrounding terminations for medical reasons are unique and differ substantially from terminations for 'social' reasons. While they remain a tiny minority of the total number of abortions carried out in Britain each year, they individually give rise to enormous pain, suffering and concern. There are more than 2,000 medical terminations carried out in Britain each year accounting for between 1 and 2 per cent of the total.

The majority of medical terminations are carried out because of foetal abnormality, discovered antenatally. Very rarely a pregnancy may be terminated because of serious maternal illness that would be accelerated or lead to death if the pregnancy were allowed to continue.

The issues surrounding medical termination are exceedingly complex, bringing together the absolute latest in scientific technology, ethics and human pain. Our aim therefore is limited to outlining a basic appreciation of some of the different factors involved and how this compares to most abortions. By adding a specialist chapter we do not aim to imply that the suffering of these women is of greater import or 'worthier' of attention than that of their sisters having social terminations. We do, however, feel that the important differences should be acknowledged and respected.

Any couple embarking on pregnancy encounter the risk of not having the perfect baby they had hoped for. According to Lachlan De Crespigny:

> It is estimated that about 4 per cent of liveborn babies have an abnormality, the cause of which is unknown in most. About 0.6 per cent have a chromosomal abnormality, 1 per cent have one of the 5000 or so rare single gene disorders and at least 2 per cent are born with a structural malformation .

. . Mental retardation is probably the most feared abnormality. It is estimated that about one in two hundred (0. 5 per cent) newborn infants are severely or profoundly retarded.

(De Crespigny 1991: 81–2)

Antenatal testing gives the opportunity for the couple to rule out, or more unhappily discover, that their baby is affected by one of the few abnormalities that can be diagnosed prenatally. Antenatal testing can detect only a minority of possible problems including chromosome abnormalities, some single gene disorders and major structural malformations; and a negative result is of course no guarantee of having a perfect baby.

The abnormality can be discovered through a variety of ways including blood tests, ultrasound, amniocentesis and chorionic villus sampling (CVS). The pregnancy may have be known to be 'high risk' and the woman offered specialist testing right from the beginning, with the knowledge that all may not be well. The commonest risk factor is that of older maternal age and this is undoubtedly related to a higher incidence of chromosomal abnormalities. Alternatively the couple may have a positive history of genetic disorder in the family or an affected child already which then gives rise to concern.

Similarly other women may have suffered a potentially damaging infection in early pregnancy, such as rubella or toxoplasmosis. They may have taken possible teratogenic drugs or been exposed to radiation before they realized they were pregnant. Most couples though have every expectation that they will have a normal healthy baby. They may be offered testing following an unexpected result during screening or an abnormality may be discovered at their routine scan. These different starting positions bring their own difficulties and will be explored further as we detail some of the specific tests available to parents.

ULTRASOUND

Ultrasound is one of the most commonly used diagnostic tests in pregnancy. This works by examining the echo pattern the foetus creates following exposure to ultrasound waves. It can be used to assess growth and can detect significant structural abnormalities. Ultrasound may be offered in early pregnancy if there is an increased suspicion of abnormality, for example, family history of neural tube defect (NTD), in which case the woman may be offered detailed scanning in a specialist centre. This detailed appraisal may also be used after amniocentesis to assess whether there are any related structural faults when the primary abnormality is known, for example, heart defects in a foetus who is known to have Down's syndrome.

However, its commonest use by far is the 'routine' scan at around sixteen to eighteen weeks, the main purpose being to date pregnancies and check for foetal abnormality and growth. Although a few couples approach this test with trepidation, it has become a customary way of catching a first glimpse of the baby and is usually looked forward to with hope and excitement. There will be times when this hope is dashed when major abnormalities are seen on the screen. A high proportion of foetal abnormalities are found in this way with no prior warning.

This will leave the sonographer with the unenviable task of having to break bad news. Jean Hollingsworth has written how this most dificult of situations could be most sensitively performed and of most help to the couple (Hollingsworth 1994). Far from being routine, a scan is one of the most acute diagnostic aids we have and women need to be aware of this fact before agreeing to the procedure. Ideally an information leaflet should be given to all pregnant women at their first antenatal visit about the purpose of ultrasound. This should include practical information and detail the further steps that would be taken in the unlikely event of a problem.

These facts would be reiterated verbally to women by the sonographer before the scan. She would inform the woman that the test aims to check the well-being of the baby, but would also very rarely expose a major problem including viability and abnormality. This allows women to acknowledge the more serious implications of the scan without bombarding the majority with unnecessary anxiety. Once the sonographer is confident of her findings and able to give most women a happy guided tour of their baby, there has at least been some mental preparation for the few who are not so lucky.

Couples who are faced with unexpected findings consistently say how important the initial communication was to them and that they would like sonographers to be honest and let them know what they see. It needs enormous sensitivity and skill for the sonographer to be open to such distress and yet still find the right words.

BIOCHEMICAL TESTS

Maternal blood has been tested for alpha feta proteins (MAFPS) at around eighteen weeks since the mid 1970s to give an indication of increased risk of neural tube defect. When the level of alpha feta proteins is found to be raised, this can be followed up by amniocentesis and diagnostic ultrasound. Approximately one in forty women will have raised MAFPs and of these one in twenty will have a pregnancy with an open neural tube defect. The MAFPS test has been determinant in reducing the numbers of babies born with neural tube defects. For example, in the west of Scotland the screening programme had contributed to a 75 per cent reduction in birth frequency of neural tube defect by 1983 (Ferguson-Smith 1983).

Much more recently the introduction of the triple test in some regions has transformed screening for Down's syndrome. In the past, screening was based purely on the woman's age and women over 37 were offered amniocentesis on the basis of a 1 in 250 risk of having an affected baby. This risk was considered to be equal to the risk of miscarriage following the procedure and therefore was perceived as justified at risks above this. This somehow made a spurious link between the widely different traumas of miscarriage or having a handicapped child. Amniocentesis based on age was only able to detect about 30 per cent of Down's syndrome babies as so many more babies are born to younger women.

The triple test involves testing the maternal blood for MAFPs as well as the hormones human chorionic gonadotrophin and unconjugated oestriol. The combination of these parameters: age, low MAFPs, low unconjugated oestriol and raised HCG give a good indication to those foetuses who are at risk. At St Bartholomew's, a fourth biological marker is used – hence this is known as the quadruple test.

Women do not need to wait long for these results, they are generally available within three working days from receipt at the laboratory. When the woman's individual risk is greater than 1 in 250 (which is the same as the 37-year-old) she may be offered amniocentesis. About one in twenty women will be in this risk group out of which one in seventy will have a pregnancy with Down's syndrome. The Triple test will detect 60 per cent of pregnancies with Down's syndrome without increasing the amniocentesis rate.

The triple test can both reassure older women that their individual risk is less than the mean for maternal age so that an amniocentesis is not indicated or herald concern for a youger woman who can then have further investigation.

These prenatal tests are not routine and any abnormal result has consequences, pre-test counselling is essential to help women making their own informed choice. The screening co-ordinator at the Kennedy Galton Genetic Service, Shona Golightly, has set out clear guidelines for health professionals working with maternal screening for Down's syndrome and open neural tube defects which are reproduced here with thanks.

Prior to the test

Clear and concise information should be provided at the first antenatal visit in order to assist the patient with decision-making and future management of the pregnancy. The following can be used as a guide:

1 a description of the condition for which they are being screened;
2 the detection rate of the test, emphasizing that the test is not a replacement for amniocentesis, it is only able to identify those at increased risk, not to make a diagnosis;
3 the likelihood of a screen positive result. About one in twenty women will come back in this category;
4 the method of testing;
5 the meaning of screen positive and screen negative results;
6 how long the result will take and how it will be given;
7 the options following a screen positive result, and the risks involved with invasive procedures.

Screen negative results

1 It is essential that women with screen negative results are informed of their results;
2 in whichever manner this is done the meaning of a screen negative result should be reiterated;
3 women should also have the opportunity to discuss their result further if required.

Screen positive results

A screen positive result not only suggests the possibility (however small) of a pregnancy with Down's syndrome: it is usually unexpected, it is not easy to understand and it can present difficult decisions for the woman concerned. This will necessarily result in anxiety, although this can be reduced by the way in which the result is initially given. It is essential that counselling support is provided for women with screen positive results.

A consultation following a screen positive result should include

1 a clear explanation of the meaning of the screening result;
2 a description of Down's syndrome;
3 an explanation of the optional diagnostic procedures, how they would be performed, the risks involved and the length of time for a result to be obtained. It should also be explained that the diagnostic test may detect other conditions than those being screened for.

Biochemical tests have revolutionized antenatal care but bring with them their own problems when used to screen whole pregnant populations. The first pitfall seems to be that women often do not receive adequate information and counselling before they are tested. Many women, and staff (Statham and Green 1993: 174–6; Smith et al. 1994: 776) do not fully understand the tests and remain ignorant about the possible implications of a positive test result. In a recent report, nearly half those offering screening said they did not have adequate facilities to counsel the women to whom the test is offered (Green 1994: 769).

The programme will therefore raise enormous anxiety in women who are positive at initial screening and have not been adequately counselled about this possibility. The aim of the programme must be to allow a woman to make an informed choice and this decision needs to be respected and supported. Without this she may find the choice becomes too much of a burden at a time when she is emotionally vulnerable already. Women sadly may end up feeling guilty and that it would be their fault if the baby was abnormal if they decide against the tests.

AMNIOCENTESIS

Amniocentesis is offered for a variety of reasons. It is able to detect chromosome abnormalities, many single gene disorders and NTD. This test involves passing a needle through the mother's abdominal wall, uterus and into the amniotic sac. A small amount of amniotic fluid is then withdrawn. The baby's cells, found in this fluid, are then cultured and two or three weeks later can be examined for genetic and chromosomal disorders. Amniocentesis is usually performed at around sixteen to eighteen weeks.

Couples are advised that amniocentesis is an invasive test and carries a miscarriage rate of approximately 0. 5 per cent. In the past women were often told that there was little point in doing this invasive test unless they were prepared to have a termination if they had a positive result. Although to some extent this thinking was logical, it did not allow for the impact the positive result would have on the couple. There is no way a couple can know in advance how the news will affect them, particularly in a couple who may primarily have been having the test for its reassurance value. There is now acknowledgement that access to testing should be for all who want it and this should be independent of their future decision. People use test results in many different ways, for some it may be important to be prepared for the birth and not an indication for termination. Some conditions that are diagnosed prenatally can also be treated. Amniocentesis is an extremely accurate way of getting information, its major disadvantage being that it is usually performed mid-trimester so that women who are found to have abnormalities and then choose to have terminations have to undergo a late abortion.

CHORIONIC VILLUS SAMPLING (CVS)

CVS is a much more recent development and involves removing a small sample of chorionic villi (the foetal placenta). This may be done either trans-abdominally or trans-cervically. CVS can detect chromosomal defects but not NTD. The major advantage over amniocentesis is that it can be done at a much earlier stage of pregnancy at between nine to eleven weeks gestation. This allows a woman to hear the outcome up to seven weeks before the results of amniocentesis would be available. CVS enables couples to avoid suffering the agony of wondering whether the baby is all right for such a long time. It also enables the woman to have an early termination of pregnancy (TOP) if she opted to have a termination following an abnormal result.

The major disadvantage of the test is that it is significantly more risky than amniocentesis. It is difficult to compare the miscarriage rate with those women who have had amniocentesis because of variables such as the natural miscarriage rate in early pregnancy (approximately 2.5 per cent of women who are pregnant will miscarry at ten weeks). However, experienced centres usually quote a 1 per cent miscarriage rate, and this may not be acceptable to many mothers. Women are known to suffer much guilt if they have a miscarriage following CVS as they attribute this to their selfishness at not being able to wait for the safer procedure of amniocentesis.

The method occasionally fails due to inadequate specimens, failure of the cells to grow or ambigious results and approximately 3 per cent may need to be repeated or have an amniocentesis. There has also been recent concern over the possibility that CVS in very early pregnancy may cause foetal limb abnormalities (Firth *et al.* 1994: 1069–71).

FOETAL BLOOD SAMPLING (CORDOCENTESIS)

Foetal blood sampling is one of the most dangerous tests, carrying a risk of foetal loss of 1–3 per cent with up to 25 per cent in high risk pregnancies. (Fisk and Bower: 1993: 143–4). The indications for this have become increasingly rare with the development of less invasive tests giving similar information. Cordocentesis is an extremely delicate procedure, with a needle being directed into the tiny umbilical vein. It can only be performed after eighteen weeks of pregnancy. Although rare, women are faced with this possibility if, for example, a fast result is requested to check the chromosomes after foetal abnormalities have been discovered on scan. Foetal blood sampling can also be used to assess whether the foetus has been infected when the mother has had a potentially harmful infection such as Rubella or Cytomegalovirus.

FUTURE DEVELOPMENTS

Prenatal diagnosis is an area of rapid development with exciting prospects for the future. New technology may soon allow much faster amniocentesis results, and by no longer needing to rely on culturing foetal cells, parents will in the future be spared waiting the two to three weeks culture time. At the same time increasingly accurate detailed scans are steadily reducing the number of invasive procedures needed by eliminating those women who are at very low risk. An example of this is the nuchal translucency thickness test on fluid that collects behind the neck of a baby that will detect a high proportion of Down's syndrome cases in the first trimester.

We may also look forward to the time when testing can be carried out on maternal blood alone. This will be made possible by analysing the tiny quantity of foetal blood cell DNA in maternal blood so that more invasive testing becomes obsolete.

Prenatal diagnosis enables a couple to make a carefully considered decision as to whether to terminate their pregnancy. It is apparent that once started on prenatal testing any abnormal result has consequences. Decisions about testing must be carefully considered at every stage so that the couple retain control and are not just carried along a medical conveyor belt. It is vital that the following scenario is avoided:

A frequent effect of prenatal care is to drain away a woman's self confidence and through medicalization of the whole experience of pregnancy and birth, to deprive her of autonomy and make her feel inadequate, helpless and often guilty because she feels if she really cares for her baby she should not mind being treated like this.

(Kitzinger 1987: 105)

DECISION-MAKING

Couples need to be given full clear information on the specific abnormality affecting the baby so they can make their own decision as to whether to terminate the pregnancy. This needs to be adequately arranged for those couples for whom English is not their first language. Their decision will be determined by the predicted level of abnormality, their understanding of how having a handicapped child would affect them, their feelings about abortion, the threat of infertility and their attachment towards their developing baby.

It is often speculated that a couple who are at risk of having an affected baby may withold bonding to the developing embryo until they have the reassurance of normal results. The theory holds that by not allowing themselves to think in terms of baby at all or to expect anything, a couple would be spared some of the pain of the decision and the resulting grief if they had a termination. This type of pregnancy has been termed the 'tentative pregnancy' (Rothman: 1988) and seems to involve psychic acrobatics. It may be that it is not that mothers do not get attached but that they are attached and then try to deny it. The decision to terminate is therefore no less of a burden but can be more complicated.

The results of antenatal testing are often not able to define the specific level of handicap a child may suffer as the abnormality may be associated with a wide clinical range of foreseeable problems. People differ widely in both the levels of risk they are prepared to take and in the extent of handicap that they feel able to deal with. These differences may also be apparent between the couple due to conflicting beliefs, capability and experiences; for example, one may have been brought up with a sibling who had died of the same genetic disorder and could not face the same fate for his or her child. The counsellor will need to use all her sensitivity and skill to help them reach a decision that they can both acknowledge and share.

Some studies have shown that the decision is easier for those couples who are told that the condition affecting their baby is lethal (Iles 1989: 784).

When counselling, the aim of the health professional involved would normally be to support a decision-making process but not to influence it. There has recently been lively debate whether a non-directive approach is possible or even ideal when foetal abnormality has been discovered. By not offering guidance are professionals merely disowning responsibility and choosing not to face the ethical dilemmas they have been instrumental in discovering? By receiving non-directive counselling the couple are urged to make their own impossible decision at a time when they are grief stricken and in emotional turmoil. Couples in this kind of situation are often desperate to be advised what to do, and being able to say 'the doctor advised us to have a termination' can sometimes be a blessed relief, but at other times it can be an example of the disempowerment by doctors that the non-directive approach has done so much to challenge.

A research paper has shown that the three kinds of professionals involved in prenatal test results give guidance at the extremes. For example, the majority of obstetricians, clinical geneticists and genetic nurses would counsel directively to continue with the pregnancy for cleft palate and directively to terminate for anencephaly. The most marked difference was in counselling for Down's syndrome. In these cases 94 per cent of genetic nurses, 57 per cent of geneticists and 32 per cent of obstetricians reported counselling non-directively. The paper uses an example of a small trial of forty cases of sex chromosome abnormalities:

> It was found that 78 per cent of parents who saw obstetricians underwent terminations in contrast with 50 per cent who saw geneticists. One possible explanation for this difference is that these groups of health professionals conducted consultations differently, giving parents different descriptions of the conditions, or using differing counselling styles. If this interpretation is correct it suggests that whether a pregnancy is terminated may depend upon which type of health professional a woman saw.
>
> (Marteau *et al.* 1994: 864)

ETHICS

Abortion raises passionate emotions on either side of the debate. These range from the sincere conviction of a woman's absolute right to choose, to the equally fixed belief of the sanctity and need to protect the rights of a foetus that is unable to speak for itself. Medical termination provokes other difficult moral dilemmas, evoking equally intense feelings. Some people may be anti-abortionists but still support termination for severely handicapped children. Others, who are in general supportive of abortion, find the terminations for foetal abnormality more morally unacceptable fearing the comparision to Hitler's eugenic programme. As one put it:

> I fully support abortion that is independent of the state of the foetus and is solely dependent on the mother's wishes. I would, however, be much more uneasy about deciding to terminate my wanted pregnancy because the foetus was not normal. Who are we to judge the quality of life of a Down's syndrome child? Do we just want a world of perfect babies? What does this say about how our society values handicapped members, is there no room for difference? Are they too expensive? Surely as a society we should do our utmost to accept, integrate and support families with handicapped members? Where does one draw the line?

In 1993, 92 per cent of cases of Down's syndrome diagnosed prenatally were aborted (Alberman *et al.* 1995: 445–7).

The birth of Domenica, born with Down's syndrome, to the journalist Dominic Lawson in summer 1995 led him to write a moving article in the *Spectator* (17 June 1995) over the sadness and elation he felt after her birth and to question the policy of termination for Down's syndrome. This fired off a furious debate, conducted in the press, about tests for Down's syndrome and the sanctity of life.

Medical terminations raise enormous dilemmas which need to be faced and are seen in their most extreme when, for example, a foetus being screened for a major chromosomal abnormality for which it is negative, is unexpectedly discovered to have a sex chromosome abnormality. In these cases it can be impossible to predict whether the baby would be entirely normal or have a serious handicap. The majority of couples once hearing the word abnormal and finding the uncertainty unbearable will decide to have an abortion based on this information. Another example of the extreme complexity of the situation is that of Huntington's chorea which leads to early dementia. A couple may decide to terminate a pregnancy because it has received a chromosome from the parent whose side of the family has the disease. In some cases the parents themselves have made a decision not to be tested as they prefer not to know. The couple therefore run the 50 per cent risk of aborting an unaffected foetus.

The reality is that there is an enormous divide with a wide middle ground between a feared eugenic programme and the avoidance of the untold agony that bringing up a severely handicapped child can cause to the parents and other members of the family. Prenatal diagnosis means that for a minority such devasting pain can be avoided and that couples are instead faced with the burden of uncertainty and choice. Far from asking for designer babies most couples just want to have a healthy baby which does not suffer and a family life that is not destroyed by the overwhelming constant strain of caring. As Madeleine Simms writes after talking to mothers of handicapped young adults born before the passing of the Abortion Act and who were therefore denied any choice: 'Two-thirds said that with hindsight, they would certainly have had an abortion had they realised what awaited them' (Simms 1991: 1268).

THE METHOD

When there has been an early diagnosis a vacuum termination can be arranged. These have the advantage that they are much quicker, simpler and are carried out before the pregnancy is visible. However, attachment to the foetus can develop extremely early so paradoxically the ease of the termination and the invisibility of the procedure can make grieving harder.

Most terminations for foetal abnormality are carried out in the mid-trimester by prostaglandin induction. With the change in the abortion law in 1990 abortion for medical reasons can now be carried out in the third trimester. As these babies may be viable after delivery it may be necessary to kill the foetus *in utero*.

The treatment of women having a medical termination has improved considerably over the last few years with increasing awareness of good practice. Support Around Termination for Abnormality (SATFA) guidelines for professionals, reproduced here with thanks, state:

1   There is a growing literature showing that terminations of pregnancy for foetal abnormality should be likened to any other perinatal bereavement, but very little evidence to show that this happens consistently.
2   When there is an indication of foetal abnormality it is essential that women are referred quickly for confirmation or refutation of a diagnosis, with the minimum of conflicting advice.
3   All hospitals should have a maternity counsellor or designated key worker, to support parents from the time of diagnosis, through the termination and afterwards.
4   It is important to give couples full and clear information about the specific abnormality to enable them to reach an informed decision.
5   All parents should be given the SATFA parents' handbook (1992).
6   If a couple do reach the decision to have a termination of pregnancy the whole process of labour and all medical procedures should be explained in as much detail as the parents require.
7   Consideration should be given to the relief of pain and the use of epidural analgesia where appropriate.
8   Couples should be given a separate room of their own and full consideration given to the woman's partner.
9   The midwife or nurse should discuss with the parents the possibility of seeing and holding their baby.
10   A photograph should be taken and either given to the couple or kept on file for the future.
11   The nature of the post-mortem and the burial of the baby should be discussed with the parents. And, if requested, help should be given in organizing a private funeral.
12   All babies, whatever their gestational age, should be disposed of with respect and dignity. Ceremonies should reflect the individual, religious and cultural needs of the parents.
13   Thorough medical and genetic follow up for the family should be carried out.
14   There should be routine follow-up by a midwife as women experience the physical changes which accompany any birth as well as any psychological problems. One home visit is essential and then as many as the midwife thinks is necessary.
15   Consideration should be given to the support needs of staff. A review of their training should be undertaken to include bereavement and support counselling.

AFTERWARDS

It is now generally agreed that having a termination for foetal abnormality evokes the same feelings as any perinatal death with the added load that this death was of course chosen. Research findings have constistently noted the high level of serious psychological sequelae (Lloyd and Laurence 1985; Donnai et al. 1981; White-Van Mourik et al. 1992).

A study that followed up eighty-four women and sixty-eight couples two years after the termination reported that:

> most couples reported a state of emotional turmoil after the termination. After two years about 20 per cent of the women still complained of regular bouts of crying, sadness and irritability. Husbands reported increased listlessness, loss of concentration, and irritability for up to twelve months after the termination. In the same period, there was increased marital disharmony in which 12 per cent of the couples separated for a while and one couple obtained a divorce.
>
> (White-Van Mourik et al. 1992: 189)

The natural mourning process is complicated by many factors. The ability to choose a termination often leaves parents feeling guilty about their decision, which may have gone against their personal beliefs and previous strongly held convictions. They may suffer extreme guilt that they were not prepared to look after their handicapped child.

In truth there are two deaths that are grieved; first the death of hopes for the perfect baby that occurred when the results were given, and later the actual death of the abnormal baby. The couple also suffer the loss of their own sense of themselves. They may no longer see themselves as an ordinary healthy couple capable of giving birth to a healthy baby. Instead there is failure and images of being diseased and only being fit to produce a diseased, abnormal baby.

There may be terrific anger and a desparate need to understand, particularly in those couples where the abnormality was unexpected: 'why us, what went wrong, what have we done to deserve this?' The sense of the world as it was before, being a safe, secure place where a wanted pregnancy automatically ensured a safe delivery has been profoundly altered. These shattered illusions may lead to a general sense of misgiving about the meaning of existence.

Some couples are able to support each other at this time and become closer as they share their pain. However, grief can also be the most lonely, 'selfish' and distant of places, with a difficulty in meeting the other, particularly when each feels crippled or in a different place. This distance is encouraged by our cultural demands and the stereotyping of male and female roles. Traditionally the woman is seen as the weak, needy, sensitive one and in this situation rightly warrants care and support. The man is seen as the one who is strong and able to give this and in doing so misses out on attention for himself. This seems fair on neither and in this case it is often the man who is isolated, needing again to once submerge his feelings, for which he may well have no language anyway. In doing so he may be both bereft and criticized for being cold.

Difficulties may be compounded by elements of blame and guilt with each wondering if the abnormality were their fault. When one of the couple is the known carrier, one of them may carry the all the responsibility and guilt, making it even more difficult just to share the pain.

Although we have described medical terminations as terminations for wanted babies, there may well be some pregnancies which aroused rather more ambivalent feelings. There may have been some intensive soul-searching before the couple decided to proceed with the pregnancy. When these pregnancies are later found to have problems the guilt may be worse and the ground is ripe for fantasies that the abnormality was indeed the punishment.

It must be stressed that in cases such as this, that evoke such deep psychological conflict and suffering, it is extremely important that health professionals who offer counselling as a secondary role also know their own limitations and that of the setting in which they work. After identifying those people who are likely to benefit, health professionals need to be able to refer on to a network of on-going counselling or psychotherapy.

The decision to terminate may have felt much more painful to one than the other for reasons which were discussed earlier in the chapter. When these have not been fully aired and tackled at the decision-making time the legacy will remain and set the scene for future problems. One of the couple, usually the woman who had the baby growing inside her, may have much profounder feelings of attachment to the pregnancy, feelings that might be quite foreign to her partner. She may suffer much more acutely and unless her partner can be sensitive to this pain, divisions between them may grow.

The couple may find it hard to break the news to their families and friends. When the pregnancy has been very 'tentative' they may have kept it secret, and in doing so they protect themselves but also leave themselves without a chance of support from others. Some couples may find discussing the termination so hard that they say the woman has had a late miscarriage. There is then the hope of some comfort but this also misses the truth.

Even when a couple have developed the courage to tell others, they are often at the receiving end of something akin to congratulations. They have discovered the baby's abnormality in time to 'get rid' of it. This honours the relief of the situation but the more difficult, painful area of death and loss may carefully be avoided. The couple may end up having to agree with other's good intent but are left alone with their grief and longing. Off-hand remarks from relatives, such as 'well, it certainly isn't from our side of the family', can be quite devastating for the couple, adding to their distress.

The bereavement will affect the couple's relationships with their other children. Some couples will respond by overprotecting and swamping their existing children while other couples lose sight of them in the pain of the loss of the unborn.

There are more complex difficulties when there is an older child with the abnormality, which indeed may have initiated the desire for prenatal testing. The couple may need to make sense of their difficult decision to terminate a similarily affected child and that it does not mean they love their first child less.

Sexual problems can develop with love making becoming connected with the pain of reproduction. There may be marked differences in the couple's attitude to sex. One may find it a source of comfort and closeness while for the other sex acts as a constant reminder of the diseased pregnancy and so becomes feared.

There may be great indecision as to whether the couple should dare embark on another pregnancy. They should receive careful follow-up and advice about their future risks of having another affected foetus. Counselling may be extremely helpful to sort out the reality of the situation as opposed to the couple's fantasies.

> Sue and Andrew attended for counselling several years after a medical termination. A very severe NTD had been discovered at routine scan and Sue had a late termination. Sue had told Andrew that she could never bear going through a pregnancy like that again, and sensitive to her distress he had agreed not to try for another baby.
>
> Recently, however, they had both come to long for a child and realized that time was running out for them. They wanted to try and come to terms with some of their feelings about the termination so as to have the hope of trying for a healthy baby. In the session they had with the counsellor, Sue spoke for the first time of the shame she had felt when she had a termination at 15. She had never talked about it again, feeling it was her wicked secret which she tried hard to forget. When she was found to be carrying a severely handicapped child she was convinced she had now received divine retribution. She felt so much guilt and responsibility for the abnormality she had been unable to share this with Andrew. It was only now in desperation that they could look at this together and begin to understand how Sue's hidden irrational fears were affecting their decision. After several sessions they were able to embark on Sue's third pregnancy.

Any future pregnancy will unfortunately have increased risks of abnormality. This may be particularly anxiety provoking when the initial identified problem was unsuspected as this undermines a couple's sense of security.

When there is a high risk of inherited disease some couples may be willing to go through with the process of diagnosis and termination two or even three times before having their healthy baby. When the new baby does arrive there may be much joy and gratitude. The couple are able to enjoy their baby without needing to have faced family life with a severely handicapped member. The stark contrast between these extremes and having the loved baby safe in their arms may also reawaken much more painful feelings about their lost baby. In the midst of the joy, grief also deserves a place to be heard.

Future infertility causes further complications and painful questioning; a couple have lost their only chance of having a baby. The study that followed-up couples for two years discovered that the couples who were still trying to conceive 'took much longer to come to terms with the TOP for fetal abnormality and 70 per cent reported continuing feelings of guilt, sadness, failure, irritability, depression and crying at the time of interview' (White-Van Mourik *et al.* 1992: 198).

DIFFERENCES

The aim of this chapter was to compare medical and non-medical terminations. There are of course striking similarities and differences: both involve the decision to terminate a pregnancy, one based on medical reasons and the other often because of a complex web of factors. Both types of termination involve one of the most important decisions a woman ever has to make.

The most striking difference that has leapt out while preparing this chapter is the sense of there being two types of abortion. The terminations for medical reasons seem 'special' compared to the 'social abortions', as though these are the more deserving abortions. The foetuses are wanted and in some way this makes the women wanted too. Although women share the experience of abortion, there is a stark contrast between women being 'forced' to reject a loved and longed for baby who is handicapped and the woman who chooses to 'abort' an 'unwanted' but presumably 'normal' foetus. Many of the feelings the women face after a termination may be identical, but these polar opposites make it hard if not impossible for the two groups to meet and share their concerns.

Medical terminations seem to encourage sympathy and understanding in others while 'social' terminations often evoke blame and even hate. While in no way do we begrudge the support and quality of service that women undergoing medical terminations receive (which anyway is still far from perfect and leaves people's needs unmet), we cannot fail to notice the disservice to other women who do not experience the same compassion. While the difference and added strains are acknowledged, we would hope that eventually all women making these kinds of decisions will be afforded the same respect.

Considerable expertise has now developed to respond to the needs of the 1–2 per cent of women having medical terminations. There are well written guidelines of how to be of most help to this minority of women. There is a respected charity, Support Around Termination For Abnormality (SATFA), that has a place on medical establishment working parties aiming to improve services. Women who have terminations for medical reasons need not be left isolated with hidden grief, they are encouraged to contact SATFA who then do their utmost to give information, support networks and offer befriending. SATFA also has a training role for professionals and has written helpful handbooks for parents and guidelines for medical and nursing staff. It is hard to imagine a similar set up that would command as much respect for women having 'social' terminations.

The two-tier treatment extends to policies about deliveries, with most medical terminations being done on the labour ward with a midwife in attendance. Many midwives feel happy about their role supporting women in this way, but would resent being involved in a mid-trimester 'social' termination.

The use of language is always important in counselling for termination. This chapter calls women – mothers and couples – parents. The word abortion, which is always difficult, seems impossible to relate to a wanted pregnancy. The most important word is *baby*. When the pregnancy is unwanted the term baby is often carefully avoided and the pregnancy discussed only in words the woman uses. In medical terminations or a miscarriage, it is always a baby that has been lost, no matter how early the pregnancy. This seems to be another factor that leaves so little commonality between the two groups.

Chapter 8

Counselling after abortion

A pregnancy that ends in an abortion is a major transition for a woman. No matter how correct or straightforward her decision was, her life has changed irreversibly.

Many women can integrate this experience, feeling secure about the decision they had to make. They are able to cope with the varied complex feelings an abortion may evoke. They can acknowledge both the relief an abortion offers as well as the pain of the lost pregnancy. They are able to live with their decision and its consequences.

However, other women, for a variety of reasons, find the experience so unsettling that they ask for the opportunity to talk with a counsellor in an attempt to gain some understanding of the gamut of feelings they are facing.

Some of these will seek out counselling in its own right, others may be discovered when they attend for their post-abortion check-up or in contraceptive consultation. There has been some concern that the offer of post-abortion counselling may create problems for women by implying that they should be experiencing some adverse psychological effects. However, the aim of this appointment is not to dig up and unearth hidden wounds but to validate a woman's experience and give her 'permission' to talk about her feelings if she so wishes.

Some women will continue to struggle on their own and do not return for follow-up appointments. Others who do attend for post-abortion counselling may never go back to the original clinic, for example, but choose to attend the more neutral ground of a completely separate counselling agency. The referring centre and hospital will always remain associated with the abortion and as well as acting as a reminder, can become instilled with 'badness' making it less likely that women want to return there. As one woman said: 'After the termination I just wanted to get out of there as fast as possible'.

Women may also not have been able to express themselves openly pre-termination, having had to keep a firm grip on themselves in order to go through with the procedure. This can make it even more difficult to return and be open to those from whom they have already had to hide their feelings. Women may be angry or have other very strong feelings about the agency, but other women find it helpful to continue working with someone who has supported them through the whole thing.

Women who may be the most disturbed by the abortion are often those who do not attend for appointments as they find it too painful to face their feelings, or think themselves so worthless that they no longer care what happens to them. This second type of non-attender is particularly at risk of returning with a request for a repeat abortion with both episodes somehow blurring into one unhappy depressive mess with no opportunity for learning and growth.

Many women feel they have no right to any help as they have brought this situation upon themselves. Indeed, society's messages perpetuate the view that women who have an unwanted pregnancy are careless, irresponsible and definitely to blame. It is as though there is a perfect contraceptive, that men bear no responsiblity and that there should be no compassion for any sexual indiscretion.

Sadly, this can be a woman's experience at the hospital as well, with some doctors giving out messages that their patients have been remiss. One woman told me of the doctor telling her, 'I never want to see you here again', after reluctantly agreeing to terminate her pregnancy. When she came to the clinic with an unwanted IUD pregnancy ten years later it was obvious that those words had remained with her ever since. She was terrified of going back to the same hospital until she was reassured that he had retired.

Some women will realize they need counselling soon after the termination. Many others will lock their pain away and to all outward appearances have dealt with the abortion, getting back to 'normal' quickly afterwards. Some time later several of these women may be affected by an event such as a friend having a baby, a miscarriage or a TV programme about abortion. These events can act as a catalyst which may expose their hidden feelings. Other women will put up with years of confused symptomology before they ask for help.

THE NEED FOR COUNSELLING

It is important to try and ascertain how many women may be distressed enough to value the opportunity to talk to a counsellor. Research into post-abortion sequelae gives contradictory results, but there is consistent agreement that abortion is beneficial to the mental health of women in releasing them from the emotional trauma associated with unwanted pregnancy. Generally studies have concluded that:

> many women who are denied abortion show ongoing resentment that may last for years, while children born when the abortion is denied have numerous, broadly based difficulties in social, interpersonal and occupational functions that last at least into early adulthood.
>
> (Dagg 1991: 578)

A literature review of abortion sequelae is confusing, and in view of this, it is incredibly difficult to give accurate statistics about how many women suffer psychologically after a TOP. An analysis of the research literature shows an amazing variation of between 0 and 41 per cent of women developing a 'psychiatric' disturbance following termination. (Zolese and Blacker 1992: 744). The limited research done so far on women undergoing either a medical or surgical procedure shows no difference between the two groups as regards short-term negative sequelae (Urquhart and Templeton 1991: 396).

Research into post-abortion problems is notoriously difficult for a variety of reasons and has been severely criticized. Much of the research has lacked any control groups or baseline assessments of the women before they became pregnant. Pregnancy itself, even in women not seeking abortion, is known to increase the incidence of psychological disturbance (see Chapter 2). Women who have an unwanted pregnancy are often emotionally distressed already and do not want to be asked many questions on how they feel. They may also be suffering from multiple other stresses as well as the pregnancy, some of which have led to the decision to have an abortion anyway. These will add enormously confusing variables to any research project. Stresses may range from a failing relationship, sexual abuse, being terrified of hospitals and operations, to being frightened of not being able to arrange a termination.

Follow-up causes particular difficulties both practically, with follow-up appointments often missed, and ethically. These difficulties are compounded when long term follow-up is wanted. Some women, who feel they have dealt with the abortion, find questioning intrusive and others, who may be coping through denial, may be unwittingly pushed into facing feelings they are unprepared for. Yet how valid is a retrospective study that invites a self-selected group, such as that used by the recently published Commission of Inquiry (Rawlinson 1994)? This put advertisements in two women's magazines and gained 136 completed questionnaires whose evidence was used, but the respondents were of course a group who would have particular needs and difficulties and were not a representative sample.

In addition to well-documented research, different lobbyists add their voices to the debate in order to promote their view. Some anti-abortionists state that all women suffer from 'post-abortion syndrome' which is extreme depression, anxiety and guilt. This is obviously not the case, as thousands of women will testify. The opposing argument originally put forward by feminists tried to minimize the emotional effect of termination on women. This appeared vital during the struggle for abortion as any discussion of ambivalent feelings or possible harmful effects could, they thought, have weakened the cause. Now that the law is in place and safer from attack, pro-choice supporters can afford to look at some of the emotional costs to women themselves.

Much distress will have been hidden in the past because of both the secrecy and stigma of abortion. The unwillingness of professionals to explore feelings, when they felt the woman had brought this upon herself and may even have considered the woman a 'murderer', may have added to this. Women also had to deny any ambivalence in case the abortion was denied and this, even now, often remains an overiding concern.

We do not intend here to argue the statistics but suggest readers may like to look at the quoted articles which give detailed findings. We believe from our own and our colleagues' clinical experience that many women, at some relevant time in their life, value the opportunity through counselling of integrating this experience and understanding what the abortion meant to them.

The research does give some guidelines as to those women who may be particularly badly affected by their experience. As Iles writes:

> Thus, there seems to be broad agreement that for the majority of women, mental state at varying intervals after termination of pregnancy appears to be better than it was immediately beforehand . . . . Nevertheless, most studies identify a variably sized group of women who do seem to experience significant psychological sequelae which are not always short lived.
>
> (Iles 1989: 773)

Factors shown to increase women's chances of developing post-abortion problems include isolation, lack of support, desertion by their partner, multiple other stresses, and cultural or religious antagonism to abortion. The woman's attitude and belief about abortion, whether she feels she was able to make her own decision or was coerced, are also significant. The very young are more at risk, as are those women who would have wanted a baby if their circumstances were different. Women who have late terminations, particularly if it involves induction of labour and delivery, are more likely to experience negative reactions. Most studies show that a previous psychiatric history or psychological disturbance at presentation were also predictive of post-abortion disturbance. One large study showed that women who had a previous history of depression were 2.59 times more at risk of depression than would be expected (Joint Study of the Royal College of General Practitioners *et al.* 1985). Even so, it is often extremely difficult to predict who will have more problems after a termination, as women who do break down can be the very ones who have always coped in the past and therefore are expected just to cope again.

THE CLIENTS

Although these facts are important to have as a baseline of theoretical knowledge, they should be put to one side when we meet the individual woman who has her own unique reaction to her experience.

The request for counselling may be precipitated by a wide variety of symptoms, any time from a few days to many years after an abortion. Themes that are common include 'crying all the time' and feelings of incredible loss, nightmares about dead babies, panic attacks, intolerable envy of women with babies, and overwhelming guilt. Women may also have distorted reactions to the abortion that may take much unravelling. These include general depression and low self-esteem, relationship or sexual problems and somatic complaints. These more complicated symptoms of course also occur completely unrelated to an abortion.

Women may arrive for counselling apprehensive, hostile, in turmoil or grief-stricken. When a woman comes for post-termination counselling, what does she need?

She usually comes with some hope that here she will have her feelings about her abortion experience honoured and respected. Basic counselling conditions are important in order for the woman to feel as safe as possible. These have been discussed before and include privacy and freedom from interruptions. Although not always possible, containment will also be found in the time of sessions and their regularity and spacing. Boundaries can give a framework which allows freedom to explore the difficult feelings that are causing such painful conflict. We also acknowledge difficulties that arise in busy places, particularly when a woman's pain arrives unannounced, and respect the work that can also be done by an air of acceptance in a hectic surgery which can enable a woman to come back.

In some cases making a contract with a definite ending date gives an added boundary. After a careful assessment counsellors at the Post Abortion Counselling Service Centre (PACS) often have a ten-week contract with the woman. This time-scale will obviously have its own resonance with a woman who has terminated an early pregnancy. She may use this boundary well, be able to work intensely, and use this experience of focused work to let go and say goodbye in a different, more helpful way. Other women, whose abortion has acted as a stepping stone to further discovery about themselves, will want longer-term counselling.

The counsellor needs to be non-judgemental and willing to fully engage with the woman so that her world can be shared in the session. The counsellor allows her the freedom and space to clarify her own feelings, however difficult, without trying to make better, reassure or placate. These painful things need to be done by the client for herself, in the accepting presence of another if she is to find her own answers and her own peace. In this way what was previously unbearable may be made bearable.

What of the women themselves? Women come for counselling from diverse backgrounds, bearing the weights of their own personal experience, history, culture, education and philosophy. They come with their own personal reasons for their abortions whether through choice, pressure or coercion. A termination of a wanted baby due to medical reasons is even more complicated with its own specific issues as discussed in Chapter 7.

Some women will have become pregnant through contraceptive failure or a passionate mistake; for others the pregnancy may have been an imagined, now failed, solution to complex unconscious conflict. Each woman comes with her own belief systems including those about the morality of abortion.

They have their own personal experience of the abortion and whether this was approached with sensitivity or with little regard for the woman's feelings; for example, being admitted to a ward with infertile women. Most women will have had their abortion carried out as a day patient, but women who need late terminations may have had to go through a painful labour and seen or felt the foetus as it was delivered. They will have also had to cope with the distaste that this type of abortion may evoke in the helper.

They come with their individual fantasies about their bodies and what having a termination has done to them and what it means for their fertility. They come in different circumstances, some women having had to keep the abortion secret, others having been supported.

They will have had different feelings about the pregnancy. Some women will have developed an attachment and think that they have destroyed their baby, the embryo being seen as a baby, no mattter how early the termination. This is not always the case; other women will have had little feeling about the developing foetus while for yet others the operation is comparable to having a diseased cancerous part of themselves removed.

The counsellor awaits each woman unknowing, in attendance to the developing story, aware only how important it is for this woman to explore her own meaning of the abortion.

THE EMOTIONAL LEGACY OF ABORTION

The first emotions, which are most likely to be witnessed by the medical and nursing staff where the termination was performed, are ones of initial relief, thankfulness and even euphoria. The woman has successfully gone through with the procedure and she is no longer anxious about an unwanted pregnancy. There is often a rapid decrease in the level of distress the woman initially presented with.

This can lead staff to be unaware of the problems that can arise later, particularly as women are discharged so quickly and there is little follow-up of them at the hospital or private clinic for the reasons mentioned earlier. The doctors who have performed the termination may also need to reassure themselves that they have done the right thing; it would be very difficult to find the woman regretted the procedure and this may make it impossible to hear the distress.

For convenience we have divided the emotional legacies under headings. This in no way indicates that things can be so neat and tidily packaged, in reality a woman may arrive with several of the consequences. Other divisions are visibly false; for example, guilt may be the result of an overwhelming depression.

Sadness and grief

One of the commonest emotions seen after an abortion is sadness. All women attending for post-abortion counselling have suffered an extremely complicated loss which may make grieving harder. The women themselves have made a decision to end a potential life and it can feel to them as though they have no right to mourn. They may also believe that if they acknowledge their sadness it could mean that they have made the wrong decision. Natural sadness may therefore be lost in the primary need to show no regret which in turn may cause blocked, stifled feelings and eventual depression. Counselling can allow the tears and validate the mixed feelings of sadness as well as relief.

Society finds any death difficult to handle and the bereaved often find themselves isolated with other people avoiding them or not knowing what to say. This isolation is compounded by the shame and secrecy that can surround abortion. Thousands of women have abortions, yet many women remain isolated and scared believing they are the only ones. Society does not allow this pain to be acknowledged. A few brave, well-known women have recently talked in public about their own experience of termination in the hope that this will in some way break the taboo of silence.

Feelings of loss are overwhelming and can be agony, they can be experienced more violently than physical pain. Grief needs to be expressed and the process of coming to terms with loss worked through. Through the pioneering work of Colin Murray Parkes (1972) and others, it is now apparent that the bereaved person needs to go through certain phases. This can sound simplistic and easy but of course remains life's hardest task. These stages can include shock, numbness, denial, pain and disorganization before eventual acceptance and reorganization. There is no neat order or timing and although this pattern is often followed, people may move in and out of these phases at different levels, they overlap, entwine or they may all be present at once. Working through loss in general means that people need to suffer before they can both internalize and let go. They cannot go back to what they were but need to integrate this painful change into their life.

One of the ways we defend ourselves against pain is to deny what has happened. This may well be an adaptive way of dealing with sudden change and loss; it is impossible for the person to take in so much pain at once so the stark reality is blocked. In the short term this can be life-saving but, at its most extreme, results in mummification, as seen in those bereaved people who leave the dead person's room just as it was before the death. In the case of abortion this seems to mean being haunted by the pregnancy for ever. Life has become stuck, there is no chance of growth and development as it is impossible to move on without working through pain.

The secrecy surrounding abortion appears to be one of the factors that make denial a particular problem. Detachment and feelings of unreality are common. The hidden experience of abortion combined with the wish to deny painful feelings helps create what can be a dream-like experience. In many cases a woman has no outward signs of pregnancy, the only thing that may make her different is a little pink circle in a pregnancy test. She goes into hospital, has a general anaesthetic, and is then sent home. Women speak of 'one moment I was pregnant the next it was gone'. 'It was like nothing happened, did anything happen, I don't feel any different? One woman spoke of having to keep awake all night before the operation in order to keep checking that she had not eaten and could therefore still have the abortion. It was as though the only marker of the event was preparing herself for the anaesthetic. Another woman told of how she welcomed the pain after an abortion as that proved something had happened. In order to mourn there needs to be an acknowledgement of the pregnancy, its meaning to the woman and the truth that a potential life was halted.

Dee, who had mild learning difficulty, attended for post-abortion counselling in a state of agony. She felt she had had the termination against her will, having been 'persuaded' by her carers that she would not cope with a baby. She was furious with everybody and felt in no way reponsible for this painful decision. The most significant part of the work with her was to help her really understand that she was no longer pregnant. In spite of her rational understanding that she had gone through with the abortion, most of the early work revolved around confirming that she felt different now she was no longer 'expecting'.

Not every woman needs to grieve but women need to be allowed to if necessary and to have the freedom to grieve for whatever the pregnancy meant to them. The level of distress and need will depend on the emotional attachment the individual woman had made to the developing embryo and whether or not it was seen as a potential person. The woman may also have identified with the foetus, becoming pregnant in the hope of nourishing that tiny foetal part of her. When this hope is dashed by the reality of the abortion, there is truly the loss of the hoped-for renaissance. The pregnancy may have been a symbol of love or hope or femininity and she may also grieve for the loss of this special meaning.

Many women find that becoming pregnant changes forever the image they have of themselves; they have discovered they were capable of becoming mothers. For some this increases their sense of femininity and sensuality, but for others choosing an abortion and denying themselves motherhood, which many women have learnt is somehow synonymous with womanhood, can lead to an enormous sense of loss. As Susie said, 'having the abortion was like losing part of myself'. Women may need the time and space to mourn the loss of both the embryonic life and also all these symbolic losses.

There is still very little public acknowledgement, a 'conspiracy of silence', the sufferers often call it, about the pain of miscarriage and the grieving that is so hard when it is due to a life not realized. There can be no focus for grief and there is so little tangible to mourn, apart from the loss of hope and dreams for this potential person. Even this acknowledgement does not extend to those women who choose abortion.

A young doctor could not understand the grief her patient was facing following the abortion the doctor had arranged. The doctor saw the distress purely as a sign of ingratitude and also felt defensive, 'She wanted it. Why is she now so upset?'

Abortion also highlights the hidden and unacceptable face of pregnancy that as a society we hide from: the paradox of death before life. The rights of mourning have been denied, condemnation often taking the place of compassion. The role of the counsellor will be to respect this process, allow the feelings a voice, and not betray women in an emotional cover-up. The importance of the loss is honoured, and the added complexities heard and respected.

Counselling for loss means being able to be alongside someone as they suffer, say goodbye and accept what happened. A woman who has chosen an abortion does not lose her right to work through this process in whatever way she needs.

The absence of any acknowledgement after abortion is one example of the way the pain of abortion is minimized, when ceremony is usually seen as an essential part of a grieving process. A counsellor may be in a position to validate the woman's need for her own ritual whether it is setting aside time, planting a tree or lighting a candle in memory.

Some women may need very focused work on the abortion as this may be the first serious loss they have experienced. It may, however, resonate with and be complicated by previous unresolved losses and/or be further confused by the impact of the break-up of a relationship. Sometimes the abortion seems to release a tide of emotion that is triggered by the abortion but truly belongs to a deep well of unlocked pain and grief from the past. Counselling in these cases will need to work backwards in order to look at the totality of the experience. Through helping someone to survive these extremes of sadness, depression may be avoided.

Panic attacks

Panic attacks are not an infrequent presentation to the counsellor. These can be associated with multiple other symptoms related to acute anxiety such as insomnia or muscle tension, and may also coexist with the knowledge that they are related to the abortion.

Sometimes, however, the woman presents denying that the attacks have any connection to the abortion. The abortion is mentioned in passing, she has got over that and cannot understand why she should suffer these paralysing attacks.

It seems in these cases that the abortion stirs up far too much disturbance for the person to deal with, and the only way the pain can be expressed is through a panic attack. Counselling can give a woman the containment needed to explore the unbearable and powerful meaning behind the attacks, allowing her the chance to integrate these dangerous feelings so that the body no longer needs to act as the window to her pain.

Eileen requested counselling to help her with the severe panic attacks she had been having for the past six months. She initially did not connect these with her abortion but volunteered that they had started two weeks after the operation. She said the decision to abort had been hard but as soon as possible after the abortion she went home and within a few minutes had forgotten all about it. She had kept busy and the abortion was not mentioned by her friends, it was all over. Two weeks later she felt she collapsed, 'I was overwhelmed with darkness, I couldn't go out, everything made me frightened, the doctor eventually put me on tranquillizers and suggested counselling'.

Very quickly Eileen started talking about aborting her 'baby'. The pain was so intense the counsellor felt they were reliving it together and felt uncertain whether she herself would be strong enough to support Eileen. The counsellor realized that she too had been trying to avoid the depths of the pain and felt quite panicky. By allowing herself to be open, she was, however, able to understand and use her own feelings in the session. In doing so she became a container for the pain. At the end, Eileen spoke of the relief of having been heard and made arrangements for further appointments.

Dreams and nightmares

Dreams, as always, act as the gateway to the unconscious and can give important indications as to the inner state of the woman. Sometimes all the feelings are hidden, a woman may think she has dealt with the operation well with no ill effect, yet have haunting dreams.

More commonly, dreams are part of the general distress and can give a clearer picture of the woman's deepest feelings. The dreams can be extremely disturbing, truly nightmarish visions of murderers attacking a baby, or of being held down and forced to have a termination against her will. Sometimes the dreams are full of persecutors in the form of her family or friends telling her she is a murderer. Other women have to face a replay of the termination each night in their dreams. Just as upsetting are those dreams when she has the baby safely yet wakes to find it was but a dream.

As counselling progresses and the meaning of the dreams becomes more available to her conscious mind and worked with, the character of the dream may change and the repetitive quality that is also common may be relieved.

Sylvie came to counselling having had a termination several months earlier. The termination had been extremely distressing. She had been so shocked by her pregnancy that she had denied it until she was sixteen weeks and then had a late termination. This had been done in complete secrecy without her parents' knowledge as they 'would have been so disappointed in me'. She tried to get back to normal immediately afterwards 'to pretend that nothing had happened'. In fact, she was unable to concentrate at school, and spent most of each day 'watching an endless replay of her time at the hospital'. She was exhausted but found no peace in sleep, her recurring dreams of holding her full term baby left her in extreme pain each morning when she found herself empty handed.

Regret

Most women make a decision that is right for them at that particular time in their life. This is not to say that women who have had a termination will not experience regret, nor does it mean that having regrets makes abortion the wrong decision. Women for whom a baby would have been much wanted under different circumstances are especially susceptible to these feelings. Those women who continue to regret the decision for the rest of their lives, but are able to admit that it was wrong for them and to live with their choice are in the minority.

Envy

Envy may be the feeling that eats away at a woman, finally driving her to ask for counselling. A woman may become painfully aware of other pregnancies and women who seem happy with their babies and children. When she sees that others are able to enjoy what she could not, life may seem cruel.

She may feel compelled to spoil others' happiness as this may be experienced as a persecution that threatens to overwhelm her. Alternatively, envy may precipitate withdrawal from the world in order to escape the constant stimulation. At its most extreme envy may become concretized in the urge to steal someone's baby. In the wake of concern over baby abduction, this extreme consequence has recently been acknowledged as a possible predisposing factor.

> Diane told the counsellor she could not understand what was happening to her. She had had a termination recently and felt tremendous relief that this had been arranged easily. She was busy with an exciting career and there was no space for a baby in her life at the moment. She had made the decision to have the abortion relatively easily and had good support from her boyfriend who had also been relieved. She said she now felt taken over with hate every time she saw a couple with a baby. She felt so angry at them she was frightened for them and wanted help so that she could feel 'normal' again.

Guilt

Guilt holds the unwelcome position of being one of the most complicated consequences of abortion to unravel. Guilt is not a simple entity but rather created by a complex web of factors including religious, cultural and societal forces, which shape women's feelings about abortion. These influences then meet with the individual woman's own make-up and the harshness of her internal world which have been modified already by these factors. A counsellor at PACS let me know that 50 per cent of the women attending for post-abortion counselling there state they have a religion; 25 per cent are Roman Catholic. This gives an indicaton as to the possible power of these forces.

At its simplest, guilt is an uncomfortable state we reach if we feel we have done something wrong, and this is the crux. Why do some women feel overwhelmed with guilt about the abortion, whilst others, subject to the same kind of background and forces, feel at peace with their decision? These hugely different responses illustrate the importance of our own individual personalities and sense of inherent goodness or badness. When a woman carries painful legacies and beliefs from childhood that some part of her is wicked, an abortion can easily become both the hook and symbol of her depravity. In this way the 'wrong' of the abortion becomes amplified many times over inside the woman's mind, making her guilt ridden. In writing this, we are not denying the ethical dilemmas surrounding abortion, but notice with great interest the apparent lack of guilt in individual women from the former USSR, where abortion is not seen as a sin or cause for remorse.

In this society many people think abortion is wrong and believe that guilt is an appropriate response. Some believe that guilt is necessary and serves a useful purpose in validating the reality of abortion and therefore preventing further unwanted pregnancies. Women who have an abortion are at the receiving end of all these feelings and often feel guilty about what they have done.

Abortion is an event about which the woman herself usually has choice and she alone is responsible for her decision. She may have had strong anti-abortion opinions beforehand and then had to act against her convictions which will make her more prone to guilt. The woman's experience at the doctor or hospital may also reinforce this guilt. Women are often made to feel idiotic or wanton when their contraception has failed, as though it were all their fault.

> Kylie came for a contraceptive consultation following a termination. She had taken the pill correctly and yet had been unlucky enough to get pregnant. She spoke tearfully of not being believed, how she had felt persecuted by the doctor telling her that was impossible. This discourse added enormously to a sense of shame, personal failure and guilt.

This hostile reception and negativity towards abortion coupled with her own feelings often adds an additional guilty burden. The woman may have turned inadvertently to a counsellor from Life for help during her decision-making time, where there is an emphasis on saving babies. If she still decides that abortion is the right choice for her, these sessions could add greatly to her sense of having done wrong. Many women also have to face the onslaught of demonstrators outside the abortion clinic. Their chants about 'baby murderers' can leave indelible self-reproach in women that may last forever.

Women also may feel guilty that they have been selfish enough to put their own needs first in choosing to have an abortion. They do not see the counter argument about the selfishness of going ahead with a pregnancy and having a baby that they feel ill-equipped to care for.

Many women expect to feel guilty after a termination as though they have sinned and should now be punished. Guilt may even be welcomed as part of the punishment, with women feeling guilty that they did not feel more guilty.

Women who have been dealt with sensitively may even complain that people were too nice or that the whole event was trivialized by kindness. When the operation has gone smoothly and there are no complications afterwards, women sometimes complain that they were not punished or that it was too easy. Staff may also have been careful to avoid emotive language; the operation may then appear to take on the same significance as having a tooth removed. The importance of the abortion may be lost for all but the woman who paradoxically may suffer more.

> Naomi was pregnant as a result of contraceptive failure. She was in her first year as a student nurse and hoped one day to be a midwife. After much soul searching she decided to have an abortion. She stated she was pleased to have had unpleasant complications following the abortion as she deserved punishment.

Guilt is an enormous issue to work through sucessfully, as though it too remains stuck in its own 'malignancy'. The Counsellor needs to respect the painful reality of the abortion and its meaning to the woman, in the context of her past life. The woman's beliefs about abortion and her general feelings about herself must first be heard so that eventually it may be possible for her to make her own links as to why the impact of the abortion should be so particularly punishing. When these issues remain hidden, the long-term legacy of guilt is severe, leading to depression and general feelings of self-disgust and shame.

As counsellors and health care professionals we need to be aware of our feelings about the morality of abortion, particularly the guilt aspect. This will be explored in detail in the final chapter.

Anger

Women often feel angry following their abortion; in many cases this seems totally appropriate. They may be angry that their contraception failed or that they had poor, insensitive treatment or that their partner was unsupportive. This kind of anger is often helpful, the energy empowering to the woman and in some cases to other women, for example, if she is able to complain about poor services which are then improved.

The anger might not be such a positive force when it is persistently focused at everyone else who is 'at fault', excepting herself. The anger can then be seen as a way of protecting herself from other more painful feelings such as sadness or confusion. By saying that everyone else is hopeless or useless she defends herself from her own hopeless/useless feelings. One of the skills needed by the counsellor would be to understand the importance of this behaviour and its function. At an appropriate time, when the relationship has proved itself and the woman is stronger it may be possible to sensitively confront the woman in a way that allows her to own her cut-off feelings. Although in the short term this process means facing the pain the woman has been so busy defending against, it is a challenge that is important to meet in order for her to move on.

> Susan asked for counselling as her relationship had ended shortly after her termination when her boyfriend had walked out saying he could not stand being blamed any more. Susan was confused and unhappy, their relationship had been good and when Susan discovered she was pregnant she was initially delighted. It took several weeks for her to decide to have a termination; she felt she could not have a baby as she was in the midst of her studies. Jason, her boyfriend, apparently would have supported her whatever decision she made. Susan had been furious with him, she hated him for having 'got' her pregnant and then just letting her choose what to do. It was all his fault that he did not use a condom that night. She had come to counselling now because since he had left, she realized how much she loved him and missed him. She was able to see how Jason had been the unlucky recipient of all her mixed-up feelings that had been channelled into anger. In counselling she was able to own her own part in not using any contraception, and the fantasy she had enjoyed about giving up college, settling down with Jason and having his babies. Reaching this point was extremely painful for Susan, losing her exaggerated self-righteous anger led her to experience a sense of deep shame and failure. It was possible to work with her in the depths of her despair and for her to realize she could accept her own decision, survive and move on. Her acknowledgement that these were her true feelings about the abortion, ones that she had tried so hard to defend herself from, allowed her to view her relationship afresh.

Just as anger may mask other more complicated feelings, anger, particularly for women, is often only found with great dfficulty under layers and layers of sadness. Due to our upbringing and position in society many women have lost their ability to recognize or be in contact with their angry feelings. When this is the case, it would be of the utmost importance for the counsellor to help the woman explore what may be behind her sad, victimized feelings. Counselling can allow the woman the ability to own her anger and become aware of how unfairly she may have been treated. She becomes less of a victim and more of a healthy, assertive woman who knows her own rights as well as those of others.

> Sonia presented not being able to stop crying or think of anything except dead babies two months after a termination. She was living with a man who treated her apallingly. She spoke unemotionally about her life and the history of neglect and brutality she had endured. She spoke as though she had no choices or opportunities and would remain a victim for the rest of her life. The doctor was suprised to feel more and more angry not only with the people who had caused such suffering but also with Sonia for allowing this state of affairs to continue. The doctor became aware of being fed up with Sonia's continual acceptance of being abused and was concerned that it was hard not to say

something unhelpful and potentially abusive. Gradually over time it was possible to start looking at how Sonia's very passivity stirred up such violent feelings in others. She was able to reach her own anger that, for so many years, had lain dormant, infecting all those around her. In doing so she became more fully alive and for the first time in her life set about standing up for herself.

RELATIONSHIPS

Some women's relationship with their partners improve after a termination. They have become closer during the difficult decision-making time. Their struggle is shared and these painful circumstances have added a new dimension to their lives. They have been through and withstood something together. For others an abortion is a turning point that leads towards the eventual break up of the relationship. This is more likely if there has been a notable difference in the couple's plans. No one can experience the abortion except the woman and no matter how involved or concerned the man, the woman alone has the abortion. The woman may feel angry and envious of his maleness and relative freedom, and the fact that he could just walk away from it all.

Sharon, a young 17-year-old, came alone to discuss her plans after discovering she was pregnant. She had been going out with Sam for two years and described him as being supportive of her. When asked what his feelings were, she said she did not really know, he had not wanted to say anything about the pregnancy as he did not feel it was his place to influence her. Sharon was left with the total burden of the decision, whereas Sam was able to avoid any conflict in the short term by abdicating any involvement. Sharon was left confused; she tried to respect his reasoning but felt abandoned at the same time.

The man may equally be awed by the power of the woman's fertility and his own potency. He may feel that she held all the control in the decision as to whether to have a termination.

He may have suffered an impossible tension between thinking that he was offering commitment if he wanted her to have the baby and rejection if he wanted a termination, with no middle road. Society encourages men to be strong, brave and practical and above all gives the message 'that big boys don't cry'. This can lead to emotional impoverishment with the only emotional recourse open to some men being anger or negation. This in turn leads to poor communication, misunderstanding and frustration between the sexes.

In particular women may resent the man if he encouraged her to have an abortion. She may disown her own decision-making process and make the man the sole holder of 'badness'. Equally some women are put in a position of having to choose between the baby or the relationship. A relationship may never recover from this kind of coercion. In some cases the man may have wanted his partner to continue with the pregnancy and been powerless and rejected as she went ahead and arranged her abortion. These painful dilemmas will need to be brought into the open so that differences can be acknowledged, worked on and maybe lived with.

These kind of problems ideally could have been helped with good couple counselling beforehand. The pregnancy and decision to terminate often forces a couple to question the very basis of their relationship and to realize the extent of their love and commitment for each other. When the answers show little confidence in the future of their relationship, the only option open to the couple may be separation. The poverty of a relationship is seen at its most extreme when the woman thinks it best to deny her partner knowledge of the pregnancy.

OTHER RELATIONSHIPS

Many relationships may change for a woman following her abortion. She may be too ashamed to tell her friends or she may confide in them and then be let down by their response. She may find that one close friend is very supportive whereas another is extremely judgemental. Some friends may be truly emotionally available for her whereas others may only be able to minimize her experience. She may be shocked by the negative response from some of her friends and may need to explore this painful impact in counselling.

> Mary told her counsellor of the awful time she had experienced after her termination. When she got back from the hospital her flat-mates hardly looked up to ask how she was before continuing with their discussion about the evening's activities.

When a young woman is still at home and she has told her parents about the abortion, there often needs to be a major readjustment within the family. Having an abortion is absolute proof of sexual activity and parents can no longer deny that their little girl is growing up. A young girl has proved her physical maturity and this needs to be acknowledged. She is separate and now capable of giving birth. This transition may be extremely hard for all of them and they may benefit from being seen altogether.

Many young women are given tremendous support by their parents but some may be less lucky and be at the receiving end of the family's projections and shame. They will need much support to withstand this attack.

When the pregnancy has been kept secret the young woman may also suffer all the imagined attacks that she would have expected from her parents. Some women may find it easy to keep the abortion secret and separate from their parents; others find it becomes yet another barrier to free communication, leading to isolation and a sense of alienation.

An unwanted pregnancy and termination may have a dramatic effect on the parent/daughter relationship, whatever the age of the woman, and whether she tells them or not. The abortion often forces painful issues to the surface. For many women having an abortion makes them feel bad and therefore unacceptable to their parents. It stirs up sad memories and the knowledge that they were not loved unconditionally but rather needed to be 'good girls' to earn their parents' approval. This is an extremely painful area that can be uncovered during counselling, leading to a reappraisal and letting go of that destructive legacy.

SEXUAL PROBLEMS

Sexual problems can develop after an abortion for a variety of reasons. Generally a woman's sexuality will be related to how she feels about herself. Following a termination when she may feel at a low ebb it is not suprising that her sexual feelings will also be affected and will improve as does her emotional well-being.

Things, however, may become much more complicated. After a termination, the carefree pre-pregnant days are gone forever; sex and pregnancy have become irretrievably connected. An abortion may lead to sex never being the same again with sex being a constant reminder of the abortion, particularly if there has been contraceptive failure and the fear that it could happen again. A woman may feel that her body has been betrayed and it may be difficult to trust again.

> Gillian was unlucky enough to get pregnant with an IUD in place. She had completed her family, and just started back at work. After much thought she decided to have a termination. For medical reasons Gillian could not use the pill and both she and her partner were unhappy about the permanence of sterilization. She decided to have another IUD fitted and was not reassured by the statistical improbability of this happening again. She said sex had become a 'nightmare' with her insisting on her husband using a condom as well and she was still not able to relax. She was terrified the week before each period in case it did not come. In the past she had taken her contraceptive safety for granted, having had three very planned children. This contraceptive failure seemed to upset her very being. It was the first time she had not felt in control of her life, since being a little girl, when her mother had died suddenly leaving her father devastated and her in the mothering role to two younger siblings. She attended the surgery three times in three months requesting emergency contraception, just in case the condom had split. Eventually her husband decided to be sterilized as he could no longer bear her anxiety and their previous enjoyable sex life had become virtually non-existent.

When the couple has not used contraception, and this results in the unwanted pregnancy, there may be other difficulties. They may feel guilt about their previous 'lack of responsibility' and find it hard to let go and enjoy themselves again. Others may resent the shackles that they see contraception impose and may deny the connection and so continue having unprotected sex with the risk of another unwanted pregnancy.

The pregnancy can alter a woman's feelings about herself, leaving her in a confusing position between non-sexual mother and lover. Her partner may also find the change from lover to potential mother difficult. This switch may act as an extreme jolt and an unwanted association that can lead to complicated difficulties surrounding the taboo of mothers and sex.

The pregnancy may make the woman feel feminine and sensual. By choosing an abortion these warm feelings about her body may dissipate and result in a cooling-off in sexual responsiveness.

Sexual difficulty may be the only way some of the unspoken agenda, anger and hurt gets expressed between the couple. In this case the body may poignantly show the aftermath of the termination. The unwanted pregnancy may have felt like an invasion, and fear of a repeat attack may lead to the 'gate coming down' so aptly demonstrated by vaginismus. Sex epitomizes intimacy within a relationship, the abortion may seem like a betrayal of that closeness, leading to enormous fears of being sexually intimate again. Great attention should be paid to the body's voice by the helper so that the symptoms can be understood for their symbolic meaning. When this pain can be understood psychically and withstood, it may no longer need to be acted out in the sexual arena.

Diana, aged 45, came to the clinic complaining that she felt she was burning inside when she had sex. This had only been since her termination a few months earlier. Physical examination showed that there were no problems but later, when she talked about the termination she spoke of the 'burning shame of getting pregnant' at her age. When these words were reflected back to her so she heard what she had said, she made her own connection. As she spent time allowing herself to grieve and forgive herself, the pain also settled.

Many women still grow up under the influence of mutiple mixed messages about sex, many of them being negative such as sex is dirty or bad. These messages may fade for a while but are reheard and taken to heart after a termination as the abortion seems like a punishment for enjoying or having sex. When these beliefs and messages are not examined and confronted they may have a devastating effect on sexuality.

Sex can also become one of the avenues through which a woman shows her true feelings about herself. The abortion may lead to increased feelings of worthlessness and depression; her lack of self respect can lead to increased promiscuity with general lack of attention to contraception and the risk of sexually transmitted diseases.

Nina, a succesful model, attended the surgery complaining of an offensive discharge. Examination revealed it to be gonorrhoea. She returned to the surgery having attended a genito-urinary clinic in the meantime. She had been treated kindly there with no hint of judgement about the many contacts that needed tracing. However, one nurse had asked if anything was troubling her. This had precipitated a crisis, stimulating Nina to ask for help. She spoke of her absolute hatred of herself, her body and particularly her genitals. She maintained her outward appearance but inside she felt she was rotting, and taking risks with her sexual health seemed to prove just how rotten she was. She spoke of an intense affair she had had with a married man six months ago. She was enraptured by him and 'forgot' her pills. The joy she felt at being pregnant quickly dispersed when he acted like it was a disaster and told her to get an abortion as quickly as possible. She had an abortion within the next week, telling no one and keeping to her busy schedule. She did not allow herself to think about the abortion but decided to 'screw' as many of those 'bastards' as she could and then hurt them by leaving. The impact of actually getting gonorrhoea helped her face her tortured feelings about herself. She realized in trying to seek revenge she was only hurting herself. She began to express her buried feelings about the abortion.

Sometimes sex may become the medium through which a woman seeks love and closeness, with intercourse filling the emptiness for a short time. This path also leads to promiscuity with the illusive hope being dashed again and again.

CONTRACEPTION

Future contraception is an area that must not be missed. Before the termination seems the most opportune time to discuss the couple's plans or any problems with contraception and allows, for example, the pill to be started immediately post-operation.

Sometimes, however, it can be extremely difficult to bring up the subject at this time as it seems so insensitive to the woman's present predicament. There may have been so much distress before the abortion that it is impossible for her to think about the future or to take in the needed information. The possibility of sex occuring ever again may be denied and any reference to contraception is seen as an attack.

In these cases, contraception must be discussed after the termination to avoid the common apalling situation of women who have undergone termination leaving health care facilities without receiving accurate contraceptive information or services (*The Lancet* 1993: 1099). The subject calls for great sensitivity on the part of the helper so that this consultation is constructive for the woman. The opportunity must not be missed, both for this empowerment and to avoid a further unwanted pregnancy.

When contraception is a problem this may sometimes signal deeper problems concerning the relationship, sexual problems or her feelings about her body which can then be given a voice.

Tania arrived for a check-up several weeks after a termination, having got pregnant due to missing some pills, and initially appeared quite reconciled about it. She gave every impression of just wanting to get out of the room as quickly as possible and made the doctor wonder just why she had come.

However when the doctor asked about contraception, every method was greeted with a disparaging remark; they were all useless and she did not want to use any of them. The doctor eventually felt led to say that it seemed then that when she had sex she would put herself at risk of getting pregnant again. This remark initially incensed Tania and then led to deep upset. She had felt so let down by her body and so angry with her boyfriend that she thought she could not stand the idea of sex ever again. Through the doctor asking about contraception Tania was able to release some extremely painful, angry feelings that had till then been hidden. The consultation ended with her accepting the offer of another appointment and asking for some 'condoms just in case'.

FUTURE PREGNANCIES

The next pregnancy and the decision to embark on motherhood is likely to have a powerful impact on women who in the past have chosen termination. No matter how different the circumstances and the length of time that has elapsed since the termination, the present pregnancy may evoke memories and feelings from the previous unwanted pregnancy.

Even when the pregnancy is planned and wanted the woman will embark on this pregnancy with a different array of feelings than if this were her first pregnancy. No matter how delighted or thrilled she is to be pregnant now, she will be forced to face that this is not her first pregnancy and may notice the stark contrast that her happy feelings this time have with her last unwanted pregnancy.

She may have been able to suppress her feelings about the new life that was inside her at the time of her previous pregnancy only to find that her pregnancy and the delivery of the new baby evokes longing and hurt for what could not be. When her feelings surrounding the previous termination are unresolved, the new pregnancy can act as a shattering catalyst that breaks through many years of a fragile peace.

A preliminary study found a highly significant association between antenatal depression and anxiety, and a history of previous termination of pregnancy (Kumar and Robson 1978). Sensitive antenatal care and counselling can help the woman begin to understand her muddled feelings of joy and sadness. Awareness allows her the space to separate and face what belongs to the past so that its harmful legacy can be quietened.

When guilt has been an unresolved issue there may be enormous concern and worry about the pregnancy. A woman may fear retribution, expecting punishment in the form of a miscarriage or by being convinced that something will be wrong with the baby. The anxieties that the pregnancy produces give the opportunity, through counselling, to look at the underlying fears and fantasies about the previous abortion that the woman has been carrying. The hope of relief comes through clients being open to these fears and understanding how their own harsh judgement of themselves leads to such painful irrational consequences.

Sometimes a termination is immediately followed by another pregnancy that is now wanted. For the doctors signing blue forms supporting women through their original decision to have a termination, this leads to great personal uncertainty. It can be hard to believe that this situation can be other than tragic.

However, there are occasions when the termination seems like an integral, unavoidable part of the process of a woman's development. Sometimes the first pregnancy and termination pushes women into thinking for the first time that they want children. The termination can lead to a woman re-evaluating her life and changing priorities to include children.

Other women may enter their next pregnancy immediately in order to deal with their uncontainable feelings of loss or guilt generated in part by their own history. Intensive pre- and post-abortion counselling may be able to prevent these painful motives from being the cause of motherhood. The urge to get pregnant again is often so powerful that such necessarily brief counselling has little impact. In trying to appease their immediate feelings about the termination, they try but fail to repair the past.

Nancy was first seen at the centre, pregnant when she was 15. She was an extremely fragile, heavily defended girl and asked for a termination. Her story was dire in the extreme: her father, who had mixed in the criminal world, had been murdered when she was 8 and this tragedy was followed by her mother's suicide two years later. Nancy had been brought up in care, separated from her only surviving relative, an older sister. She hated most members of the caring professions and had in the past always refused the offer of counselling. The doctor was virtually unable to do anything other than arrange a termination for Nancy. She did not want to talk and could not be drawn into taking up the many careful invitations to explore the meaning of this pregnancy.

Three months later she returned to the clinic, this time delighted to discover she was pregnant. She said she had been forced into having the termination, but a baby now was just what she wanted and would make everything all right. Over the next two years Nancy was seen rarely, coming in to the centre only in crisis; she was unable to take up any offer of sustained help, but she and her baby son seemed to be managing.

Then a third pregnancy brought Nancy back requesting a termination. Now 18, Nancy seemed more able to think a little about herself: 'Sam was the best thing that had ever happened to me', but she knew she could not manage another baby. She seemed excited about the chance to come regularly for counselling and to somehow face the mutiple losses she had endured. She admitted that her life was a 'mess', she was living with a violent man and she herself spent much of the time in a drug-induced retreat. Once again she was unable to keep any appointments but came to the clinic two months after her termination now pleased to be pregnant. She said she had been unbearably depressed following the termination, had considered suicide but her own memories of being deserted as a child had somehow enabled her to go on living for the sake of Sam. Her decision to get pregnant had been impulsive, as a compensation for the tremendous feelings of loss that had completely overwhelmed her. Her unreal excitement left the doctor desperate. By the end of the pregnancy social services had to be involved and the two children taken into care leaving their mother abandoned and despairing. It remains to be seen whether there can be any salvage for Nancy as she returned to have counselling in an attempt to get her children back.

The next pregnancy may also be met with ambivalence. Particularly significant are those pregnancies that are a result of a still-unresolved unconscious conflict. Some women will choose a second termination (see Chapter 6: Repeat abortion). Other women will decide to continue to term as they feel they could not go through with another abortion. It would be helpful for these women to be given the space both to become aware of the pregnancy's meaning and to be able to separate their feelings about this future baby from those that belong to their last pregnancy.

Any woman who is pregnant has the added trial of being asked about their previous obstetric history which will include any abortions. If her previous abortion has been a closely guarded secret she may read into this request much more than the simple need for medical information. It may suddenly seem that the secret is out and written all over her notes for everyone to see, acting as a constant reminder. This may be the cause of unease and anxiety particularly when her present partner is also unaware of it. The forced openness does, however, allow another opportunity for the woman to recover her feelings about her previous termination in a safe setting and work through them.

WHEN THINGS GO WRONG

This heading includes infertility, spontaneous miscarriage and termination for medical reasons. The common linking feature between these three personal tragic events is that they may well all have added meaning to those women who in the past have had a termination.

The loss of an actual or potential pregnancy, perhaps without the hope of children ever, has an added poignancy when a previous pregnancy has been terminated. These losses may precipitate renewed grief for the life that the woman chose not to have which is interconnected with her present sadness.

The loss of a pregnancy also leaves a wide berth for fantasy as to the reasons for this event. The simple reality that many early pregnancies miscarry and one in six couples have difficulty conceiving may seem irrelevant. When there has been a termination in the past where guilt and self-blame are such frequent features that fantasies about retribution and punishment may germinate and flourish. These can be unbearable and much painful work will be need to be done in counselling to uncover their malignant roots and alleviate their distressing consequences.

Anna was discovered to have blocked tubes and was therefore infertile. It was suspected that this was a consequence of a termination years earlier which was unfortunately complicated by an episode of pelvic inflammation.

When she was told this tragic news, she became absolutely convinced that this was a just punishment for her abortion. She attended for counselling as her marriage had also failed and she felt bereft. She spoke of her early years, her strict upbringing with constant punishment for any minor misdemeanour. Infertility became infused with her mother's voice and thoughts of getting her 'just deserts'.

DEPRESSION

We will define depression as a severe disorder of mood which results in disturbed thoughts and behaviour. At its worst depression is an inner sense of absolute hopelessness and despair. There is often no focus and no connections, just an utter knowledge of emptiness and worthlessness. The world seems an abyss, the person believes that nothing can be done to relieve the pain and there may be no end in sight.

Although this state is agony and the pain alive, the reality of depression is that it occurs when we push down our feelings so we are unable to work through them, so that depression becomes an alternative to grief. As Bowlby writes:

So long as there is active interchange between ourselves and the external world, either in thought or action, our subjective experience is not one of depression: hope, fear, anger, satisfaction, frustration or any combination of these may be experienced. It is when interchange has ceased that depression occurs.

(Bowlby 1961: 246)

Later he goes on: 'In general it seems likely that the more persistent the disorder from which a person suffers the greater the degree of disconnection present and the more complete is the ban he feels against reappraising his models' (Bowlby 1981: 249).

Depression is therefore incredibly difficult to disentangle. As the pain is so disconnected how can we prove it is the abortion that has caused the depression? Is it more likely that the abortion just acted as a trigger and the depression would have happened anyway?

One thing we do know, however, is that the secrecy and stigma surrounding abortion make it more likely for depression to occur and that for some women depression that has been present for years is lifted as they face their losses and make those missing connections.

For other women the abortion triggers a resonance with deeper losses which makes the mourning process more complicated and engenders a greater possibility of pathological mourning which can lead to depression. This explains some of the research findings about depression mentioned earlier.

Women may also be more prone to depression when they have identified with the foetus, which becomes that part of themselves that is not yet born, and which symbolically carries hope for their future. When they choose for rational reasons to have a termination and lose that tiny foetal part of themselves the grief can be overwhelming. As this usually remains unconscious, the feelings are inexplicable and remain hidden, making it more likely for depression to develop.

> Helen had been depressed for several months when she came to counselling. She said her life had no meaning, she wanted to die and said that the only thing that was stopping her killing herself was concern for her family. She had had periods of time in the past when she had been depressed but had never felt so 'empty' as now. She said she had become depressed after a termination; she had had a 'meaningless' one night stand and had not bothered to use any contraception. It would have been 'madness' to have a baby, 'she had nothing to give it'. She remembered how excited she had felt to have something good growing inside her and how she had pushed those thoughts away before her termination. Since then she had been crippled with guilt, 'I am worse than a murderer who kills anyone, this baby was entrusted to me, I should have looked after it, not killed it, I have lost my soul'.

GROUP WORK

We have been discussing themes that seem to recur when a woman attends for post-abortion counselling. The expectation is that these women have been seen individually. However, group work, originally pioneered by Mira Dana at the Woman's Therapy Centre, has a powerful and uniquely rewarding role to play in helping women. Many women feel isolated and ashamed after an abortion. The very fact that they meet with others who have also shared this experience is on it's own incredibly therapeutic.

Group work is intense and needs excellent facilitating in order to contain the pain. The impact of the group can lead to dramatic expression and relief of suffering. Intense two-day groups and short-term groups lasting for two hours over several weeks are both successful models.

The small group provides a unique setting where it is possible for women to explore the meaning of the abortion to them. They are usually structured so that each woman has the space to tell her story, to hear other women talk and to realize that they are not the only ones who have had an abortion and are still struggling with painful feelings.

The group enables women to focus on their experience of the abortion, other women in the group may act rather like springboards, so that emotions that may have been too difficult to face alone can be shared. A woman may be able to reach more inaccessible feelings by seeing them acknowledged and respected in another.

A group may be enough for the woman to come to terms with the abortion or it may just be the first step of a therapeutic journey.

GROWTH

An abortion is frequently seen as a purely negative act whereas in reality it may act as an opportunity for the woman to understand herself and develop. The abortion may be seen by the woman as an extremely positive decision that will affect her future life. She may enjoy tremendous feelings of relief at not needing to bring an unwanted child into the world. She has been able to make a choice, maybe her first choice, and in doing so is making a very powerful statement about herself and her hopes and dreams. She has been able to say no to something that was wrong for her at that particular time and can use this experience to think about what she does want to do with her life.

During their therapy the women may reach an understanding of what was going on in their life before they got pregnant. There is time to reflect on the meaning of the pregnancy which is particularly important when the pregnancy is in part the result of unconscious conflict. New conscious awareness offers enormous potential for learning and growth.

> Kathy looked as though she had only just managed to get it together to turn up for her follow-up appointment. She had decided to take the pill. She couldn't bear the idea of having another abortion. She seemed to be in total disarray, but somehow it had mattered enough not to get pregnant again. She cared about herself a tiny bit so as not to go through that turmoil again. This seemed to be the first step she had taken to actively looking after herself and thinking about herself and her plans. She described a home situation of uncaring absent parents who never bothered about her and she herself never once believing she was worth bothering about. She had had the abortion as she had been terrified of her parents' reaction to her pregnancy as though it would be confirmation that she was worthless.
>
> Returning for contraception was the first step for Kathy to see herself as a separate person with her own needs and desires. She came to counselling for several months during which time she was able to leave home and enrol on a college course in child care. She left her boyfriend who had treated her as badly as her parents, using her when he wished. This was an act of tremendous courage and seemed to mark a turning point when she actually saw herself as being worth more than being a doormat.

Some women may initially use this experience of abortion to perpetuate their belief that they are a failure and cannot look after themselves. The abortion just adds to their general feelings of low self-esteem and poor self-worth.

Post-abortion counselling can be the door through which a woman grasps the chance to find out who she is and what she wants from her life. More than 70 per cent of women having counselling at Post Abortion Counselling Service have never had any experience of counselling before, and this figure is virtually 100 per cent in the young people's agencies where we work. Hence abortion can be the means through which a woman is catapulted to challenge some of her basic assumptions about herself. The abortion itself may just be the tip of the iceberg which then acts as a catalyst for the woman to look at her basic self.

Chapter 9

The effects of abortion work

Choosing to end a potential life through abortion is not easy. The workers' role is complex, they need to be alongside and supportive of women who have to make a decision in a very short space of time. They often have to give information and arrange future contraception. Additionally the workers are sensitive to the terrible suffering of women that has been caused by their pregnancies and their social and emotional circumstances. In the health professional's case, taking part in the abortion itself will give an added burden.

When we have counselled many women as they decide on abortion or have taken part in the procedure itself, it can be tempting to switch off and not think about what happens or our own part in it. It is difficult to stay involved with such raw pain. As one nurse who said, 'if we thought about what we were doing, we couldn't do it'.

This chapter aims to help us to face what we do, so that we can work more openly and therefore more beneficially with our clients. In order to do this we need to examine our own feelings about abortion and what feelings the work evokes in us. We must also be prepared to look after ourselves. In this way we may avoid burn out and perhaps even enjoy the rewards of feeling fulfilled about the work we do. The worker has the opportunity to help a woman surface through pain and loss to being able to take charge of her life. In the midst of the mess there is also hope and potential for growth. This alone offers the worker riches.

OUR OWN BELIEFS

Ideally, anyone involved in abortion should have a clear idea of their own beliefs and feelings about abortion. These may be at any position between the extremes of, at one end of the spectrum, feeling that any abortion is murder, to, at the other end, believing absolutely the absolute belief in a woman's right to choose with no acknowledgement of any difficulties that could arise.

Most of us fall somewhere between these polar opposites, most counsellors (straw poll) hold the general view that the woman's wishes are paramount but cannot deny the moral issues. It may be important to check your own value system and ask yourself some basic questions to help you clarify your own ideas.

How do you view abortion? For yourself? For others? Should it be available on demand? If not available on demand, in what situations, and who do you feel should make the decision? If a woman is refused an abortion, are you concerned about the risks she may be prepared to take to get rid of her pregnancy? Do you feel differently about late terminations? Are there any situations when your own feelings about abortion (either for or against) could influence a woman, for example, when working with a very young/disabled/disturbed client who you feel (from your viewpoint) would not be able to cope with the demands of motherhood? Are there other times when you feel resentful of a woman's seemingly cavalier attitude to abortion?

Do you see some women as more deserving than others? Do you ever find yourself condemning or judgemental? What do you feel about women who have repeated abortions? Do you think that women should feel guilty after a termination? Do you think choosing an abortion is too easy a decision for some women? Do you feel swamped by images of abortions or are you able to acknowledge and survive the losses that are involved?

The results of our small survey sent to health workers and counsellors working both in the NHS and in a selection of private agencies showed varied responses to the question 'Can you tell us how you feel about abortion for other women?' Overwhelmingly the majority felt it was the woman's right to choose. Responses ranged from 'entirely the woman's decision, good quality counselling extremely important beforehand' to 'I never thought it was *right* but never condemned women who had abortions. I was always guided by my religion (RC)'.

The response to the question 'Can you tell us how you feel about abortion personally?' was poignant as those who had been most supportive of a woman's right to choose were also most aware of how difficult the decision would be for them. The constant exposure to abortion in no way eased any personal dilemmas. In some cases, they appeared more acute: 'I feel I would find it unbearably traumatic and am not certain I could proceed with a termination myself'. 'In the past OK – now I would be unhappy about it.' 'I have been fortunate, I have not had to face that choice – I cannot believe that at any stage it is an "easy" decision or that it is ever an "easy" option.' 'I never felt I would be able to have an abortion but I am unsure as I have never been in the situation.'

One gynaecologist answered:

I feel that abortion involves taking a human life, irrespective of the gestation. I feel that there are circumstances where it is clearly inhumane to ask a woman to carry on with the pregnancy, for example, if child abuse or rape had occurred. Having decided that taking a life by abortion is sometimes the lesser evil, I do not feel able to judge between one woman's need and another – this would be completely unacceptable ethically. I would also find it personally difficult to wash my hands of a woman wanting abortion just in order to protect my own moral purity. I will therefore do any abortion at any gestation if the woman is sure herself that abortion is her only option. I think that I would not find an abortion possible for myself, and would not have antenatal screening for foetal abnormality.'

A few of the workers found their views about abortion generally had changed since they started work. They replied, 'I have become more liberal under twelve weeks but more restrictive over twelve weeks'. 'I am more understanding to my patients needs and feelings – I will perform abortion more readily.' 'No, only the shades of grey – the areas around decisions have increased.'

Several of our female respondents owned that they had had a termination themselves and how this had affected them. One writes: 'The whole experience, the decision, the operation and the memories afterwards overtook my life. Because of my own experience my values and beliefs have altered. I have a deeper appreciation of life and human relationships.'

A high proportion mentioned the difficulties of involvement in mid-trimester abortions. One consultant gynaecologist wrote: 'I find the process of mid-trimester abortion of a normal foetus very disagreeable and (if done by D & E) nauseating.'

It is important that nobody should work in this field unless they feel comfortable with the reality of abortion, both for their own sake and for their clients'. Several women attending for post-abortion counselling tell of the hurt caused by unsympathetic, even hostile staff. Strong anti-abortion feelings in workers can give rise to lectures on irresponsible behaviour and lax morals that can cause considerable distress. Only a little less disturbing is the counsel of sympathetic staff who cannot identify and accept their own difficult feelings about abortion, and therefore try to give them (through projection) to their clients. Women are told that they will feel guilty and have regrets after their abortion; this by 'caring' helpers who put themselves in the other's shoes rather than empathizing and accepting the difference of the other, which is of course a much more difficult task. While women occasionally distort what was said or meant, in many cases projections can leave scars. The worker must be self-aware and able to own her own feelings. The woman will have enough of her own issues to face without having to take on the unresolved feelings of the worker.

While the counsellor enjoys the relative luxury of being able to remain independent, health care professionals are of course unable to absent themselves from taking part in the procedure. Doctors particularly have enormous power and responsibility. Women are totally dependent on their willingness and skill in order to obtain their abortion. It is here at the cutting edge that it is so vital that staff are comfortable with what they do. Agreeing with a woman's right to choose changes from theory to practice and the reality of practice may challenge those idealistic beliefs.

Non-surgical doctors are also in the position of signing the blue form. Two doctors need to sign this for the abortion to go ahead, in the case of abortions on the NHS this usually means the GP and the surgeon. One GP said:

I believe absolutely in a woman's right to choose and I will do my utmost to help arrange this. I often end up feeling a hypocrite as I know I could never do one myself, in fact I have never seen one done. I have some difficulty signing the blue form. I don't like having that power over someone's destiny. I always wonder if it is the right decision. I used to worry about it a lot but I think I now give back much more responsibility to the woman and see myself just as her agent.

The position of moral guardian often hangs heavy and begs change. One doctor wrote in the *BMJ* of feeling unable to sign a blue form.

The patient was 38 and had a husband, three chidren, a large house, and a marvellous nanny. She wanted a fourth child but not quite yet. They had a skiing holiday booked for Christmas. Next spring would be a good time to get pregnant . . . I am a feminist. I have marched and lobbied in support of a woman's right to choose and would do so again. But I am not a rubber stamp. I am a thinking and feeling professional and I must live with the clinical and ethical decisions I make. I, the doctor, also have a right to choose.

(Greenlagh 1992: 371)

The resulting correspondence pointed out the contradiction 'in fighting for a woman's right to choose abortion if you then unilaterally invent criteria for rationing that so called right'. When one doctor in the practice holds strong anti-abortion views they have no responsibility to sign the form but should refer the patient to a willing partner and not sabotage the request.

Many health care professionals struggle. Surveys have consistently pointed out the low level of empathy and the judgemental attitudes among nurses, in spite of the fact that standards of care were often high. Others have found that nurses do not talk to the patients. They get the job done but leave the anguish unrecognized.

Frequently gynaecologists are forced into a role they do not want. One let us know that, 'The termination service was taken on as part of the overall service, not through choice. Therefore aspects of other parts of the job motivate me to continue.' They may have entered the speciality in order to deliver babies and hold strong anti-abortion views. Refusing to be involved in abortion may have ruined job prospects whereas prevarication and acting as a moral guardian only resulted in damaging women.

In one hospital where I worked the only compromise the gynaecologist could work for herself was to limit herself to two abortions a week. Somehow this limit salved her conscience, but was completely disconnected to the actual needs of the district and the many women whose lives were made a misery. She may have been able to offer a different more appropiate service if she could have faced her ambivalence and worked it through.

When a health worker objects to abortion, they have a legal right to refuse to participate. Section 4(1) of The Abortion Act 1967 states: 'no person shall be under any duty . . . to participate in treatment authorized by this Act to which he has a conscientious objection'.

The only area, however, from which a conscientious objector may be exempt is participation in any destructive procedure or the active administration of abortifacients. A midwife cannot allow harm to come to a woman because of lack of care, even though he or she may object to the procedure of abortion.

While the conscience clause protects some workers from needing to participate, the majority of professionals do not seek to opt out but continue to work in what for many is a difficult area. There may also be concern over being denied a career or promotion in gynaecology, or resentment from those who then have to do more than their fair share.

WHAT THE WORK DOES TO US

Those working in a counselling capacity

We are assuming that most people who choose to work in this field have no enormous objection to abortion, but that this area of work cannot fail to affect us. We are all individuals and will experience different feelings but some will be common to most of us.

Working with abortion, staying aware and available to women can have a huge impact on us. Indeed, if we are human, how could it be otherwise? The emotional cost to the involved worker can be high. As well as dealing constantly with life-and-death issues we are in contact daily with large numbers of women for whom life is harsh and for whom we can do little. 'I find I am from time to time profoundly affected by the isolation and helplessness of the women seen. I also find I sometimes share their grief in considering a termination.' 'I find it draining and exhausting, I become tired to the point where I do not want to relate to anyone, especially my family who may be in need of emotional support. I feel I sometimes suffer from burn out.' 'I think I must switch off my emotions, I have become hardened.'

Working with unwanted pregnancy always involves loss, either of the pregnancy or of the woman's future intentions. There is usually no clear-cut, right decision and we therefore have to cope with constant ambivalence and sometimes helplessness.

The worker knows that any choice the woman makes involves pain and she faces that pain with her so that a decision is possible. It can be hard to remain with the client's distress, and yet still feel that something helpful has happened in the session. Women are often desperate for someone else to tell them what to do. The counsellor may be put under intolerable pressure to give advice. She mustn't let herself fall into the trap of complying with this demand as any short-term relief the woman gains is inevitably followed by loss of responsibility and ownership of the self. The position of counsellor should be far from being a powerful influence, it's power lies in the ability to remain with the feelings.

Many counsellors said that women's indecision was one of the most stressful parts of their job, as this selection of replies illustrates: 'A client who just cannot decide whether to keep the pregnancy or to seek termination. The scales are level – working together you cannot seem to achieve a decision – there is no positive result.' 'When people are undecided themselves, or want the decision to be made for them, or made easier by something I say. That makes me anxious about what I say in case I sway them unduly.' 'Having to ensure that the final decision is the patient's, when they obviously want the counsellor to suggest what they should do.' 'Feel as though I should know the right answer.' 'When the woman finds it impossible to make a decision there are often long-term underlying issues which time pressures make it difficult to deal with.'

Day after day, the counsellor may be left with unanswerables. One day it may be the pregnant homeless teenager who she just wants to take home and mother instead of sending back to a King's Cross hostel. It could be the girl who denied her pregnancy for so long and came requesting a termination only after feeling foetal movements. She threatens that she will kill herself unless this is arranged for her.

We get in touch with our own powerlessness when we see the same women come back for a second or even third or more termination. What went wrong, what was missed?

How does it feel when a woman comes back after you had counselled her three months earlier when she had a termination? She is now delighted to be pregnant. She says she should never have had the termination and this pregnancy is to replace the baby she lost. At the least this makes us question the quality of our counselling, at the extreme it can send us into a spiral of despair and inadequacy. It is in cases such as this that supervision and therapy are essential.

Sue had worked for a short time in a young person's clinic, she was conscientious and tried her utmost to help the young women make a choice right for them. She was extremely upset after a session with one of her clients (Jane) who was now pregnant for the second time and planning to keep the baby after a recent abortion. Sue came to supervision visibly shaken, wondering what important communication she had missed. However, far from being a learning experience, this incident had awakened all her feelings of inadequacy and of being no good. She seemed to think this turn of events would never have happened if someone else had seen her. She appeared to be blaming herself for the unnecessary death of a baby. Meanwhile Jane was making happy plans for her pregnancy with no sense of poignancy or sadness. Sue, because of her own 'no good feelings' had been the hook for all of Jane's confusion and remorse. This needed to be untangled in supervision before it could be understood and learnt from.

There are often particular issues that stir up feelings in different people. There are so many ways that workers can be tested, suprised and caught out. It can be difficult to give ourselves space and time to reflect when pushed by so many triggers. Without this space, disturbed by our own feelings about abortion, we impulsively react and easily become attacking, so that a woman sadly may get the confirmation she was unconsciously looking for, that she is to be despised.

For David, a usually sympathetic GP, it was the ones who 'mucked me about' that made him angry. By this he meant the occasional woman for whom he would make an appointment at the hospital who then didn't turn up but later rang to ask for another. David thought he had worked hard on her behalf and felt unappreciated and furious at having to reschedule appointments. He became unable to see the meaning behind any prevarication, and in his self-righteous anger lost any opportunity to understand.

A normally placid doctor, usually deeply concerned for the welfare of her young clients refused to see a girl again. The girl had been sullen and uncommunicative in the session, and seemed unable to take any responsibility for her pregnancy although she had been having unprotected sex for months. She wanted a termination but when this was arranged did not turn up. She came back to the clinic saying she had overslept. The doctor had to rebook her appointment at the hospital with difficulty and apologetically. On her follow-up visit she vandalized the centre. The doctor felt unable to work with her, she thought Jane was totally irresponsible and showed no sign of any connection with the sadness over her abortion. It was not until she saw a new doctor that Jane was able to talk of the pain of having to choose an abortion or lose her boyfriend. She felt she was a murderer, and her only way of coping with those feelings was through acting them out.

Many counsellors find that they have difficulties with women who request late terminations although they are able to support them if this is their decision. This was mentioned specifically by a majority of respondents. 'Personally I feel as long as the woman involved makes the *best* decision for her then the abortion should be granted.' 'I feel sad that it has to happen but it's much sadder for a child to be brought up by carers who don't really want it and can't meet it's needs. That's more damaging for all concerned.' 'It's not easy to decide on a cut-off point, but it's important not to be sentimental. The reasons women have left it late just show their confusion.' 'I do not feel that the number of weeks plays an important part in the feelings I have – in some cases it makes it harder for the client – in others perhaps taking time to make that decision is recompense.' 'I do not feel that there is any moral difference between an abortion at six or thirty-six weeks, and do not have any different attitude or emotional response dependent on the gestation.' 'My cut-off point is eighteen weeks, I feel the emotional implications for late terminations are often not addressed by women opting for one.'

Counsellors who have little difficulty in supporting a woman having an abortion under twelve weeks may find facing the loss of a perfectly formed foetus unbearable. 'I know what it feels like to have a foetus moving inside.'

'One counsellor mentioned how concerned she was 'that my unease doesn't show, and upset the woman'. Another, 'tried to deal with this in supervision so my personal feelings do not come into the counselling'.

> Marilyn came as an emergency. Her aunt had noticed that she looked 'fatter. Marilyn had been taking the pill and had not suspected she was pregnant until now. She requested a termination. On examination by the doctor she appeared to be at least twenty-six weeks, which is over the legal limit for most abortions. They faced this together in shock, then Marilyn begged for it to be taken away. The doctor felt outraged that Marilyn could still want to reject her baby and initially lost the capacity to view this as anything other than barbaric. Later she was able to reflect that Marilyn's plea was not about 'murdering' a baby but was the only possible solution she could face in her desperate state of denial. There was, however, little opportunity for this to be further explored and faced as Marilyn fled the centre hoping to find a doctor who would help her.

There are few happy endings in this work. As well as coping with painful choices, there are many instances when clients do not return and we end up not knowing what has happened. This uncertainty can be a continual worry.

> Lorraine, aged 16, came to a young person's clinic when she was ten weeks pregnant. She was distraught, saying her parents would kick her out if they discovered the pregnancy. She was suffering from terrible sickness and thought her parents suspected. She was adamant that she could never let them know or the consequences would be dire. An appointment at the hospital was arranged for her which she did not attend. She had left strict instructions that no communication was allowed via her home, nor had she given any alternative contact address.

> A 30-year-old married woman came requesting a termination. She had two children already, had a serious drink problem and felt there was no way she could give a baby the care it needed. She had come secretly fearing that if her husband found out there would be no way he would allow her to have an abortion and that she would never get back on her feet. She could not entertain the idea of discussing her fears with her husband, as she said he would hit her.
>
> She begged for the termination to be carried out as swiftly as possible. She never returned to the centre to be told the arrangements and never took up her appointment. No home contact was allowed.

> Aisha, aged 16, was referred by the school; she had confided to a teacher that she was pregnant. She was found to be nearly sixteen weeks pregnant. She wanted a termination and an appointment was arranged as quickly as possible. As it was a late termination she had to stay overnight at the hospital but she could think of no way to explain her absence to her strict Bengali parents. She phoned the doctor asking her to phone her parents saying she

was a teacher and that a school trip had been arranged. When the doctor regretfully explained that she could not agree to this request, Aisha rang off and made no further contact.

The woman may respond to the burden of choosing a termination by blaming the counsellor. 'Didn't you know that I really wanted to keep the baby? You forced me to agree to a termination.' It is as though she is desperately trying to dump the guilt and terrible feelings about the abortion onto the counsellor. In order to withstand this attack, the worker needs to retain her own truth and firm boundaries.

Abortion counselling is rarely straightforward, the role of the counsellor often involves a multitude of tasks. This was cited as a difficulty by several respondents who at times were caught up sorting out social problems and legal issues. 'The many facets of the situation, that is, the moral, legal aspects as well as the many emotions it arouses.' As previously mentioned in Chapter 5, an acutely troublesome aspect was coping with some of the questions raised by the women. 'Sometimes answering very specific questions about procedures such as will the baby feel pain, what happens to the foetus and so on.'

Several workers were extremely concerned over the sheer volume of work they were reponsible for. 'The work I find can be physically and emotionally tiring and frequently exhausting.' 'The heavy caseload and the repetitive nature of the work.' 'There are constant difficult beginnings, few happy endings, and rarely the satisfaction of long-term work.' A few felt so pressurized by their impossible brief (for example, being the only counsellor for a district gynaecology service) that they could not in any way provide an adequate counselling service. In some cases this was combined with inadequate resources, often completely outside their personal control, such as having to tell desperate women that there was a four-week wait for a termination. This left many counsellors in the position of never being able to give what was needed, leading to low morale and constant compromise of themselves.

Counsellors often gained much support from their colleagues (see next section), but others worked in isolation. 'Since I am the only one actively engaged in termination counselling I do feel quite isolated. I do not feel part of a close team with medical and nursing staff' (hospital social worker). Unfortunately, a sizeable proportion of counsellors mentioned that poor staff relationships led to increased stress. 'Working with other staff members who are clearly stressed and unable to deal with it.'

Some workers found that they took the distress home with them. Others were more able to keep a boundary round their private life. All pregnancies may become associated with disaster and destruction; it can be hard to disentangle the distress and recover a sense of wonder and awe about the miracle of pregnancy. Is it still possible to experience pure joy for a friend's longed-for pregnancy when other images are jostling for attention? One counsellor spoke of how hard it was for her to believe that men could be anything other than bastards, having shared and identified with the pain of many women.

Certain conditions in the counsellor will affect the relationship. How does it feel to be pregnant, maybe even at the same stage as your client, and discuss termination? Does this lead to feelings of insecurity about your own pregnancy? How does it feel for both client and counsellor when the counsellor is visibly pregnant? How does it affect the counsellor's baby? One recently first-time pregnant doctor who was very much involved in referring young women for abortion said that her pregnancy, 'gives me much more sympathy to women who decide against all the odds to continue with their pregnancies'.

Jenny had just had a miscarriage and came back to work shortly afterwards. She said that her own therapy enabled her to differentiate her own desire for a pregnancy from those of the women who were deciding on abortion. The baby she had wanted and lost was her baby and she did not have any difficulty continuing her work.

This was not the case for Suzanne who after trying to get pregnant for several months discovered that she was infertile. It became impossible for her to continue working; it was as though every termination she arranged after that was her own baby's. Her infertility stirred profound self-doubts and a belief that she was being punished for her previous active involvement in the abortion campaign.

One of our respondents, a general clinic nurse in gynaecology out-patients, also spoke of the enormous pain she experienced when women requested termination since discovering her own infertility ten years earlier. She writes: 'Because of my personal circumstances I find this work very distressing. If I find I cannot cope another nurse takes over from me so that the woman requesting abortion is dealt with in a fully professional manner.' She found the most stressful parts of her job 'hearing the woman have to say why she wants the abortion and the examination of the pregnant womb – knowing the content is to be destroyed'. She admitted that she had no supervisory support at work and stated that she took care of herself by, 'crying when alone and getting relieved of looking after that patient by colleagues at work'.

When the worker has felt unwanted herself or has even been adopted, a sense of existential precariousness can develop. 'If termination were legal, would I myself be here?' Identification with the unwanted foetus may be extreme, and the apparent ease with which some women are able to opt for termination may be particularly painful.

Health professionals involved in the termination

Health professionals have the task of carrying out the termination. This may cause problems for some and is related both to their beliefs and also to the reality of the procedure.

A study by Wendy Savage, champion of women's rights, confirms that professionals are unhappy about their abortion work. In her paper she pointed out the ambivalence and denial that permeates this field as a way of coping 'with unpleasantness in life'. The ambivalence around abortion was demonstrated by the fact that although many doctors agreed with the legal limit of abortion, only a tiny fraction would be prepared to carry these out at the upper limit. Denial was demonstrated by gynaecologists believing that they carried out many more of the abortions in their district than was the true case (Savage 1992: 51).

The gynaecologists who responded to our survey seemed to confirm this, and also managed to rationalize their part of the drama. There is little space for doubts when one is terminating a life. The very nature of the demands and magnitude of the job can force distance and cutting off.

When asked how the work affected them, several doctors responded: 'Not at all, it is necessary'. One writes poignantly: 'I have been doing abortion for years and have no physical or emotional reaction. I worry this means that I don't have any respect for human life.' One notes: 'I occasionally feel pangs of remorse and have to remind myself of the consequences of the woman's continuing with the pregnancy'.

A gynaecologist who is truly able to own her struggle wrote in the *BMJ*:

> I can now say openly that I do think I am ending a life every time I do an abortion, but I do it as someone who has a certain skill which is put at the disposal of a woman who does not want her pregnancy to continue. I do not regret all the agonising – it has helped me to understand the problems that each woman faces when deciding about her abortion.
>
> (Anonymous 1984: 1377)

In the book *The Unconscious at Work*, Anna Dartington (1994) examines the coping strategies of hospital nurses. Her summary is of acute relevance here. She argues that workers need opportunities to mobilize appropriate defences against pain and anger. When these are not available we resort to either breakdown or breakout solutions as demonstrated in sick leave or psychosomatic symptoms. The other alternative and the one most common to doctors is the development of a protective shell:

> Which serves to deflect and anaesthetize emotion. This is largely an unconscious development. If such a shell becomes a permanent feature of the personality, it is at great cost to the individual, who can no longer be fully responsive to his or her emotional environment. The resulting detachment is dangerous to clients, patients or colleagues who will sense the potential cruelty inherent in the indifference. Appropriate defences are those which are mobilized in the recognition that a situation is painful or downright unbearable. They involve attempts to protect oneself from stress in order that the work task be preserved. Pathological defences are those which are mobilized in order to deny reality, to allow a really mad or unbearable

situation to continue when in fact it needs to be challenged in order to preserve both the workers and the work task.

(Obholzer and Roberts 1994: 107)

Apart from the surgeon, pre-operatively the procedure involves different people from other disciplines. This includes the sonographer who has to date the pregnancy using ultrasound. She witnesses the vibrant life in the womb and knows it is to be terminated. From our meeting with women who report their conversations, this is not easy. Women say they have been congratulated on having twins, other women are congratulated on still being pregnant after a threatened miscarriage. A woman told me with horror her story of a failed early abortion. She had an ultrasound which confirmed she was still pregnant and was told how lucky she was that the foetus had not been harmed.

Nurses are also in the position of watching and assisting during terminations and caring for women afterwards. A survey in 1994 questioned nurses about their feelings over early medical or surgical termination. This showed that 'medical termination' provoked mixed reactions amongst gynaecology ward nurses; 60 per cent found caring for women undergoing medical abortion to be a negative experience but 23 per cent had the opposite opinion. 'The main reason given for dissatisfaction with medical abortion was distress at seeing recognizable products of conception.' The paper noted the extreme distress experienced by some nurses when caring for women undergoing medical terminations and recommends:

Nursing staff who care for women undergoing medical abortion should be carefully recruited, and should be committed to this method. They should receive specific instruction, not only in counselling women who opt for medical abortion, but also in dealing with their own feelings. The same principles apply to medical staff.

(Marwick *et al.* 1994: 8–10)

Late terminations evoke powerful feelings in staff. Nurses find handling the foetus extremely distressing. A study by Kaltreider (Kaltreider *et al.* 1979: 235–8) on nurses compared mid trimester terminations carried out either by surgical evacuation under general anaesthetic as opposed to medical with intra amniotic prostaglandin terminations. This showed that nurses:

reported medical terminations to be 'difficult', emotionally disturbing and a symbol of abandonment by medical stafff. However, nurses involved in surgical procedures seemed to be more positive about their role, possibly because primary responsibility for performing the abortion lay with medical staff.

(Kaltreider *et al.* cited in Marwick *et al.* 1994: 10)

We have received some rather harrowing letters from nurses whose experience on the gynaecology ward has left them unsupported and flooded with emotions as, for example:

The unplanned abortion was shameful and it was her decision (maybe her fault). Sympathy was on a different level and understanding very difficult to assess. But because nurses did not talk about it, how could any nurse truly help these women? Or indeed really develop any worthwhile skills. Skills that were not just hands-on care but that of trust, consideration, good nurse/patient relationship? . . . I did not notice any real team work between the nurses in this department. They did not support each other, they did not air their feelings . . . They did not talk to the women. The hardest, biggest decision most women had to face they faced alone, even separate from their named nurse. The nurses remained unattached, perhaps that was good nursing care! Not to get involved.

Other nurses wrote to us of how caring for women having abortions constantly opened up their own wounds:

I had no idea when I took up my new staff nurse position of the emotional impact this area of work would have on me. My termination was a year beforehand, I was over it. I knew how these women would feel, what they would require. Did I? I had to constantly relive the event and confront my reasons and excuses again.

One nurse ends her letter with a *cri de coeur*:

Is training the answer? Can you train for emotions whether for the nurse or for the patient? The ward staff need to get together. They have to support each other. Be non-judgemental, not only of their patients but also of their colleagues.

On this note we move on.

HOW DO WE LOOK AFTER OURSELVES

Looking after ourselves starts with a belief in what we do. Gaining fulfilment and job satisfaction leads to a sense of self-worth and pride. Wendy Savage clearly shows her belief in her role of surgeon. She asks 'How can one then deal with being the person who destroys the potential and kills the developing fetus, which should be secure in the womb?'
She answers herself:

The positive aspect of abortion work is seeing the relief of the woman and knowing that a young woman's life is not ruined by a birth before she is ready, or that a family continues to survive, when another child would make this unlikely or impossible . . . I learnt from bitter experience that women, even young and intelligent, will take their lives in their hands and die in the attempt to rid themselves of a pregnancy that comes at the wrong time, or they may damage themselves and never be able to have children when they want to.

(Savage 1992: 54)

Our respondents let us know dramatically what kept them motivated and excited about work:

Enjoy counselling and the working environment. I like working with women.

My own experience and sympathy with these women.

I feel counselling is so important. I find the work satisfying as I feel I am making a positive contribution to the woman's decision.

The relief that most of our clients feel when we give them a caring service seems to balance out against the difficult aspects.

Mostly I am pleased to be able to facilitate access to a provision that is crucial for women and has a major impact on their lives.

A feeling of doing valuable work. It is important to me to be working with people who may not normally have access to a counsellor. I am especially motivated to work with young people. I quite often get the feeling that I have had a positive effect on a person's life and that encourages me to carry on.

I know that I can perform the procedures well technically with a low rate of complication. I think I do a reasonably good job. I also know that I am sharing in women's problems rather than hiding from the bits of life I don't like.

No matter what the satisfaction, working with abortion can cause much grief. In order to face this impact, and not resort to glossing over, we need to look after ourselves. There is so much potential for unhelpful and potentially damaging interaction with patients that looking after ourselves becomes essential. We need to find our own ways of recovering from this work dependent on how it affects us. It should not be our bodies, or family or patients who have to bear the brunt of our undigested emotions.

We are often attracted to working in areas that are meaningful to us. Our hidden motives for choosing to work in the caring professions and specifically abortion work are important and may have extreme significance and influences of which we are unaware.

Why be a nurse, counsellor or doctor? Why should we wish to care for others? We may be attracted to this work by the need to repair something from our own past. This is not necessarily harmful, as we are all driven by these powerful factors. However, it can be harmful when our issues also invade the relationship with the client. Our unresolved wounds can lead to over-zealousness, assumptions and blind spots. This can be helped by training, supervision and therapy.

Anne had always felt unwanted by her family. Before becoming a pregnancy counsellor, she had worked in a children's home with what she described as 'unwanted children'. When she started work, it appeared to others that she was on a personal mission to prevent any child again from feeling unwanted.

Barbara, a counsellor, was very disturbed by Tessa who had initially decided on a termination. Tessa had said she definitely did not want a baby but was in fact unable to go through with an abortion and hence decided to continue with the pregnancy. Barbara reacted extremely powerfully when she heard this. She was overwhelmed by her reaction to this potentially unwanted baby being born. Eventually, Barbara was able to make links with her own impoverished, deprived background. She was born just before the abortion act made legal abortion possible, her mother's most frequent remark was how she wished she had got pregnant later so an abortion could have been arranged. Barbara's identification with the foetus made it hard to bear the thought of another unwanted child coping with that pain. In her own therapy she was able to see that this foetus was separate to her and could see how Tessa in fact accepted and grew to love her developing baby.

Susan's therapist helped her understand that her way of trying to make everything better was in fact counterproductive. Her clients' pain was real and needed honouring, not placating. Susan's mother had been chronically depressed and Susan had spent most of her childhood trying to make her happy. In her choice of profession and in her day-to-day work this impossible mission had continued.

Stress management

The way we react to pressure is personal to us, dependent on how the external stressors connect with our inner being. We will be affected by the general workload as well as more specific issues related to abortion. We may develop more control over our workload by such techniques as prioritizing and time management. Learning assertiveness skills will also be helpful if we find it hard to say no. We may join pressure groups or work politically in order to improve the service. In this present 'caring, financial market climate' the hardest tasks may be to know one's personal limits and to bear the feelings of helplessness.

Many people are able to withdraw from the pressures at least on a temporary basis. Specifically helpful are meditation, yoga and relaxation.

I use hobbies, interests to distract me and to make home life very separate from work. I use yoga and meditation to relax, and have a massage periodically to deal with any build-up of tensions. I have a number of close friends I can talk to about life in general and I have weekly psychotherapy. I work part time.

I live in the country by the sea – I garden and walk.

Work environment peer support

The environment in which we work is extremely important. Is the work we do valued and is this reflected in the pay and conditions of service? Is management supportive of the workers, fostering good relationships between staff and striving towards equality in the work-force? Does management recognize that stress exists and acknowledge the need for support? Is there good liaison between team members, whose differing roles are respected? Are the needs of all individuals attended to? Are there opportunities to discuss protocols and the management of difficult cases? For example, how do we respond to the needs of people with learning difficulties or those who do not speak English? These optimal conditions exist but rarely, nevertheless peer support and the sharing of difficult times was quoted in our survey as making the job more bearable. 'We try to take time to discuss counsellings which have been "difficult", we tend to lean on our colleagues as long as we are not all stressed together.' 'We have a great deal of support from our team.' 'I find discussing the situation with another health care professional helps.' 'I am able to discuss and off-load on to my close colleagues.' Equally it was poor staff relationships, isolation in the work-force, on-going divisions and poor communication that led to low morale.

> One of the doctors at a youth counselling agency had great difficulty with referring for late abortion. Reception staff somehow managed to feed these to the other doctors to protect her. The other doctors who had their own emotional reaction to late abortion grew resentful, there were many undercurrents and a denial of the valuable contribution she gave. The clinic was one of the only centres were young women felt safe enough to admit to their concealed pregnancies. The atmosphere grew worse, as though the doctor was carrying all the awful feelings that belonged better to the abortions. In the end a meeting was arranged and the pain of the work could be faced and everyone's distress heard. The situation remained difficult but was no longer invidious.

COUNSELLOR TRAINING

Another way of recognizing the unique demands of working with abortion would be in the selection and training of future workers. While some of the abortion charities run their own in-house training and induction programmes most counsellors (for example, social workers in hospitals) will just be thrown in to this field. In the end they need to rely on their intuition and experience. 'They learn from their mistakes', although there may be nobody available to check these out. Our experience of running workshops for counsellors in the abortion field showed their eagerness to talk through their beliefs, share thoughts on good practice and common difficulties.

London Brook run an intensive training programme involving at least twenty-four' hours induction time where there is the opportunity for learning. The senior counsellor responsible for recruitment said:

> We aim to let applicants know exactly what their job entails so that they are clear about the purpose, scope and range of issues they may be dealing with.

They need to know they will be continually working with loss and to think about that impact. Apart from a basic competence level in counselling, the single most important thing is their attitude and sensitivity to women with unwanted pregnancy. During the induction important issues such as confidentiality, cross-cultural work, assessment, deciding what help is needed and referring on, are topics that are invariably discussed. We also aim for the counsellor to feel that she belongs to a team and that she feels supported in that.

NURSE TRAINING

Several studies have noted concern over the unkind and punitive attitudes held by nursing staff towards women who had chosen to terminate their pregnancy. Nurses often held condemnatory attitudes to abortion and abortion patients and often disliked this aspect of their work. More abortions are now being carried out in specialist units where workers are selected because of their commitment to women's right to choose. Most, however, are still taking place on the ordinary gynaecology wards where they may be the least-enjoyed part of the job.

In practice this gives important indications for nurse education. Webb talks of 'providing appropriate knowledge and skills for nurses to make their own decisions and to carry them out in a way which preserves their dignity and leads to optimal patient care'. She asks that training should include five key areas:

First a sound basis in the biological aspects of reproduction and sexual functioning is clearly needed and this should be complemented by a critical examination of psychological and sociological aspects of sexuality and their relationship to biology. This should include a study of gender roles, varieties of sexual expression and cultural differences in sexuality as well as their implications for individual life style and health.

Epidemiological studies should focus on differential access to and use of health services according to social class, gender, geograhical region and other variables, and comparative studies of different options, for example termination of pregnancy versus adoption. Fourth, a study of moral philosophical questions including definitions of life, human rights and criteria for decision making should provide the grounding for clarification of personal values and decision taking. Communications and counselling skills are the fifth area, and are needed both for working directly with patients and also for nurses themselves to feel confident and able to give their views about patient care and their own role in it's delivery.

(Webb 1985: 47)

Webb suggests that this training is carried out through experiental methods and group discussions led by staff who are active in the work. She suggests that this kind of initiative would improve the care of women and relationships between staff. Eventually the following situation may be avoided:

In the area in which I worked it was very difficult to relieve stress. The process of the ward's daily work load did not allow for time for nurses' problems. The abortion concept, by social standards, was rarely discussed for fear of a nurse saying something that others might disagree with. The only protection was to work in a rather blasé manner – to do the necessary nursing and try to rise above any thought or consequences that one might feel. Another way to relieve stress was the unkind manner in which nurses treated each other. Often abrupt and hostile towards colleagues.

These revolutionary suggestions for training could also of course be applied to medical staff. As Savage writes: 'My own feeling is that a doctor who feels he is wrong in performing a termination is doing neither the woman nor himself a service by doing the operation' (Savage 1992: 55).

SUPERVISION

The British Association of Counselling (1995) is clear about the need for counsellors to bring their work to supervision. Its code of practice states:

B.3.1. It is a breach of the ethical requirement for counsellors to practise without regular counselling supervision/consultative support.
B.3.2 Counselling supervision/consultative support refers to a formal arrangement which enables counsellors to discuss their counselling regularly with one or more people who have an understanding of counselling and counselling supervision/consultative support. Its purpose is to ensure the efficacy of the counsellor–client relationship. It is a confidential relationship.
B.3.3. Counsellors who have line managers owe them appropriate managerial accountability for their work. The counselling supervisor role should be independent of the line manager role. However, where the counselling supervisor is also the line manager, the counsellor should also have access to independent consultative support.
B.3.4. The volume of supervision should be in proportion to the volume of counselling work undertaken and the experience of the counsellor.
B.3.5. Whenever possible, the discussion of cases within supervision/ consultative support should take place without revealing the personal identity of the client.

Supervision should give an opportunity to reflect on the work we do, in a safe supportive environment. Most counsellors agree that supervision is essential both to their work and for their development as counsellors. It helps to be able to look at our work, as we struggle with the demands of clients and make sense of our conflicting feelings. Supervision should not be so threatening as to lead to withholding and numbing. Equally, when supervision is too cosy, little creative learning takes place.

Although the boundaries with personal therapy are sometimes grey, in supervision the focus is always on the service to the client.

Many agencies do not offer supervision. We asked our respondents what support or supervision they recieved. 'I have no formal laid-down support or supervision.' 'We do not have much time for supervision unless as a special request.' 'We have very little support though the work was clearly explained and the procedures, but personal communication was limited.' The overwhelming majority thought that more supervision would help them. They asked for: 'Senior counsellor support on a more regular basis.' 'supervision on a regular basis however short the time.' 'More time to discuss individual clients – those who caused us heartache, to share our feelings.' Several counsellors cited a peer support group as a particularly useful: 'Group support from counsellors doing the same work.' 'I would like peer supervision.'

London Brook have very clear guidelines over group supervision which takes place twice a month for two hours. The aim is to provide the best service for their clients. This includes:

1 the presentation of material;
2 issues appropriate to supervision to be accurately identified and managed;
3 to provide an appropriate balance of challenge and support for counsellors;
4 boundaries between supervision issues and personal therapy are identified, as supervision cannot provide therapy;
5 personal issues for counsellors that may be affecting their counselling work, it is legitimate for these to be addressed and shared so the counsellors can be fully effective and be helped to take these issues to counselling/therapy outside the group when appropriate;
6 counsellors are encouraged to look at their practice and any areas for improvement;
7 the counsellor is helped to explore and develop the ways in which theory informs practice;
8 the counsellor is helped to identify good practice and this recognized and acknowledged;
9 time to look at the functioning of the counselling group and the relationship within it, to enable the counsellors to remain effective.

The guidelines also give clear instructions for action when there is concern over the standards of a counsellor's work or their physical or emotional wellbeing.

Susan found she disliked supervising Diane's work. Supervision was far from being a creative experience as Diane attended the sessions with trepidation. Diane was always terrified, any suggestion or comment by Susan was seen as a put down. Diane's deep sense of inferiority made her unable to see the supervisor as anything other than critical. Being made to feel like this dragon disturbed Susan and felt strange to her. She was eventually able to discuss this with Diane and was able to direct her towards her own personal therapy where this damaging trait could be more usefully adressed.

Samantha brought a client who she called Jade to supervision; Samantha was furious and said she never wanted to see her again. Jade had been rude and missed appointments, causing much administrative work and apologetic grovelling on Samantha's behalf. She spoke of how Jade seemed to have such a careless attitude to everything, the only thing that was making her agree to see her again was to avoid another unwanted pregnancy. This was incredibly unusual for Samantha as she usually enjoyed meeting with her young clients. Samantha started being able to look at how she had reacted to all of Jade's 'I'm no good messages'. She began to see how her 'careless attitude' and rudeness were ways in which Jade proved her worthlessness and invited rejection. Samantha also began to understand the ambivalence behind her missed appointments. Supervision allowed her to put her judgements aside and to see Jade with new eyes. When Jade was next seen, late as usual, it was possible to look past the anger to the despair.

Sally was a young 16-year-old. She was Catholic and had a 1-year-old baby, the result of an earlier concealed pregnancy as she did not agree with termination. She came to the centre six months after the birth, pregnant, having stopped the pill for no obvious reason. This time she had an abortion as she said she could not have coped with another baby. After the termination she spoke of her guilt which had been stirred further by demonstrators outside the abortion clinic. She took the pill again but then arrived pregnant six months later. The doctor was so distressed and puzzled that she lost the opportunity to understand and find any meaning in her recurrent pregnancies. She was able to bring Sally to supervision and begin to explore if an important communication had been missed and reflect on her interaction. She was also helped to bear the pain.

There are many ways of receiving supervision. Two of the most common are one-to-one or group supervision with an experienced counselling practitioner. Both have their advantages and disadvantages. The supervisee having individual supervision enjoys the luxury of undivided attention but misses peer support and the benefits of other views. In group supervision, there is the pleasure of sharing and learning with others but there is less time for one's own cases. The dynamics that develop within each group can be both productive if harnessed or potentially damaging.

Sally supervised a group of four members. Two of the members had an antipathy towards each other and several sessions were spent fruitlessly by their constant undermining. Supervision in the group became virtually impossible until the dynamics and underlying rivalry were explored.

The benefits of supervision among the majority of nurses and doctors remain unknown and in some cases threatening as though it were an attack on professional competence. Most gynaecologists responded to our question about supervision along these lines: 'I do not at the moment feel in the need of any support', which we felt confirmed a defensive attitude. The gynaecologist who had been open enough to question her respect for human life was able to write of the benefits she had experienced in a group: 'As part of the structured teaching within my training I have in the past had group sessions with other members of the department, led by a psychotherapist where some of these issues were discussed. They were very helpful', she adds wistfully, 'more of this might be useful'.

Some nurses were very aware of the lack of support and asked for 'counselling for those that require it, more openness about experiences and feelings, maybe training and development of communication skills towards fellow work-mates, patients and relatives'.

COUNSELLING

Self-awareness along with compassion are perhaps the most important qualities a counsellor can have. As Hillman writes, 'The purpose of training analysis is not merely to heal the personality of the analyst, but to open his wounds from which his compassion will flow' (Hillman 1993: 132). Compassion, of course, is a human quality not dependent on whether we have had counselling. However, our own therapy can also permit us to have compassion for those we previously would have found it easier to judge. When we see in others those bits that we cannot accept and hate in ourselves condemnation may be our only recourse. Our own counselling helps us connect with those parts of ourselves that if still hidden could be potentially unhelpful to clients.

> Anne had a difficult relationship with women who presented as victims and allowed themselves to be down trodden and unable to take responsibility. Her sessions with those clients tended to be abrasive with 'a pull your socks up, what are you doing to yourself' message. This confronting attitude was often so brutal and unhelpful that it left no space for the women to discover their potential for themselves. In Anne's case, she held a deep terror of her own inadequate feelings, of which she was unaware and this made her punish all those other victims out there.

Through our own counselling we are able to protect clients from these kinds of projections. We bring ourselves to our counsellors where there is time to explore and have our shadow honoured and contained. In turn we are then able to travel with our clients to their depths. We now dare face pain and can remain open to anything that the client needs to bring. We no longer wipe away our experiences by hiding and keeping distant and are able to mourn and rejoice in our common humanity.

As we continue our own therapeutic journey and personal development, we often are put more and more in touch with our infantile self. Paradoxically, therefore, as we become more sensitive to others, and more life-loving, abortion work becomes harder and increasingly painful. It is, however, only through honouring that pain, that women's voices are heard.

Bibliography

Abramsky, L. and Chapple, J. (1994) *Pre-natal Diagnosis: The Human Side*, London: Chapman & Hall.

Ades, A.E., Parker, S., Berry, T., Holland, F.J., Davison, C.F. Cubitt, D., Hjelm, M., Wilcox, A.H., Hudson, C.N. Briggs, M. Tedder, R.S. and Peckham, C.S. (1991) 'Prevalence of maternal HIV-1 infection in Thames regions: results from anonymous unlinked testing', *The Lancet* 337: 1562–5.

Alberman, E. and Dennis, K.J. (1984) 'Late abortions in England and Wales: report of a national confidential study', London: Royal College of Obstetricians and Gynaecologists.

Age of Legal Capacity (Scotland) Act 1991 Section 2(4).

Alberman, E., Mutton, D., Ide, R., Nicholson, A. and Bobrow, M. (1995) 'Down's syndrome births and pregnancy terminations in 1989 to 1993: preliminary findings', *British Journal of Obstetrics and Gynaecology* 102: 445–7.

Allaby, M. (1995) 'Contraceptive services for teenagers: do we need family planning clinics?' *British Medical Journal* 310: 1641–3.

Allen, I. (1982) 'A study of the factors affecting decison making in women seeking TOP', unpublished manuscript.

—— (1985) *Family Planning, Sterilisation and Abortion Services*, London: The Policy Studies Institute.

—— (1990) *Family Planning and Counselling Projects for Young People*, London: Policy Studies Unit.

Annex, A. (1974) *Extracts from 'Section K of Lane Committee's Report on Counselling and Assessment', (HC (77) 26)*.

Anonymous (1984) 'Personal View', *British Medical Journal* 289: 1377.

Ardenne, P. and Mahtani, A. (1989) *Transcultural Counselling in Action*, London: Sage.

Ashton, J.R. (1980) 'The psychological outcome of induced abortion', *British Journal of Obstetrics and Gynaecolgy* 87: 1115–22.

Ashurst P.M. and Ward D.F. (1983) 'An evaluation of counselling in general practice', final report of the Leverhulme Counselling Project, London: Mental Health Foundation.

Baldo, M., Aggleton, P. and Slutkin, G. (1993) 'Does sex education lead to earlier or increased sexual activity in youth?' paper presented at the June 1993 conference of the WHO Global Programme on AIDS.

Benedek, T. (1959) 'Parenthood as a developmental phase', *Journal of the Psychoanalytical Association*, 7: 389–417.

—— (1980) 'The psychological outcome of induced abortion', *British Journal of Obstetrics and Gynaecology* 8: 7.

Berer, M. (1993) 'Abortion: a woman's perspective', in *Progress Postponed; Abortion in the 1990's*, Newmann, K. (ed.) London: International Planned Parenthood Federation European Region.

Bibring, G. (1959) 'Some considerations of psychological process in pregnancy', *Psychoanalytic Study of Child*, 14: 113–21.

Bibring, G., Dwyer, J., Huntington, D.S. and Valenstein A.F. (1961) 'A study of the psychological processes in pregnancy of the earliest mother–child relationship', *Psychoanalytic Study of the Child* 16: 9–32.

Birth Control Trust (1994) 'Model Specification for Abortion 1994–1995', London: Birth Control Trust.

Bond, T. (1993) *Standards and Ethics for Counselling in Action*, London: Sage.

—— (1994) 'Counselling, confidentiality and the law', Rugby: British Association of Counselling.

Bounds, W. (1994) 'Contraceptive efficacy of the diaphragm and cervical caps used in conjunction with a spermicide – a fresh look at the evidence', *British Journal of Family Planning* 20: 84–7.

Bourne, G. (1974) *Pregnancy*, first published 1972, London: Pan.

Bowlby, J. (1961) 'Processes of mourning', *International Journal of Psychoanalysis* 42: 317–40.

—— (1981) *Attachment and Loss, Volume 3: Sadness and Depression*, Harmondsworth: Penguin.

The Brandon Centre Annual Report 1994–5, available from The Brandon Centre, 26 Prince of Wales Road, Kentish Town, NW5 3LG.

Breen, D. (1974) *The Birth of a First Child: Towards an Understanding of Femininity*, London: Tavistock.

—— (1981) *Talking with Mothers: About Pregnancy Childbirth and Early Motherhood*, London: Jill Norman Ltd.

British Association of Counselling (1990a) 'Recognition of counsellor training courses', Appendix B, p. 21, British Association of Counselling: Rugby.

—— (1990b) 'Code of ethics and practice for counsellors', first published 1984, B4-B8.2, Rugby.

—— (1995) 'Counselling and psychotherapy resources directory 1995', Palmer, I. (ed.) p. xv, Rugby.

British Medical Association (1994) 'Confidentiality and under 16s for GPs', supported by the General Medical Services Committee, Health Education Authority, Family Planning Association, Royal College of General Practitioners and Brook.

Brook (1995) *Under 16's, the Law and Public Policy on Contraception and Abortion in UK, 1995*, London.

Callahan, D. (1970) *Abortion: Law, Choice and Morality*, New York: Collier-Macmillan Company.

Caplan, G. (1970) 'Crisis intervention as a mode of brief treatment' in Roberts, R. and Nee, R. (eds) *Theories of Social Casework*, Chicago: University of Chicago Press.

Christopher, E. (1987) *Sexuality and Birth Control*, London: Tavistock.

—— (1993) 'Appendix' in Guillebaud, J. *Contraception Your Questions Answered*, London: Churchill-Livingstone.

Condon, J.T. (1987) 'Altered cognitive functioning in pregnant women: a shift toward primary process thinking', *British Journal of Medical Psychology* 60: 329–34.

Corney, R.H. (1990) 'Counselling in general practice – does it work?', *Journal of Royal Society of Medicine* 83: 253.

Dagg, P. (1991) 'The psychological sequelae of therapeutic abortion – denied and completed', *American Journal of Psychiatry* 148(5): 578–85.

Dana, M. (1987) 'Abortion: a women's right to feel' in Ernst, S. and Maguire, M. (eds) *Living with the Sphinx: Papers from the Women's Therapy Centre*, London: Women's Press.

Dartington, A. (1994) 'Where angels fear to tread: idealism, despondency and inhibition of thought in hospital nursing' in Obholzer, A. and Roberts, V.R. (eds) *The Unconscious at Work*, London: Routledge.

—— (1995) 'A very brief psychodynamic counselling of young people', *Journal of Psychodynamic Counselling*, 1(2): 253–61.

Davies, V. (1991) *Abortion and Afterwards*, Great Britain: Ashgrove Press.

De Beauvoir, S. (1949) *The Second Sex*, first published 1949, London: Penguin.

De Crespigny, L. with Dredge, R. (1991) *Which Tests for My Unborn Baby: A Guide to Prenatal Diagnosis*, Australia: Oxford University Press.

Department for Education (1994) 'Education Act 1993: sex education in schools', HMSO, Circular 5/94.

Department of Health (1990) 'A guide to consent for examination or treatment', HMSO, HC(90) 22.

—— (1992) 'The Health of the Nation: a strategy for health in England', London: HMSO.

Department of Health and Social Security (1986) 'Health Service Management. Family Planning Services for Young People', HC (86)1; Welsh Office Guidance whc(86)10; (whc)FP(86)10; woc(86)15.

Deutsch, H. (1944) *The Psychology of Women: A Psychoanalytic Interpretation*, New York: Grune and Stratton.

Di Salvo, P. and Skuse, T. (1993) 'The really helpful directory for pregnant teenagers and young people', London: Trust for Study of Adolescence/Maternity Alliance.

Donnai, P., Charles, N. and Harris, R. (1981) 'Attitudes of patients after genetic termination of pregnancy', *British Medical Journal* 282: 621–2.

Doppenberg, H. (1994) 'Abortion – a necessity to be limited', Forum for Family Planning Conference – Can we Learn from the Dutch?.

Drife, J.O. (1993) 'Deregulating emergency contraception', *British Medical Journal* 307: 695–6.

European Collaborative Study (1992) 'Risk factors for mother-to-child transmission of HIV-1', *The Lancet* 339(8800): 1007–12.

Family Planning Association (1992) 'Abortion: Statistical Trends', Fact Sheet 16A.

Fairweather, D.V. (1968) 'Nausea and vomiting during pregnancy', *Obstetrics and Gynaecology Annual* 7: 91–105.

Ferguson-Smith, M.A. (1983) 'The reduction of anecephalic and spina bifida births by maternal serum AFPs screening', *British Medical Bulletin* 39(4): 365–72.

Firth, H.V., Boyd, P.A., Chamberlain, P.F., Mackenzie, I.Z., Morris-Kay, G.M. and Huson, S.M. (1994) 'Analysis of limb reduction defects in babies exposed to chorionic villus sampling', *The Lancet* 343: 1069–71.

Fisher, N. (1994) *Your Pocket Guide to Sex*, Harmondsworth: Penguin.

Fisk, N.M. and Bower, S. (1993) 'Fetal blood sampling in retreat', *British Medical Journal* 307: 143–4.

Franz, W. and Reardon, D. (1992) 'Differential impact of abortion in adolescence and adults', *Adolescence* 22: 161–72.

Furedi, A. and Paintin, D. (eds) (1994)'Running an early abortion service' in proceedings from a conference organized by Birth Control Trust, London: 16–18, 30–2.

General Medical Council (1995) 'Duties of a doctor: confidentiality', series of four booklets, London.

Ghetau, V. (1978) 'L'Evolution et la fecondité en Roumanie', *Populations* March–April 33(2): 525–39.

Giannakoulopoulos, X., Sepulveda, W., Kourtis, P., Glover, V. and Fisk, N.M. (1994) 'Fetal plasma cortisol and B-endorphin response to intrauterine needling', *Lancet* 344: 77–81.

Gillick v *West Norfolk* and *Wisbech AHA* (1985) AC 112.

Gillman, R.D. (1973) 'The dreams of pregnant women and maternal adaptation' in Shereshefsky, P.M. and Yarrow L.J. (eds) in *Psychological Aspects of a First Pregnancy and Early Post Natal Adaptation*, London and New York: Raven Press.

Goldberg, D., MacKinnon, H., Smith, R., Patel, N., Scrimageour, J., Inglis, J., Pentherer, J., Urquhart, G., Emslie, J., Covell, R. and Reid, D. (1992) 'Prevalence of HIV among childbearing women and women having termination of pregnancy: multidisciplinary steering group study', *British Medical Journal* 304: 1082–5.

Green, J. (1994) 'Serum screening for Down's syndrome: Experiences of obstetricians in England and Wales', *British Medical Journal* 309: 769–72.

Greenlagh, T. (1992) 'The doctor's right to choose', *British Medical Journal* 305: 371.

Greer, G. (1984) *Sex and Destiny: The Politics of Human Fertility*, London: Secker & Warburg.

Group for the Advancement of Psychiatry (1986) *Crises of Adolescence. Teenage Pregnancy: Impact on Adolescent Development*, New York: Brunner/Mazel, Inc.

Guillebaud, J. (1993) *Contraception Your Questions Answered*, London: Churchill-Livingstone.

Hanford, J. (1968) 'Pregnancy as a state of conflict', *Psychological Report* 22(3): 3–42.

Hansard (1987), vol. 110, no. 49, col. 147 (p.65).

—— (1990) 21 June, vol. 17, col. 1158.

Hare, M.J. and Haywood, J. (1981) 'Counselling of woman seeking abortion', *Journal of Biological Science* 13: 269–73.

Henshaw, R.C., Naji, S.A., Russell, I.T. and Templeton, A.A. (1994) 'A prospective economic evaluation comparing medical abortion (using mifepristone and Gemeprost) and surgical vacuum aspiration', *The British Journal of Family Planning* 20: 64–8.

Heywood, L.,J. (1994) 'The law of consent', *The British Journal of Family Planning* 20: 63.

Hillman, J. (1993) *Suicide and the Soul*, USA: Spring Publications.

HMSO (1987) 'The Cleveland Enquiry Report', London: HMSO.

—— (1991) 'Working together under the children act', London: HMSO.

Hollingsworth, J. (1994) 'The sonographer's dilemma' in Abramsky, L. and Chapple, J. (eds) *Prenatal Diagnosis The Human Side*, London: Chapman & Hall, 106–15.

HSG (95)37 'Guidance on Fundholding Purchased of Terminations of Pregnancy', NHS Executive 1995.

Hudson and Ineichen (1991) *Taking it Lying Down: Sexuality and Teenage Motherhood*, Hong Kong: Macmillan Education Ltd.

Human Fertilisation and Embryology (1991) 'Code of Practice', HFEA; London.

Iles, S. (1989) 'The loss of early pregnancy' in *Balliere's Clinical Obstetrics and Gynaecology* 3 (4) London: Balliere Tindall.

Imrie, J. (1995) 'No time to waste', Barnado's Child Care Publications.

International Planned Parenthood Federation Medical Bulletin (1992) International Medical Advisory Panel Statement on Abortion Vol. 27.

Jacobs, J.L. (1992) 'Pregnancy Outcomes', *Journal of Child Sex Abuse* 1(1): 103–12.

Jarrahi-Zadeh, A., Kane, F.J., Van De Castle, R.L., Lachenbruch, P.A. and Ewing, J.A. (1969) 'Emotional and cognitive changes in pregnancy and early puerperium', *British Journal of Psychiatry* 115: 797–805.

Johnson, A., Wadsworth, J., Wellings, K. and Field, J. (1994) 'Sexual Attitudes and Life-styles', Oxford: Blackwell Scientific.

Johnstone, F., Brettle, R., MacCallum, L., Mok, J. Pentherer, J. and Burns, S. (1990) 'Women's knowledge of their HIV antibody state: its effect on their decision whether to continue the pregnancy', *British Medical Journal* 30: 23–4.

Joint Study of the Royal College of General Practitioners and the Royal College of Obstetricians and Gynaecologists (1985) 'Induced abortion operations and their early sequelae', *Journal of the Royal College of General Practitioners* 35: 175–80.

Jowell, R. (ed.) (1990) *British Social Attitudes: The 7th Report*, Aldershot: Gower.

Kaltreider, N.B., Goldsmith, S. Margolis, A.J. (1979) 'The impact of mid trimester abortion on patients and staff', *American Journal of Obstetrics and Gynaecology* 135: 235–8.

Keenlyside, R. (1994) 'HIV infection in women-epidemiology and heterosexual transmission', *British Journal of Family Planning* 20: 44–5.

Kitzinger, S. (1987) *Freedom and Choice in Childbirth*, Great Britain: Viking.

—— (1877) *Law of Population*, London.

Kumar, R. (1990) *Motherhood and Mental Illness*, London: Academic Press.

Kumar, R.,and Robson, K.,(1978) 'Previous induced abortion and antenatal depression in primiparae: preliminary report of a survey of mental health in pregnancy', *Psychological Medicine* 8: 711–15.

Kumar, R., Brandt H.A. and Robson K.M. (1981) 'Childbearing and maternal sexuality: a prospective study of 119 primiparae', *Journal of Pyschosomatic Medicine Research* 25: 373–83.

The Lancet (1993) 'Post abortion family planning: reversing a legacy of neglect', *The Lancet* 342: 1099.

Lane Committee (1974) Report of the Committee on the Working Party of the Abortion Act, 3 vols, London: HMSO.

Lazarus, R.S. (1996) *Psychological Stress and the Coping Process*, New York: McGraw-Hill.

Lewis, E. (1979) 'Inhibition of mourning in pregnancy: psychopathology and management', *British Medical Journal* 2: 27–30.

Liley, A.W. (1972) 'The fetus as a personality', *Australian and New Zealand Journal of Psychiatry* 6: 89–105.

Llewellyn-Jones, D. (1994) *Fundamentals of Obstetrics and Gynaecology*, London: Mosby.

Lloyd, J. and Laurence, K.M. (1985) 'Sequelae and support after termination of pregnancy for fetal malformation', *British Medical Journal* 290: 907–9.

London Brook Advisory Centres Annual Report 1994–5, available from London Brook Advisory Centre, 233 Tottenham Court Road, London, W1P 9AE.

Luker, K. (1975) *Taking Chances: Abortion and the Decision Not to Contracept*, Berkeley: University of California Press.

Mansour, D. and Stacey, L. (1994) 'Abortion methods' pp. 29–38 in Paintin, D. (ed.) 'How the NHS can meet the needs of women: abortion services in England and Wales', London: Birth Control Trust and Pregnancy Advisory Service.

Marcus, R.J. (1979) 'Evaluating abortion counselling', *Dimensions in Health Service*, August: 16–18.

Marris, P. (1974) *Loss and Change*, London: Routledge & Kegan Paul.

Marteau, T.M., Drake, H. and Bobrow, M. (1994) 'Counselling following diagnosis of a foetal abnormality: the differing approaches of Obstetricians, clinical genetists and genetic nurses', *Journal of Medical Genetics* 31(11): 864–7.

Marwick, D., Anderson, M., Henshaw, R., Naji, S., Templeton, A. and Russell, I. (1994) 'A comparision of surgical vacuum aspiration abortion with medical abortion using mifepristone (RU486) and Gemeprost: implications for nursing staff', *British Journal of Family Planning* 20: 8–10.

Massey, D. (1994) *Family Planning Today*, third quarter edition of journal.

Medical Defence Union 1991, 'Consent to Treatment' (Section on Termination of Pregnancy), DMU.

Moore, S. and Rosenthal, D. (1993) *Sexuality in Adolescence*, London: Routledge.

Muir, R. (1982) 'The changeling myth and pre-psychology of parenting', *British Journal of Medical Psychology* 55: 97–104.

Murphy, S. (1994) 'The impact of HIV infection on women in the UK', *The British Journal of Family Planning* 20(2): 31–2.

Murray Parkes, C. (1972) *Bereavements: Studies of Grief in Adult Life*, London: Tavistock.

Nicoll, A., McGarrigle, C., Heptonstall, J., Parry, J., Mahoney, A., Nicholas, S., Hutchinson, E. and Gill, N. on behalf of a collaborative group (1994) 'Prevalence of HIV infection in pregnant women in London and elsewhere in England', *British Medical Journal* 309: 376–7.

Oakley, A. (1980) *A Woman Confined: Towards a Sociology of Childbirth*, Oxford: Martin Robinson.

Obholzer, A. and Roberts, V.R. (1994) *The Unconscious at Work*, London: Routledge.

O'Brien, B. and Newton, N. (1991) 'Psyche versus soma: historical evolution of belief about nausea and vomiting in pregnancy', *Journal of Psychosomatic Obstetrics and Gynaecology* 12(2): 91–120.

Office of Population and Census Surveys (1995) 'Legal Abortions 1994: residents of regional and district health areas', Monitor AB 95/8, London: HMSO.

Orbach, S. and Eichenbaum, L. (1982) *Outside In, Inside Out*, Harmonsworth: Penquin.

Osler, M., Morgall, J.M. and Jensen, B. (1992) 'Repeat abortion in Denmark', *Danish Medical Bulletin* 39(1): 89–91.

Parker, R. (1995) *Torn in Two: The Experience of Maternal Ambivalence*, London: Virago.

Payne, S. (1991) *An Introduction, Women's Health and Poverty*, Harvester Wheatsheaf.

Petchesky, R.R. (1986) *Abortion and Woman's Choice*, London: Verso.

Phoenix, A. (1991) *Young Mothers?* Cambridge: Polity Press.

Pines, D. (1972) 'Pregnancy and motherhood: interaction between fantasy and reality', *British Journal of Medical Psychology* 45: 333–43.

—— (1993) *A Woman's Unconscious Use of Her Body*, London: Virago.

Popay, J. and Jones, G. (1988) 'Gender inequalities in health: explaining the sting in the tail!' paper presented to Social Policy Association. Annual Conference, Edinburgh.

Potts, M. and Diggory, P.P.J. (1977) *Abortion*, Cambridge: Cambridge University Press.

R v Bourne 19391KB687.

Raphael-Leff, J. (1980) 'Psychotherapy with pregnant women' in B.L. Blumb (ed.) *Pregnancy, Birth and Bonding*, New York: Human Sciences Press.

—— (1993) *Pregnancy the Inside Story*, London: Sheldon Press.

—— (1994) *Psychological Processes of Childbearing*, London: Chapman & Hall.

Rawlinson, P. (1994) 'The physical and psycho-social effects of abortion on women', a report by the Commission of Inquiry into the Operation and Consequences of The Abortion Act.

Rayment, B. (1994) 'Confidentiality: developing confidentiality policies in youth counselling and advisory services', London: Youth Access.

Redman, C. and Walker, I. (1992) *Pre-eclampsia: The Facts*, Oxford: Oxford University Press.

Rich, A. (1977) *Of Woman Born: Motherhood as an Institution*, London: Virago.

Roberts, J. (1994) 'Surgeon general resigns in masturbation row', *British Medical Journal* 309: 1604.

Robson, K.M., Brant, H.A. and Kumar, R. (1981) 'Maternal sexuality during pregnancy and after childbirth', *British Journal of Obsterics and Gynaecology* 88: 882–9.

Rothman, B.K. (1988) *The Tentative Pregnancy: Prenatal Diagnosis and the Future of Motherhood*, London: Pandora.

Samaritans (1995) 'Behind the mask: men, feelings and suicide!' report designed and produced by Ex Cathedra.

SATFA (1992) *A Handbook for Parents When an Abnormality is Diagnosed in their Baby*, Great Britain: Good News Press.

Savage, W.,(1986) *A Savage Enquiry: Who Controls childbirth?*, London: Virago.

—— (1992) 'The nurse, the gynaecologist and the trainee: feelings about late abortion', paper given to Institute of Psychosexual Medicine, second international conference Cambridge.

—— (1994) 'Abortion in the NHS', The *Diplomate* 2(1): 7–10.

Scottish Office (1995) 'Scottish Abstract of Statistics 1994', Edinburgh: The Scottish Office.

Seligman, M.E.P. (1975) *Helplessness: On Depression, Development and Death*, San Francisco: WHF Freeman.

Selwyn, P.A., Carter, R., Shoenbaum, E., Robertson, V., Klein, R. and Rogers, M. (1989) 'Knowledge of HIV antibody status and decisions to continue or terminate pregnancy among intravenous drug users', *Journal of the American Medical Association* 261(24): 3567–71.

Sharpe, S. (1987) *Falling for Love: Teenage Mothers Talk*, London: Virago Press.

—— (1991) Letter to *The Lancet* 338: 1268.

Sloane, E. (1993) *Biology of Women*, New York: Delmar.

Smith, D.K. Shaw, R.W. and Marteau, T.M. (1994) 'Informed consent to undergo serum screening for Down's syndrome: the gap between policy and practice', *British Medical Journal* 309: 776.

Smith, T. (1993) 'Influence of socioeconomic factors on attaining targets for reducing teenage pregnancies', *British Medical Journal* 306: 1223–35.

Sobolm, M. and Daly K.J. (1992) 'The adoption alternative for pregnant adolescents. Decision making, consequences and policy implication', *Journal of Social Issues*, Fall 48(3): 143–61.

Statham, H. and Green, J. (1993) 'Serum screening for Down's syndrome: some women's experiences', *British Medical Journal* 281: 452.

Sunderland, A., Minkoff, H., Handtes, J., Moroso, G. and Landesman, S. (1992) 'The impact of HIV serostatus on reproductive decisions of women', *Obstetrics and Gynaecology* 79(6): 1027–31.

Thomson, R. (1993) 'Religion, ethnicity, sex education: exploring the issues', London: National Children's Bureau.

Turner, M. (1994) 'Consumer survey: provision of young people's health services in Camden and Islington', London: Camden and Islington Health Promotion Service.

Tylden, E. (1968) 'Hyperemesis and physiological vomiting', *Journal of Psychosomatic Research* 12: 86–93.

Uddenberg, N., Nilsson, N. and Almyren, P.E. (1971) 'Nausea in pregnancy: psychological and psychosomatic aspects', *Journal of Psychosomatic Research* 15: 269–76.

UKCC (1992) 'Code of professional conduct', London: United Kingdom Central Council for Nursing, Midwifery and Health Visitors.

Urberg, K.A. (1982) 'A theoretical framework for studying adolescent contraceptive use', *Adolescence* 17: 527–40.

Urquhart, D.R. and Templeton, A.A. (1991) 'Psychiatric morbidity and acceptability following medical and surgical methods of induced abortion', *British Journal of Obstetrics and Gynaecology* 98: 396–9.

Webb, C. (1985) 'Nurses attitudes to therapeutic abortion', *Nursing Times* 81(1): 44–7.

Weideger, P. (1982) *Female Cycles*, first published 1978, London: Womens Press.

White-Van Mourik, M.C.A., Connor, J.M. and Ferguson-Smith, M.A.(1992) 'The psychological sequelae of a second trimester termination of pregnancy for fetal abnormality', *Prenatal Diagnosis* 12: 189–204.

Wolkind, S. and Zajieck, E. (1981) *Pregnancy – A Psychological and Social Study*, London and New York: Academic Press.

Zolese, G. and Blacker, C.V.R. (1992) 'The psychological complications of therapeutic abortion', *British Journal of Psychiatry* 160: 742–9.

Index